MW00712065

IBM's Local Area Networks

POWER NETWORKING AND SYSTEMS CONNECTIVITY

IBM's Local Area Networks

Power Networking and
Systems Connectivity

W. David Schwaderer

VNR Van Nostrand Reinhold
_____ New York

TRADEMARKS

IBM is a registered trademark of International Business Machines Corporation.

The following are trademarks of International Business Machines Corporation: Personal System/2, PS/2, Operating System/2, and OS/2.

The following are trademarks of Sytek, Inc.: Local Net PC, Link Access Protocol, Reliable Stream Protocol, Datagram Transport Protocol, Session Management Protocol, user Datagram Protocol, Diagnostic and Monitoring Protocol, and Name Management Protocol.

Advanced NetWare/86 is a trademark of Novell, Inc.

Scout is a trademark of Computer Insights.

Copyright © 1989 by Van Nostrand Reinhold
Library of Congress Catalog Card Number 88-17420
ISBN 0-442-20713-1

All rights reserved. No part of this work covered by the copyright hereon may be reproduced or used in any form or by any means—graphic, electronic, or mechanical, including photocopying, recording, taping, or information storage and retrieval systems–without written permission of the publisher.

Printed in the United States of America

Van Nostrand Reinhold
115 Fifth Avenue
New York, New York 10003

Van Nostrand Reinhold (International) Limited
11 New Fetter Lane
London EC4P 4EE, England

Van Nostrand Reinhold
480 La Trobe Street
Melbourne, Victoria 3000, Australia

Macmillan of Canada
Division of Canada Publishing Corporation
164 Commander Boulevard
Agincourt, Ontario M1S 3C7, Canada

16 15 14 13 12 11 10 9 8 7 6 5 4 3 2 1

Library of Congress Cataloging in Publication Data

Schwaderer, W. David, 1947–
  IBM's local area networks.

  Bibliography: p.
  Includes index.
  1. Local area networks (Computer networks)
2. IBM Personal Computer.   I. Title.
TK5105.7.S38   1989   004.6′8   88-17420
ISBN 0-442-20713-1

To my family: Barbara, Greg, and Melissa,

and to

IBM's PC Network Development Group in Boca Raton, Florida.

You knew what it would take.
You know what you have done.

I wish I could have been with you to create
the soul of a new network.

Godspeed in your journeys.

Contents

Preface

Work for this book began in July 1985. Its scope was necessarily limited to IBM's only announced Local Area Network (LAN) offerings, the IBM PC Network Broadband LAN's initial hardware and software. Since the book's launch effort, IBM announced the IBM Token-Ring LAN, the IBM PC Network Baseband LAN, new adapter frequencies for IBM PC Network Broadband LAN adapters, the IBM Personal System/2 family, as well as significant new LAN software products. Consequently, the original scope has been thoroughly expanded and updated to include appropriate material related to these LAN product offerings.

However, the original book's extensive original material on broadband technology intentionally remains because broadband technology continues to be misunderstood by and mysterious to many candidate users. The situation is exacerbated by a remarkable absence of readable information on the subject as compared to, say, on the IBM Token Ring LAN. Hence, this book is my attempt to rectify this unfortunate situation; it reflects my opinions on the subject of LANs, not those of IBM's.

I initially intended to write a book devoted solely to the IBM PC Network, but during my research I stumbled into the realization that the IBM PC Network is only part of an even larger, more exciting story.

In short, I discovered the astounding potential and remarkable implications that broadband networks have for truly simplifying establishment communications. If you are tired of the effort and expense of pulling special wires and cables in your establishment each time a new data communication, telephone, video, fire alarm, security, public address, energy management, or other system comes along, you also need to be aware of broadband networking's good news.

To be sure, good books need good subjects; IBM's Local Area Network offerings are one of the finest subjects an author can have. I hope you find the book useful, informative, and as illuminating as it deserves to be.

I am periodically asked if the IBM PC Network LAN family is a temporary, interim network with limited applicability, design, and economic life. If IBM's April 2, 1987 and November 3, 1987 announcements did not provide a resounding "NO" to the question, I believe the facts presented in this book squarely address the question and speak for themselves.

Acknowledgments

The following people were instrumental in the creation of this book, and I am deeply indebted to them for their efforts.

Rosemary Morrissey of IBM's Boca Raton Entry Systems Division Communications Group

Bill Selmeier of LanTel Corporation

Phillip K. Edholm of Sytek, Inc.

Bert Moldow, visiting Associate Professor of Iona College

Paul M. Onushko of BRAND-REX TELECOM, a division of BRIntec Corporation

Howard Vipler, Telecommunications Marketing Manager in IBM's North Central Marketing Division

David C. Baker of IBM's PC Local Network Program Group in Austin, Texas

Bob B., Art G., Ed K., Kim L., and Glenn N. of the IBM PC Network Baseband development team in IBM's Boca Raton Entry Systems Division

Jorge A., Ron B., Lou D., Happy D., Noel F., Tony G., Matt K., Brian M., Ozzie O., Bill O., Bob S., Marty Z., and other members of the IBM PC Network development team in IBM's Boca Raton Entry Systems Division

The Sytek F8000 ROM group: R. Bernstein, I. Chang, G. Ennis, M. Gang, A. Gomez, J. Haver, B. Lieberman, M. Maiten, J. McCrae, P. Olmstead, J. Pinsky, J. Rezelman, F. Simoneau, and D. Stevens

Ellen Thro and Dr. Lance Leventhal, who edited a preliminary manuscript

The book reviewers were Dick Sloan and Ralph Cruikshank; Phillip K. Edholm of Sytek, Inc.; Bill Selmeier of LanTel Corporation; Noel Fallwell and Matt Kaltenbach of IBM Boca Raton; David C. Baker, Howard Vipler, Roy Heistand, Bert Moldow, and Nick Trufyn. They all made a difference.

Though the book has been reviewed by many, I accept full responsibility for any remaining errors. Please call them to my attention; thanks in advance.

IBM's Local Area Networks

POWER NETWORKING AND SYSTEMS CONNECTIVITY

Section 1

Local Area Networks—A Key to Increased Productivity

Chapter 1

Local Area Networks: What They Are, What They Do

The IBM Personal Computer (PC) has become a significant element in the quest for personal productivity on the job since its introduction in 1981. At the same time, people have increasingly noticed that the PC, like other microcomputers, sometimes seems a bit too personal. Scaling up and extending productivity from the personal level to the group or organization level can be a challenge.

Take a written business report. The text might be drafted more quickly on a PC than by other methods. But once completed, it is often retyped by a secretary. Figures must be added from accounting, and illustrations from the graphics department. Then someone must check the draft and approve it. Or the final version is carried down the hall on a diskette to an underused, and expensive, high-quality printer for printing and distribution. Or else the work is transmitted over a telephone line at a pedestrian 120 characters per second (four pages per minute).

Regardless of the delivery method, once the initial novelty of PC ownership diminishes, users often regard the exchange or delivery of PC data as slow, awkward, or both.

In a different organizational context, it is not uncommon for coworkers to debate diametrically opposing positions on a subject, buttressed by contradictory spreadsheet analyses. Why? Analysts are unable to obtain recent data from other systems without a batch printout and manual entry on the PC. Or different data and individual analysis can produce different conclusions, with organizational productivity often the casualty.

Similar instances occur in other organizations: A police dispatcher may have difficulty learning the status of all cars; a hospital nutritionist may require updated information about patients who need special diets; and the results of special tests must be entered into the patients' records as soon as possible.

As these cases indicate, organizations work most efficiently when the employees have a uniform view of the organization. A catalyst in promoting this, avoiding both isolation of production of information and the lack of timely availability of data, is a computer network.

NETWORKS AND PRODUCTIVITY

Virtually any group that functions in an organized way can make use of a computer network—a college department or campus, a warehouse, a manufacturing plant, a hospital, a military installation, an airport, a farm, or a bus station. To refer to any such group, I use the word *establishment*. Establishments must quickly transform data to meaningful information if they are to remain competitive. They also need an effective way to provide the information conveniently to all users.

One type of network, known as the IBM PC Network, first made public in 1984, addresses the problem of adapting the PC for establishment-wide communication. Where an individual PC is used in isolation, the PC Network permits the PC to be used as part of a system, implying organizational rather than personal use.

In addition, the network's flexibility offers increased organizational productivity to establishments with a few PCs or many, with a small office or a large corporate headquarters. Using IBM products exclusively, it can serve as many as 72 workstations in a circle with a 2,000-foot diameter. By adding other equipment and custom cabling, the network can be enlarged to handle 3,000 workstations within a 30-square-mile area—larger than most big-city downtowns or college campuses. The PC Network was IBM's first type of network known as a local area network (LAN). Since its announcement, IBM has announced two other LAN offerings: the IBM Token-Ring and the IBM PC Network Baseband.

WHAT IS A LOCAL AREA NETWORK?

There is no precise definition of what a local area communications network is, but for our purposes we can say that a LAN:

- Is privately owned and operated
- Operates in a geographically limited area (usually less than a 15-mile radius)
- Transmits at high data rates (say, hundreds of thousands of characters per second)
- Uses inexpensive communications and wiring (say, costing $.50 per foot or less)
- Allows a variety of devices to be used either singly or with each other by means of a standard connector for reliable communication

This "fuzzy" definition raises several issues that must be addressed by anyone planning to use a LAN.

Security

Security of data is a major consideration for any establishment. The fact that a LAN is privately owned and operated may reduce somewhat the need to encrypt data before transmitting it. Most establishments have information that should be kept secure: personnel files, information relating to research and development, and the establishment's financial records are just three examples. But security should always remain a primary consideration for anyone designing, installing, or owning a LAN. Consider the following IBM statements:

IBM Statement 1

On page ii, the Token-Ring Network PC Adapter Technical Reference Manual states:

Note: This product is intended for use within a single establishment and within a single, homogeneous user population. For sensitive applications requiring isolation from each other, management may wish to provide isolated cabling or to encrypt the sensitive data before putting it on the network.

User homogeneity may prove difficult to achieve on a departmental basis, much less on an establishment-wide basis. Even establishing user-homogeneity measurement criteria is likely to prove an interesting exercise.

IBM Statement 2

On page 1-4, the IBM NetBIOS Application Development Guide Introduction states:

It is the responsibility of the operating system or application program to make sure that data or devices are secure on the network as network security is not built into the NetBIOS.

Private Nature

Because it is private rather than public, a LAN need not be regulated by governmental agencies (such as the the Federal Communications Commission in the United States). However, a LAN usually requires installation of wiring and may be subject to local building codes. Finally, a LAN's private nature prohibits it from gaining arbitrary right-of-way access over public thoroughfares and private land. Such right-of-way access may prove costly or difficult to secure.

Geographical Limitations

A LAN operates in a geographically limited area, such as a building, campus, or business complex. In practice, this limitation is useful both technically and economically because of the nature of establishment communication patterns. Studies have shown that 50 percent of all information remains within the group that generates it, 75 percent remains within a 600-foot radius, and 90 percent never leaves the establishment. Of course, some LANs are vastly smaller than others. And the "local" network that becomes "too large" (variously defined) is a "wide area network."

Speed of Data Transmission

A LAN's data transmission rate is related to its geographic range because of the characteristics of the medium of transmission. As a rule of thumb, the farther a LAN extends, the more expensive it becomes to maintain a high data rate. This is true whether you are starting with a large network or expanding a small one significantly.

In most cases, the LAN's data rate is constant across the network. This means that selecting a high data rate requires more expensive equipment, which can take advantage of it. Selecting equipment by price affects speed. As a result, large LANs may run more slowly than small ones because the large ones require more components, whose cost must be taken into account. Remember: Extending a network usually requires keeping the speed constant. So a small network that eventually will require major expansion should be built with the necessary network equipment the expanded network will need.

Interconnecting LANs

If a LAN's geographic scope proves too limited, it can be extended by creating a second local network and linking the two with what are called *network bridges*. Even two different types of networks can be connected by *gateways*.

Transmission Media

Establishments without networks frequently transmit data internally by means of modems and telephone lines or even hand-carried data disks. LANs use inexpensive transmission cables of various types, which are discussed in detail in Chapter 3. Transmitting data over a LAN can reduce the number of telephone lines and associated modems required while allowing a far higher-transmission rate.

Flexibility

LANs allow, but do not require, autonomy of workstation operation. This option is entirely consistent with current trends in computer operations toward what is called *distributed processing*—allowing the processing elsewhere of data from overworked central processing units. But it also increases the requirement for effective high-speed data communication.

Different Types of Computer Equipment

Finally, a LAN should support a variety of workstation types that, although not generally part of it, can be attached to it. Using common LAN hardware connectors allows flexibility in selecting equipment and preserves the benefits of a unified approach to wiring.

Chapter 2

Selecting a Network: What to Look for

A LAN is an establishment-wide communication catalyst that quickly becomes part of your establishment's day-to-day operations in subtle as well as obvious ways. Once acquired, the LAN is your establishment's resource for a long time—for better or worse. So its selection is a critical business decision the importance of which it is hard to overstate.

WHAT SIZE ORGANIZATIONS BENEFIT FROM LANS?

LAN connectivity offers a modular workstation-based alternative to the traditional approach of centralized computing. An organization's work can be spread across multiple independent workstations that coordinate their activities over a LAN. As parts of the work load increase, the power of the individual workstations handling the additional work can be increased selectively.

Thus, small organizations, such as a department, can use LAN-oriented computing approaches in lieu of centralized computers and their so-called "unintelligent terminals." On the other end of the scale, LANs can help large organizations to communicate with existing centralized computers and can interconnect independent departments' LANs to form establishment-wide communication networks. This helps solve the chronic headache of building wiring.

WHY IS BUILDING WIRING SUCH A BIG HEADACHE?

Consider the following historical perspective on the traditional practices of wiring a building for centralized computing environments. This casts light on the reason building wiring is such a chronic problem.

Wiring has historically been installed on an as-required, informal basis. As a result, wires were not marked with information that would allow later identification. Nor were general maps or wiring plans maintained.

If a terminal was moved, a new cable would casually be installed at its new location. The original cable was disconnected but usually not removed because of labor costs. However, because the original cable was not marked, its use and points of origin and termination were often forgotten. Thus, even if a terminal of the same type were later reinstalled, a new redundant cable would also be installed. On a global scale, the problem of wiring was repeatedly being solved on a case-by-case basis.

On a small scale, the existence of redundant cable posed no problem or exorbitant expense. However, as the use of teleprocessing accelerated, the wires accumulated and establishments soon discovered their sheer physical weight and tendency to tangle prohibited their removal. In some situations, this made further expansion of teleprocessing applications difficult.

One major aircraft firm found that its only conduit under a public thoroughfare became clogged with cables, even though it was 2 feet in diameter. A nationally prominent research organization found that it had to reinforce its building's ceilings because of the crushing weight of accumulated cable. A development organization's roof support beam cracked, forcing an emergency building evacuation and causing the loss of many years of productivity before the beam was repaired. (See Figs. 2-1 through 2-4 for examples of how bad wiring problems can become.)

As the wiring problems compounded, they began delaying terminal installations. Because establishments depended on teleprocessing to assist them in daily operations, it was not uncommon to delay establishment reorganizations until adequate teleprocessing support could be provided for new organizational

Figure 2-1 Wires extending through a ceiling fire wall. Generally, such wires should be plenum cable (flame-resistant) but aren't in this instance. Thus, if the wires ignite, they burn with a wick-effect through the fire wall, rapidly spreading the fire and generating dangerous smoke.

Figure 2-2 Typical ad-hoc wire routing in ceilings

structures. Ominously, the installation of terminal wiring began to inhibit an establishment's reorganization capabilities and, hence, its ability to compete on a flexible basis. What was previously a second-thought activity quietly became a potential major obstacle to business operation.

Exacerbating this situation was the increasing requirement for organizational flexibility. Staff reassignment and turnover volatility dictated that any establishment support system be rapidly and easily reconfigurable to the dynamic needs of the organization; existing wiring tended to be static.

It was not unusual to construct or remodel a building for a group, only to have the group be redirected in mission or location before the building was occupied, rendering the best-laid wiring plans useless. Thus, wiring had to be flexible in function and support varieties of devices in ways traditional wiring could not.

As the pace of business became increasingly competitive, it required greater synchronization between organizational functions, resulting in unprecedented requirements for information exchange and unified connectivity through establishment wiring. Business techniques such as "just before needed"

Figure 2-3 Ceiling wire accumulation near a wiring closet

manufacturing required accurate synchronization of activities from manufacturing to procurement to accounts payable.

In turn, this dictated that establishment members have a uniform perspective of the organization and its resources. However, since a specific type of wiring tended to be supported on a subsystem basis only, various departments could be using two different subsystems that had inconsistent data.

As technology extended the techniques and feasibility of distributed processing to the PC level, the potential for data inconsistency grew commensurately. Finally, something had to be done to address the widespread proliferation of PCs within establishments that would unify them into a cohesive network and allow them to communicate in a productive manner. Good network design was the answer.

"DO WE NEED A LAN?"

There is no specific way to determine whether your establishment will benefit from the installation of a local area network. But ask yourself these questions:

Figure 2-4 Ceiling wire converging into a wiring closet

- Does the physical distance between our personal computers interfere with information flow?

- Do we have computers that need to communicate with each other: PC to PC, PC to mainframe, or mainframe to mainframe?

- Will it be valuable for us to be able to share stored information, programs, and devices, such as hard disks and printers?

- Is our volume of computer processing increasing, so that it would improve the flow of information to have distributed processing (away from a central processing unit)?

If you have answered yes to one or more of these questions, you can probably make good use of a LAN. Virtually any establishment will find that a LAN is an expediter of organizational information, whether it has a few personal computers or uses a time-sharing system or any arrangement in between.

"WHAT QUESTIONS SHOULD WE ASK?"

If you are a newcomer to LANs but have started looking into acquiring one, you may feel uncertain discussing the subject with potential vendors. Here are some questions they should be able to answer to your satisfaction:

How easy is it to move and reattach devices on the LAN?

The answer should satisfy your need to move people and equipment throughout your establishment.

Can the LAN wiring support different services to facilitate establishment reorganization?

For instance, one LAN might use twisted-pair wiring (like telephone wire) to carry digital data only, while a different LAN might use coaxial cable (the type used for cable TV) that can carry sound and video pictures, as well as data.

How much does it cost to install a LAN?

Remember to ask about labor costs, as well as the cost of materials. Fiber-optic systems must be installed by high-priced experts, whereas coaxial cable can be installed by semiskilled laborers.

How fast can it transmit data?

Look for high transmission rates, with a wide bandwidth (frequency range), for high-speed, efficient operation. However, be aware that high transmission rates do not necessarily mean superior performance. To better understand this, think of transmission speed as travel speed. For example, you may be able to travel quickly on an expressway. But the speed may not make up for the time spent driving to and from the expressway, waiting at toll booths or metered entry points, and passing through detours or construction zones. You may do better on the surface streets, despite their lower speed limits and traffic signals.

Several key factors apart from transmission speed determine a network's efficiency. Analysis of operating LANs reveals a hierarchy of bottlenecks. In decreasing order of severity they are:

- applications software
- interface between the workstation and its network adapter
- network protocol
- medium transmission speed

Clearly, transmission speed must be balanced with many other factors. These include communication session setup delay, message transmission delay, error recovery efficiency, and message receipt acknowledgment procedures. Also, higher speed usually means reduced geographical coverage, higher equipment costs, or both.

In the final analysis, a LAN's transmission rate does not, in itself, play the major role in determining how fast a network application will execute. So, a network with a slower transmission rate may actually suit your needs better than a faster one.

How many different devices will this LAN support?

Again, it must meet your needs.

Is isolation one of its characteristics?

If one device on the network fails, it should not shut down the entire system. Conceptually, your system should work like Christmas tree lights: individual light bulbs are isolated from one another so if one burns out, the others can still function properly.

How available is maintenance for the LAN?

Repairs and servicing should be made quickly and inexpensively.

REQUIREMENTS FOR A LAN

The best way to approach selection of a local area network is to determine what you want it to do for you. Many establishments have found that the most useful LAN provides the following features.

Useful and Easy-to-Use Services

Once operational, your LAN must support a variety and varying number of devices economically and effectively. The individual workstations should be able to use the network equitably and efficiently, without encountering electronic "gridlock" (network paralysis due to blockages).

One of a LAN's most important services is its near instantaneous transmission of data. Under the best circumstances, this means a minimum of missed business opportunities due to the loss of the information's time value.

A LAN also provides quick and easy access to shared resources, such as printers, data storage devices, programs, and modems. You should keep in mind that it is often the expensive, one-of-a-kind resources that are shared and that this situation may be temporary. For instance, today an establishment might have one $20,000 laser printer in the graphics department; in 5 years, the price of laser printers may be low enough that every office can have its own. On the other hand, a $300 fixed disk may be shared, so everyone is using the same level of programs and data.

High Reliability

A LAN should be reliable, a characteristic that assumes many forms:

1. Ideally, it should be available for general use 100 percent of the time. Disruptions for maintenance or reconfiguration should be eliminated or at least minimized.
2. A LAN should have a very low rate of errors—usually less than one per 10 trillion characters transmitted—both in transmitting individual messages and in general operation.
3. It must be easily maintained. When failures do occur, the failing component must be easy to identify and isolate from the rest of the network. That implies that the network be robust under failure (versus failing robustly) and degrade "gracefully" in the event of failure. For this to happen, moderately trained individuals must be able to identify the failing component. Even better, the LAN itself should be able to predict when components are approaching failure, allowing removal or repair before failure occurs.

    For large and complex LANs, this may require a network support center with an administrator and staff to provide management services. For smaller networks, a contract with an outside consultant may serve the same purpose.

Uniformity

A LAN should provide a uniform interface to both users and equipment. An employee should be able to use any LAN workstation with a single set of procedures. Access to the LAN's services should be by an intuitively understandable menu or other consistent method.

The equipment should have uniformity of data transmission speed, data format, and transmission procedures (message protocols). A single type of attachment, known as a *multidrop direct cable* with a standard hardware adapter, should connect the workstations to the network.

Such uniformity allows higher transmission speeds with greater reliability. It also permits diverse types of equipment that provide a variety of functions to be integrated into the network.

Consistency in use and connections results in an establishment-wide image of uniform data and service systems. It does this while insulating users from any rearranging of LAN devices and services. It also provides an architecture for future enhancements. Finally, it preserves an establishment's investment in user training in two ways—it makes training easier for more people, and it extends the usefulness of the network's devices.

Ease and Economy of Installation

A LAN must be easy and economical to install. This implies the use of inexpensive cable, workstation connections, and low-skill labor, even for custom-designed networks.

Ease of Reconfiguration

It must be easy to add, remove, or move devices with little or no impact on the LAN's wiring. Initially, users do not generally know what they need or how they will eventually use the network. You may want to add more PCs, minicomputers, laser printers, or other devices as their costs come down. And relocation of offices or changes in layout usually include movement of network devices, as well.

Such changes should be insignificant to the operation of a LAN. For instance, a small LAN should even be connectable to another network, with little or no disruption of either one.

Price Performance

A LAN should be cost-effective. Many people's first impulse is to measure this in terms of the instantaneous transfer rate, such as 250,000 characters per second versus 1.25 million characters per second. But this figure is misleading, because it is not an adequate measure of performance. You must also include the processing requirements, message propagation and staging, error recovery, synchronization, and general network housekeeping. The cost-effectiveness of these functions is determined by the LAN's architecture and its software programming.

The LAN also should have a useful life, measured in decades, comparable to that of a cable TV network. While such a protection against obsolescence preserves an establishment's investment in the network, prudence should prevail. As Keynes once aptly quipped, "In the long run, we are all dead."

Ease of Expansion

It is always wise to assume that you will be expanding any LAN that you install. For one thing, your establishment may grow in size. Or your volume of information and communication may grow. After installation, a LAN must be expandable quickly and inexpensively, requiring little effort and minimal network disruption. An easily expandable LAN allows smoother growth and affords a longer, useful life for the system. Expandability depends in part on the flexibility of the wiring design, or topology of the LAN's wiring.

Independence of Environment

Finally, a LAN should be insensitive to environmental problems, such as rodents, radio frequency interference (RFI), and electromagnetic interference (EMI). In addition, it should be relatively insensitive to corrosion, conduit flooding, humidity, and extreme temperatures.

EVALUATION CRITERIA

Now that you are familiar with the general requirements for a LAN, you should examine a number of criteria that can help you decide whether a particular LAN addresses your current or future needs. The following checklist may prove valuable in making your decision.

Does a LAN have ample initial excess capacity for future expansion?

Initial excess capacity should exist for geographic coverage, number and type of devices that can be attached, and transmission bandwidth. How much is necessary depends on future needs, which, of course, are unpredictable. In other words, buy as much as you can get. The LAN should be flexible enough to grow along with your organization and its future needs.

Say's economic law, "Supply creates its own demand," applies to a LAN in an establishment. Once users become familiar with a LAN's operation and advantages, they often adapt their procedures to capitalize on its presence. As with new highways, this, in turn, may lead to further expansion of the LAN or its use. In summary, you should insure that the LAN does not itself become a subsequent organizational pressure point or bottleneck.

Is the LAN compatible with the way your business is conducted?

An organization comes to depend on the LAN and, as with the telephone, always assumes its services are available. If your establishment must operate around the clock—for instance, a hospital emergency room, a car reservation service, a police station, or a 24-hour restaurant—can the LAN be maintained, expanded, or modified without unacceptable disruption of service?

Remember, a LAN exists to meet your establishment's communication patterns and operating requirements. It is not an independent institution that exists for your establishment to service! Noticeable shifts in establishment operating procedures often occur, once a LAN is installed. But you should not have to radically change your fundamental operating procedures merely to accommodate a LAN's characteristics.

Does the LAN software address your business needs?

Does the LAN permit more than one unit to provide access to a printer or other shared device (provided by special network nodes called *servers*)? If not, does the software prevent monopolization of the single server by one user or group of users?

Does the LAN provide a level of data integrity your establishment merits?

Does the LAN software allow multiple access to data? For example, two users may try to update the same information. Will the second update request reflect the first's activity, or simply ignore it, resulting in a data integrity problem? If multiple access of records while preserving data integrity is not possible, do normal provisions prohibit such access?

Does the LAN medium support all the necessary types of services (video, voice, and data) that you, or perhaps the inheritors of your facility, will conceivably need?

The presence of a powerful, functional, and operating LAN is identifiable as an attractive asset. As a result, buildings under construction are often wired for LANs that support video, voice, and data, to attract a spectrum of tenants at premium prices.

Does the LAN have sufficient data security?

Every establishment will have a unique answer to this question, in terms of both data and programs. As an example, many programs cannot be used indiscriminately on a LAN without a license from the publisher. They must be protected from unauthorized access by unlicensed LAN users. If the LAN does provide an adequate level of security, it is appropriate to ask whether there is a reasonable trade-off between security and usability. If the LAN's level of security is not adequate, you should know whether you can add procedures to supplement those provided, in order to achieve an acceptable level.

What are the LAN's maintenance characteristics?

What are the LAN's records for mean time between failures (MTBF) and mean time to repairs (MTTR)? These records (long for MTBF and short for MTTR) should be well established in operating environments that are similar to yours or even more stringent than yours, such as cable TV networks which have existed since the early 1950s.

Ideally, a LAN is able to identify components that are near failure or fall outside of operating tolerance. This feature facilitates repair or replacement under warranty before failure occurs. In addition, the administrator or operator of a network should be able to address any problem with adequate diagnostic and maintenance tools and a minimum amount of skill and training. And, when failure strikes, a LAN should be repairable without unnecessarily interrupting unaffected users. Servicing people should be able to isolate most problems from the rest of the network, with gradual degradation being the worst consequence.

What kind of vendor support is available?

Vendor support and vendor independence are important and related. A hardware vendor should offer technical assistance in the form of manuals and classroom training. The hardware should be readily available from a number of convenient sources for two reasons: to provide your establishment with a measure of independence and to decrease the amount of hardware you must keep in inventory. Finally, a LAN with an open or standard architecture offers obvious advantages in useful lifetime and extended support.

Because LAN software is usually revised periodically, you need to know what the provisions are for upgrading. And is the software usable only on current hardware, or can it migrate to future machines similar to the way the IBM PC family incorporates software compatibility with the PS/2 family?

How much does the LAN cost?

There are two kinds of costs, initial and deferred. Initial costs include those for hardware (including computers and other devices), software, and wiring. The cost of the connecting media includes the cabling and connectors, as well as labor for designing the layout, installation (the most significant), and certification that the network was designed and installed properly. Media costs vary widely: One LAN's media alone may cost as much as another LAN's media plus installation.

Deferred costs include connection and removal of devices, LAN maintenance, user training, expansion, reconfiguration, and any network support center. Economies may exist in this category, depending on your selection, since a LAN providing intuitive ease of learning and operation requires less user training.

On the other hand, economies in initial cost can create a large deferred cost in later years—a LAN that supports only a small number of devices may require complete replacement, if you need a modest expansion. The possible result: a substantial cost at an inconvenient moment. You should not have to "buy another train to get one more seat."

The cost of a LAN is usually dominated by the cost of the devices. Typically, a LAN's media cost 2 to 5 percent of the total network cost, and adapters cost 10 to 15 percent.

ADMINISTERING THE NETWORK

No discussion of networks is complete without examining the duties of network administrator, and how the costs of performing these services are shared throughout the establishment. As with a car pool or a law partnership or a condominium association, a network needs an administrator to assure that the system functions smoothly. Also, plan network administration formally. It is a thankless job and needs to be assigned, or it receives as-available attention.

A network administrator has a variety of responsibilities, namely:

- Recognizing the difference between hardware or software failures and knowing whom to call after performing preliminary problem analysis and isolation procedures
- Training other associates to perform network administration tasks in the network administrator's absence
- Maintaining service history records for each network component
- Documenting and monitoring how the network is being used, including network addresses and location of equipment by room
- Establishing disaster bypass and recovery procedures
- Overseeing the system's security by assigning and periodically changing passwords
- Reassigning passwords when someone leaves the establishment, voluntarily or by being fired
- Monitoring use of licensed software on the LAN
- Making backups of network files (programs and data)
- Defragmenting shared network disks to increase shared disk server performance
- Refereeing disputes regarding priorities and use of shared network devices such as shared disks, modems, printers, and printer paper
- Cancelling print jobs in progress to permit sudden, top-priority jobs to go through
- Monitoring mischief, such as changing network device names or cancelling jobs
- Updating network software by making sure all nodes and program version levels are compatible
- Determining access procedures
- Maintaining wiring plans and labeling the origin and termination of network wires
- Insuring new LAN hardware does not violate wiring distance or connection considerations
- Allocating costs of time and work to each department using the LAN

CONCLUSION

A LAN should exhibit many of the user-friendly qualities associated with home telephone service: It should allow intuitive and consistent use with minimal training, regardless of the type of device. Both attributes promote the transfer of skills among as many employees as possible. Finally, it should be easy to install and modify without obtrusive disruptions.

After all, how useful would the phone system be if you had to learn a new operating procedure every time you used a different phone? Or if phones in Los Angeles, California (population approximately 3 million) were inoperative because of line problems in Mercury, California (population exactly 3)?

Section 2

Local Area Networks and IBM's LAN Offerings

Chapter 3

Local Area Network Technical Overview

This chapter provides a general technical introduction to local area networks. You need not be familiar with this information to use a LAN, but terms and concepts introduced here appear in the rest of this book. This chapter also provides technical information for those who want to know more about the design and operation of LANs. The topics discussed include the roles of communications devices in a LAN, types of LANs, layered architecture, and LAN speed.

In the final analysis, a LAN user does not need to know which medium, signaling technique, or access method a network uses. These attributes should be "transparent," or invisible. However, inappropriate use of one of them could lower the network's reliability or performance. Knowing something about their characteristics helps you understand their strengths and weaknesses. This knowledge also helps you make the correct buying decision.

Virtually all media, signaling techniques, and access methods can be used with each other. But because of affinities between specific types of media, signaling techniques, and access methods, they are not easily discussed out of context.

COMMUNICATION DEVICES IN A LAN

This section discusses nodes and servers, the two roles that communications devices can play in a LAN.

Nodes are devices on a network. Each has at least one name, consisting of a hardware setting, a number, or an ordinary symbolic name.

Nodes

A LAN transforms individual devices, known as *nodes*, into an interconnected communication system. To distinguish one node from another, each has at least one unique name or identification. This name is one of three types:

- A setting determined by switches within the node
- A number, much like a serial number, electronically imprinted in the hardware during manufacturing. The manufacturer guarantees that these are unique. Thus, you can always distinguish network nodes this way, as long as you stick to one manufacturer.

- An ordinary or symbolic name, such as "GREG" or "MELISSA," which is clearly easier for users to recall. However, these are not necessarily unique, nor are they intended to be. Some names may even be used simultaneously, allowing a single network to define groups of nodes, perhaps those within a department, that are somehow related.

Symbolic names are convenient and let a node take the name of its principal user. This method is convenient, of course, if the user is Tom, Dick, or Harriet, but less so if he or she is Rumplestiltskin, Thumper, or BeagleBarker. In addition, unattended nodes can be identified by their functions—DEPT-L43-PRINTER or DEPT-L43-DISK, for example. The network software then relates the symbolic names to the hardware addresses.

Specialized nodes, called Servers, let other nodes share fixed disks, printers, or other scarce establishment resources. Some servers also act as independent nodes. Others are dedicated to a single purpose, such as printing.

Servers

Some nodes provide special hardware or software services to other network nodes referred to as *client nodes*. For example, print servers are nodes that let client nodes use one of their printers, and file servers are nodes that share fixed disks and the data stored on them.

Different LAN servers have different capabilities. Some may be able to do background processing, such as organizing a queue of files and printing them while running a spreadsheet in the foreground. Other LANs require a print server to be completely idle before it can accept a printing request.

File servers share files. Disk servers share portions of a disk, and client nodes create their files there.

File servers provide two types of file storage: private volumes, which have restricted access, and public volumes, which are generally accessible. Each type has its role. Files on public volumes can contain common data and current versions of programs and other information. Private volumes provide file security because they can be accessed only by a single specified client node. Servers that provide only private volumes for single nodes are called *disk servers*. Those that permit sharing, reading, and modification of data by multiple nodes are called *file servers*.

Dedicated Servers

A server whose sole function is to provide services to other nodes is a *dedicated server*. It may be a general-purpose machine, such as an IBM PC AT. Or it may be a specifically designed machine that performs just one function, such as file sharing, perhaps better or faster than a general-purpose machine could.

Dedicated servers are often preferable to nondedicated servers for two reasons. First, the dedicated server's total capabilities are always available for network tasks. This is important because servers can be the primary bottlenecks of a LAN. Switching between foreground and background processing takes time and effort. Dedicating a server eliminates foreground processing, allowing background processing to proceed unimpeded. Larger networks usually have several servers of the same type to reduce competition.

Second, rebooting of nondedicated servers can cause undesirable and unpredictable events, such as programs not being available to clients. For this reason alone, it is a good idea to place dedicated servers in secure areas. You do not want one user to turn off or reset a server machine and thereby disrupt its possibly several clients.

Regardless of function, all servers should receive periodic data maintenance. This should be the responsibility of the network administrator. The administrator should back up and update shared programs, data files, and directories, and assign network names and passwords to users.

Virtual or Logical Devices

Programs (and users) cannot tell that shared devices are attached to server nodes and not to their network nodes. To programs running in nodes, local phantom devices seem to exist that behave just like real devices. We call these *virtual* or *logical* devices. As an example, the space a disk server shares may be a virtual diskette to a client node.

Like real devices, virtual devices have local names associated with a shared device on a server. When a program requests a service from a virtual device by using its assigned local name, a process called *redirection* reroutes the request to the appropriate server for execution (see Fig. 3-1).

For example, we might call a virtual printer LPT1. A user command would associate this name with a specific network printer. It might, for instance, be a central high-speed laser printer. A local request to print a file on LPT1 would cause the file to be printed on the server.

Gateways connect networks of different types. Bridges connect the same type of networks. Repeaters support part of a larger LAN.

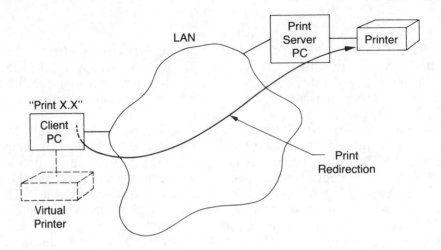

Figure 3-1 Virtual devices and redirection

Gateways, Bridges, and Repeaters

A communications server connects the devices of two networks. If networks are of the same type, a *bridge* creates the connection. A bridge would be used, for example, to connect two IBM Token-Rings. Bridges typically only transfer messages that need to be routed onto the adjoining network. This keeps unnecessary traffic from appearing on the bridge-connected LAN.

If the networks are of different types (for instance, an IBM PC Network and an IBM Token-Ring Network), we call the server that connects them a *gateway*. For example, a telephone modem, to allow other network nodes to connect to the telephone network, could serve as a gateway.

Repeaters are used to receive and retransmit messages within parts of the same LAN. This "purifies" a LAN's signals by removing accumulated network noise. The signal regeneration provides "isolation" between LAN segments and has the effect of extending a LAN's geographic coverage, which might otherwise have been limited for noise considerations. However, unlike bridges, a repeater retransmits every message it receives to the LAN section it supports, while bridges are selective in what messages are retransmitted onto an adjoining LAN.

THE ROLE AND EFFECTS OF TRANSMISSION MEDIA

Nodes communicate by sending signals over a medium. If a medium carries data in only one direction, it is *unidirectional*. If it carries data back and forth, it is *bidirectional*.

The most commonly used media are air, wire, and fiber-optic cable. The specific medium is critical, because it affects the LAN's cost, maximum operating speed, and error rates. LAN media generally should be durable, rodent-proof, reliable, inexpensive, immune to noise, and easy to install, maintain, and reconfigure.

Media differ in their ability to carry signals. For example, over long distances, fiber-optic cable can transmit tens of millions of characters per second, while copper wire is limited to thousands of characters per second. Thus the choice of medium plays a role in determining a LAN's operating speed.

Characteristics of the medium can also limit its maximum usable length within the LAN. Faster transmission speeds can dictate smaller networks. For example, a short wire may be able to handle at a rate of millions of bits per second, while a longer wire of the same type requires a much slower data rate. Though the speed varies with the type of wire as well as its length, the following rule generally applies: The longer the transmission distance, the lower the maximum speed.

The nodes may also limit transmission speed. For example, the wire in most telephone installations can transmit data much faster than the telephone company can accept it with today's equipment. In this instance, the speed of the nodes rather than the medium lowers the effective speed of the network.

Reflections, or Through the Looking Glass

You have undoubtedly noticed reflections from windows and lakes. Simply put, light is diverted from its original direction when it strikes and ricochets off a surface. Before impact, light travels through air. At the point of impact, it encounters a new medium, say glass. Some light continues into the glass, but some reflects because of the difference in densities between air and glass (Fig. 3-2).

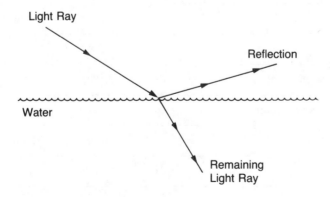

Figure 3-2 Reflection of light off water

While the amount of reflected light can be predicted mathematically, you need only remember that signal reflections occur when a characteristic of the medium, such as density or temperature, changes. For example, higher media temperatures can cause attenuation, or loss of signal strength. Signal strength losses result in weaker arriving signals.

Transmission Media Types

As you read the following descriptions of different media, refer to Table 3-1, which summarizes their characteristics.

Air

Some LANs transmit data by radio waves or by infrared or laser light. Such systems eliminate the expense and inconvenience of installing cables or wires. They also eliminate the need to buy or lease expensive rights-of-way. In addition, infrared and laser transmissions do not require the governmental approval often needed for microwave or FM signals.

Of course, infrared and laser transmissions have disadvantages as well. First, laser light travels only in a straight line, so it needs an unobstructed line-of-sight path between nodes. Today's unobstructed path may disappear with

	Twstd Pair	Shielded Twstd Pr.	Coaxial Cable	Fiber Optic
cost per foot	Low	Middle	Middle	High
installation skill level	Low	Low	Middle	High
bandwidth	Low	Low	High	High
external interference immunity	Low	High	High	High
difficulty of tapping/splicing	Low	Low	Middle	High
security from emissions	Low	High	High	High
connection costs	Low	Middle	Middle	High

Table 3-1 A summary chart of media and their characteristics.

tomorrow's new construction or foliage. Second, light signals are susceptible to interference from fog, haze, and smog. Don't count on good results if you live in London, San Francisco, or Los Angeles. And, finally, data transmitted through the air can be intercepted, creating a potential security problem.

Twisted-Pair

As its name implies, twisted-pair wire—the medium used in most telephone lines—consists of two insulated wires twisted together (see Fig. 3-3). Many sets of twisted-pair wire may be bundled to form fat cables, such as those found in many homes and other buildings.

Like any metallic medium, twisted-pair wire picks up electrical "noise" and interference from the environment. However, the twisting tends to expose each wire in the pair to the interference uniformly, permitting use of a simple, inexpensive process to eliminate noise.

Twisted-pair is the second most commonly used wire; only electrical power wiring surpasses it. Twisted-pair offers three primary advantages. It is readily available in many forms at low prices, relatively easy to install, and, especially important, it is used extensively by telephone companies, which may allow you to run networks through telephone lines, perhaps easing right-of-access problems.

On the other hand, while the problems of undesirable signal absorption (signal ingress) and radiation (egress) are common to all media, twisted-pair's high susceptibility to electromagnetic interference can cause data errors. Moreover, signals easily radiate from the wires, subjecting adjacent sets of wire to a form of electromagnetic interference called *crosstalk* (Fig. 3-4).Thus, twisted-pair also presents security problems as well.

In addition, the quality of different forms of twisted-pair can vary radically, resulting in different degrees of success at noise removal. This variance in quality makes it difficult to ensure uniform signals of acceptable quality with already installed wire.

Finally, twisted-pair has difficulty transmitting high-frequency signals over long distances. The range of usable frequencies of a communications connection, called its bandwidth, ultimately determines the maximum transmission rate. Because twisted-pair's bandwidth is narrower than that of other media, its maximum transmission rate is commensurately slower.

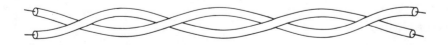

Figure 3-3 Twisted pair wire

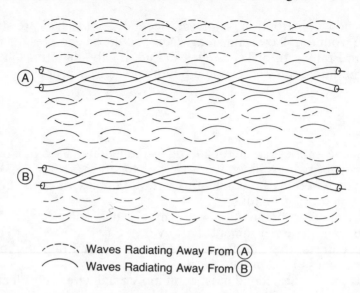

Waves Radiating Away From (A)
Waves Radiating Away From (B)

Figure 3-4 Crosstalk between sets of twisted pair wires

Shielded Twisted-Pair

Shielded twisted-pair is a high-quality variation of twisted-pair wire. It differs from ordinary twisted-pair in that

- Its individual wires must meet rigid manufacturing standards and must have high-quality insulating polymer to limit signal ingress and egress
- The twisting of the two wires is carefully controlled during manufacturing to facilitate noise removal
- The pair of wires is shielded with a metallic mylar foil that further limits signal ingress and egress
- The entire cable is insulated with metallic braid to further limit signal ingress and egress and then is sealed with polymer

Besides the advantages of ordinary twisted-pair, shielded twisted-pair provides improved immunity to environmental interference and crosstalk, and better system security. Of course, these features make it more expensive (Fig. 3-5).

Coaxial Cable

Coaxial cable is the type used in commercial cable TV networks (Fig. 3-6). It is the third most commonly used cable and comes in various qualities. The

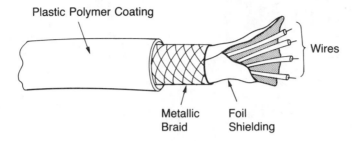

Figure 3-5 Shielded twisted pair

highest quality coaxial cable has enormous transmission capability, with a bandwidth second only to that of fiber-optic cable.

Coaxial cable comes in a variety of exterior colors, the predominant ones being black, white, and beige. Other colors require coloring materials that have not been studied as extensively as the popular ones. As a result, the aging and color-retention characteristics of these other colored cables may not be as predictable as those of the popularly colored ones. While the cable's usefulness may not be affected, over a 5-year period a red cable may fade to purple, for example, complicating visual identification and repairs. In addition, a colored cable exposed to extreme heat may be susceptible to premature cracks in its exterior plastic sheath.

The connectors required for coaxial cable are widely available and can be easily installed by semiskilled labor. Another advantage of coaxial cable is the natural rigidity of some of its forms, which may let it be installed without conduits or cable trays.

Fiber-Optic

Fiber-optic cable consists of a hair-thin strand of spun glass or plastic covered with opaque protective insulation (Fig. 3-7). It has extremely low rates of signal loss and high immunity to radiation, crosstalk, lightning, and corrosion.

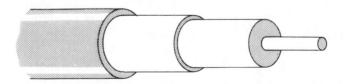

Figure 3-6 Coaxial cable

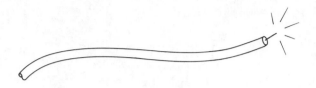

Figure 3-7 Fiber optic cable

As with twisted-pair wire, telephone companies use fiber-optic cable extensively, so using it in a network may facilitate right-of-way access through the telephone system.

The transmission capability of fiber-optic cable is virtually unlimited. Its bandwidth is constrained only by its ability to generate light signals of uniform frequency and to keep the signal traveling in as uniform a path as possible. The thinner the cable, the easier it is to control the light signal's path. The light is generated by lasers or by light-emitting diodes (LEDs).

Fiber-optic cable is difficult to tap and does not radiate emissions, so it offers greater system security. In addition, it may not need protection from lightning. Its installation is made easier by its small size and light weight. But splicing sections together and connecting nodes to the network may require highly skilled technicians and special equipment.

As a result, the number of LANs using fiber-optic cable has been limited. As its price decreases and its technology improves to ease installation, its role as a network medium is likely to grow—primarily because of the ease with which a fiber-optic LAN's transmission rate can be increased to meet future requirements.

The only significant exclusively fiber-optic LAN is the so-called Fiber Distributed Data Interface (FDDI), defined by the American National Standards Institute/Computer and Business Equipment Manufacturers Association (ANSI/ CBEMA) X3T9. 5 committee.

BANDWIDTH

Just as a highway consists of traffic lanes, the medium connecting two nodes provides one or more "lanes," or channels, for data traffic. Through each channel flows an independent stream of data that is carried by a transmission signal within the channel's frequency range. The signal's frequency is described in cycles per second, or Hertz (Hz) (see Table 3-2.)

Each channel has its own bandwidth, or range, of signal frequencies that it can transmit. For example, a typical home telephone line's channel can transmit signals between 300 Hz and 3,300 Hz. Its bandwidth is thus 3 KHz (3,300 Hz minus 300 Hz).

Cycles Per Second	Frequency	Abbreviation
1	1 Hertz	1 Hz
1,000	1 Kilohertz	1 KHz
1,000,000	1 Megahertz	1 MHz
1,000,000,000	1 Gigahertz	1 GHz

Table 3-2 Frequency terminology.

Although telephone wire could handle a larger bandwidth than 3 KHz, telephone exchanges do not use it because of cost restrictions and historical legacies. A bandwidth of 3 KHz is considered limited or narrow, because it severely restricts the range of transmitted frequencies. Evidence of this limitation is the poor fidelity of music transmitted over a telephone circuit.

In contrast, an FM radio station usually has a bandwidth of 150 KHz. The increased bandwidth allows more information to be transmitted per second, resulting in increased signal fidelity.

The range of frequencies available to a medium's specific channel, called its *frequency spectrum,* is determined partly by the medium used. This is important, because the frequency spectrum ultimately limits a LAN's transmission speed, just as the lack of bandwidth limits music's fidelity over the telephone. The discussion later in this chapter on LAN speed explores this subject in greater detail.

CONNECTION PATTERNS, OR TOPOLOGIES

The pattern of node connections is called the *physical LAN topology,* or *topology* for short. It may be naturally suggested by the locations of the nodes.

LAN software may let the nodes behave as if they were connected using a topology different than the network's physical topology. We call this topology a LAN's *logical topology* (see Fig. 3-8).

A LAN's topology plays a key role in determining wiring costs. Designers must choose a topology carefully, especially if the LAN will be expanded later. Typical LAN topologies are "stars," "rings," "buses," and hybrids.

Topologies
Star—connects nodes to a central point
Ring—connects nodes in a circle
Bus—attaches nodes to one trunk or to branches from a trunk

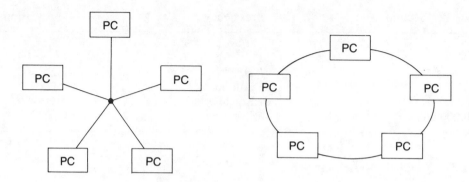

Figure 3-8 Physical and logical topology example

Star Topology

In a star topology, all nodes are connected to a central point that is often called the *hub*, which is located within a wiring closet (Fig. 3-9). Star topologies are commonly used in private branch exchanges (PBXs). One also finds them in centralized computer systems with terminals that have no computing power of

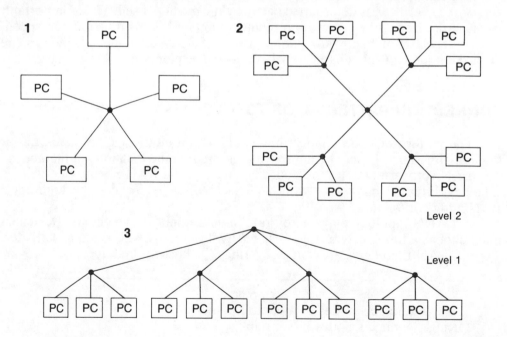

Figure 3-9 Star topologies

their own (so-called unintelligent terminals). In these examples, the central point actively controls the network, resulting in what we call an *active star*. If the central point does not actively participate in the network, the star is *passive*.

In the star topology you can easily identify and remove failed nodes. In addition, small star networks are usually easy to install and reconfigure. However, a star network generally incurs high wiring costs, because it needs long bidirectional cables from each node to the central point. Another drawback is that a failure in the central point can immobilize the entire network. Generally, this type of network-vulnerable device is called a single point-of-failure. Moreover, the central point of an active star can become a bottleneck which reduces the speed of the entire network.

Finally, note that star networks can be connected together by other star networks. Such combined networks are called *hierarchic star networks*. The second and third diagrams in Figure 3-9 are actually the same hierarchic network redrawn differently. But to the network electronics, they are identical.

Ring Topology

A ring topology results from point-to-point node connections in a circular pattern, with no central point (Fig. 3-10). It has two basic advantages: easy identification of a severed medium and suitability to fiber-optic cable. As for cost, a ring network generally uses less cable than a star network but usually more than a bus network.

Because the nodes are connected point to point, they can be unidirectional, reducing connection costs. However, bidirectional connections can provide a backup contingency capability (Fig. 3-11). Finally, some rings, called *counterrotating* rings, normally operate using two transmission paths that allow

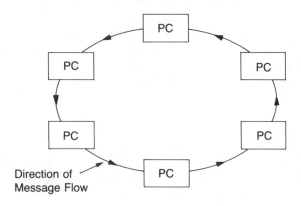

Figure 3-10 Ring topology

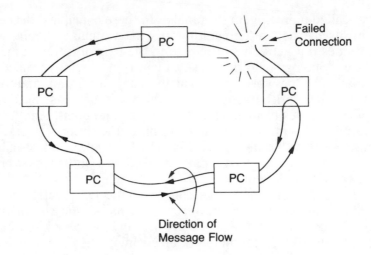

Figure 3-11 Bidirectional backup in a ring topology

independent messages to travel in opposite directions. When one path fails, the other path assumes the work of the failing path.

Rings also have shortcomings. Each node must regenerate every message it receives and send it on around the network. Signal regeneration can slow the network's operating speed. It can also limit the distance between nodes and makes each node a potential point of failure that could disable the entire network.

There are several ways to reduce the impact of single-node failure. One approach, used by the IBM Token-Ring, connects each node to a central wiring concentrator, so that a failed node can be removed and the operation of the remaining nodes can be restored. Concentrators can also be connected to other concentrators, allowing a ring to have the physical topology of a star network while retaining the logical topology of a ring (Fig. 3-12). Though this configuration may require extra wiring, its advantage is simplified network problem analysis and the ability of the undamaged portion of the network to continue operating when part of the network fails.

Bus Topologies

A LAN may have all its nodes attached to a common medium, called a bus. In such topologies, nodes connect to the bus at points called *taps*, or *tap points*, using drop (or multidrop) cables. (See Fig. 3-13.)

The actual shape of the bus can vary, allowing bus topologies to use the least amount of cable. The two most common configurations are the single trunk and the branching tree.

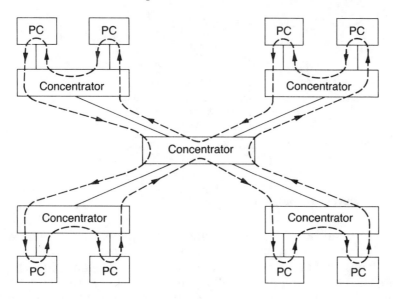

Figure 3-12 Wiring concentrations in a ring

Single-Trunk Bus Topology

This topology uses a single main cable, or trunk cable, to which all nodes connect with drop cables (Fig. 3-14). Thus the bus must extend to a tap within the reach of each node.

Because of LANs' length restrictions, extending the single-trunk bus to

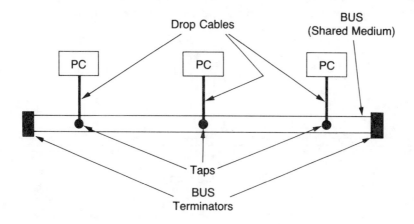

Figure 3-13 Bus network

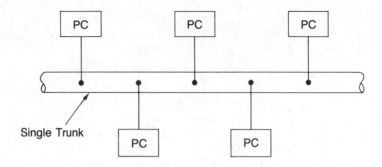

Figure 3-14 Single-trunk bus

every tap point can pose problems, unless the nodes are in a small area. Also, cable breaks and short circuits can be difficult to locate.

Single-trunk bus networks may allow bidirectional signal flow (Fig. 3-15). If signals are broadcast bidirectionally, you must keep the taps a minimum distance apart (how far apart depends on the specific LAN design). Otherwise, the signals of nearby nodes will drown the weaker attenuated signals of distant nodes. Bidirectional traffic also introduces signal reflections, which can cause significant problems.

Wire and the House of Mirrors

You have probably been in a popular amusement attraction called the House of Mirrors. Reflections from the mirrors make it difficult to find your way out (and give you a rousing headache, as well).

The same situation can occur on a single-trunk bus LAN that allows bidirectional signals. As Figure 3-13 shows, each node connects to the bus at a

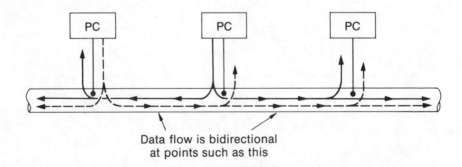

Figure 3-15 Bidirectional data flow on single-trunk multidrop bus

tap point. The actual tap is usually constructed in one of two ways, as a T-tap or as a pressure (vampire) tap (Fig. 3-16).

Attaching a T-tap involves cutting the cable and adding a connector. This substantially alters a critical characteristic, the impedance, of the cable at the point of insertion. The result is an electronically reflected signal similar to the reflection of an image from a window.

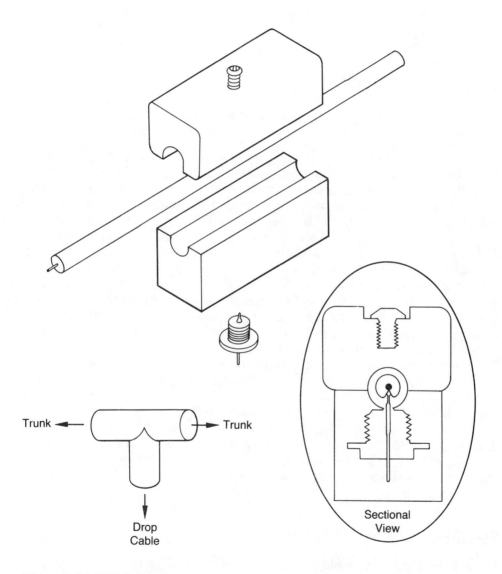

Figure 3-16 T-Taps and pressure taps

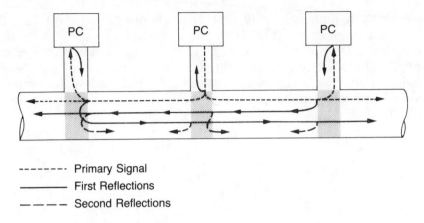

-------- Primary Signal
———— First Reflections
— — — — Second Reflections

Figure 3-17 Signal reflections on a single-trunk multidrop bus

If you have ever stood between two mirrors that face each other, you may recall the many images trailing off, each smaller and darker than the previous one. Similarly, with signals on a bidirectional single-trunk bus network, a reflection travels in a direction opposite to that of the original and generates more reflections as it passes through subsequent taps. These reflections travel in the same direction as the original signal and generate reflections themselves—and so on (Fig. 3-17). The result can be electronic signal chaos, much like colliding ocean waves in a choppy sea.

To minimize the electronic chaos, single-trunk bidirectional networks must use specially designed taps, limit the number of allowable network taps, restrict tap spacing, and/or reduce the allowed geographical scope of the network. For example, bidirectional single-trunk coaxial media networks can use a type of tap known as a *pressure tap*, which disturbs the bus less at the point of insertion. While this partially addresses the signal reflection problem, reduced geographic coverage and careful spacing of taps is usually required to make the reflector problem somewhat more manageable.

As a historical note, some early Community Antenna TV (CATV or cable TV) companies originally tried using T-taps and pressure taps in bidirectional single-trunk coaxial networks. They were eventually forced to abandon them because of the reflection problems, the logistics of tap spacing, and the requirement for large geographic networks.

Branching-Tree Bus Topology

A branching-tree topology is another example of a bus topology. In contrast to the single-trunk topology, with its one main trunk, here the main trunk is split

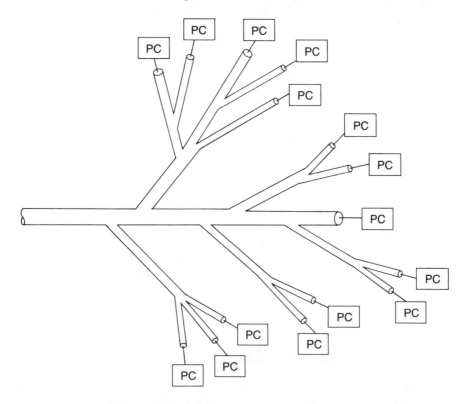

Figure 3-18 Branching tree topology

into large limbs, which are subdivided into branches. Branches can be further subdivided (Fig. 3-18). Branching makes it easier to extend the bus to every node but introduces the potential for signal reflections at each of the many node and branch connection points.

To minimize this problem, most branching-tree LANs contain directional components, which force all messages to travel in one direction from the node to a central point. We call this point the *headend* or *central retransmission facility* (CRF). At the headend, the signal is re-amplified and retransmitted as a second, higher-frequency signal. This second signal also travels in a single direction, that is, away from the headend to all nodes (Fig. 3-19).

The process of retransmission at a higher frequency is called *translation*, and the difference between the frequencies of the first and second signals is the network's *frequency offset*. The directional components are designed to virtually eliminate signal reflections. Thus, while a given signal can travel only in one direction, bidirectional traffic (the original signal and the translated signal) is made possible by the directional components and the headend (Fig. 3-20).

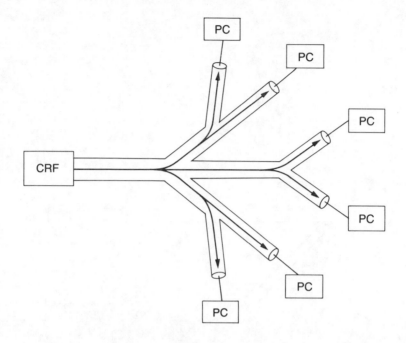

Figure 3-19 Signal directionality in a branching tree network

Most branching-tree networks are balanced. That is, they are adjusted until the signal strength from any transmitter to any receiver is the same (balanced) throughout the system (Fig. 3-21). This balancing or alignment results from careful initial network design and planned expansion.

Because each node can attach at only one point, its unique path from the headend facilitates the determination of problems, maintenance, and quick location of breaks in the medium. Finally, failing branches can be temporarily removed from the network electronically for service or restoration of network operation for the remainder of the network.

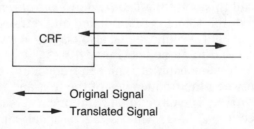

———— Original Signal

— — — ➤ Translated Signal

Figure 3-20 Direction of travel

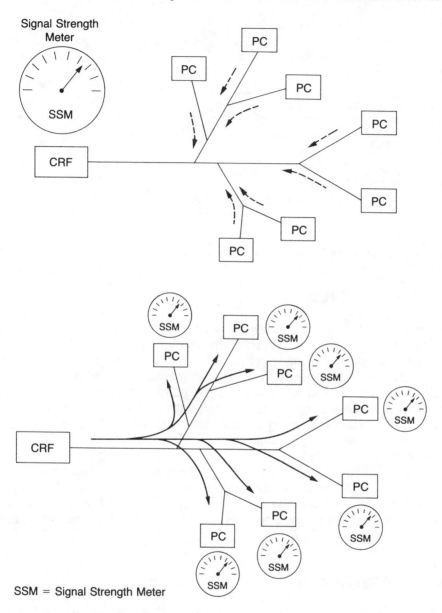

SSM = Signal Strength Meter

Figure 3-21 Signal strength on a balanced network

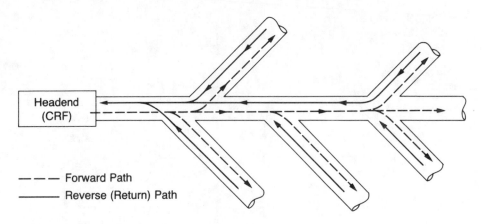

Figure 3-22 Forward versus reverse (return) path

THE HEADEND, OR CRF

Messages travel from sending nodes to the headend on what we call the *return* or *reverse* path, and travel from the headend to nodes on the *forward* path. Headends are the direct consequence of the directionality of signal flow (Fig. 3-22). Under proper provisions, a branching-tree network can have multiple headends to avoid a headend being a single point of failure.

Just as all network messages traveling on the return path converge on the headend, so does all network noise and signal distortion. You can reduce noise and distortion by using high-quality cables and amplifiers, which is particularly important in large networks.

However, using the best amplifiers often improves the signal quality by only 10 percent. So other methods have been designed to boost branching-tree LAN signals. These methods include electrical "scrubbing" of the signals of a group of nodes by a channel processor before they proceed to the headend. (See Section 5 for more details.)

CABLE CLASSIFICATION

The branching-tree topology uses cables hierarchically (Fig. 3-23). This hierarchy is similar to that of freeways, off-ramps, city streets, and driveways.

The cables that originate at the headend are called *trunks,* as are any cables that transport signals between amplifiers. Trunk cables are usually at least 0.5 inch in diameter and are clad in aluminum to provide electrical power to amplifiers farther from the headend. Trunks correspond to freeways in our analogy.

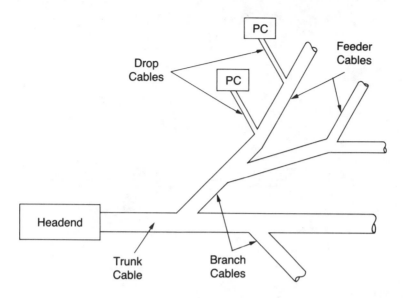

Figure 3-23 Hierarchy of cable sections in a broadband network

Branches extend from trunks to the vicinity of node outlets (like off-ramps). Trunk and branch cables together constitute the *network backbone*. Branches typically use 0.5-inch cable.

Feeder or distribution cables split from the branches and are typically less than 0.5 inch in diameter. Signals carried on feeder cables (city streets) usually require amplification for long distances, which vary with the network.

Drop cables (driveways) connect distribution cables to network outlets. Because they tend to be short, they can have a smaller diameter than trunk cables. However, they generally constitute the major percentage of network wiring. So they should be heavily shielded and of high quality to minimize interference.

SINGLE-CABLE AND DUAL-CABLE BRANCHING-TREE NETWORKS

In a branching-tree network, each direction of travel can occur on its own dedicated cables. Or signals can travel in both directions on the same cable (Fig. 3-24). If a single cable is used, the signal's frequency determines its direction of travel. The directional components force lower-frequency signals toward the headend and higher-frequency signals away from it.

A dual-cable network has a separate cable network for each direction. In such a network, the entire frequency spectrum of each cable can transmit

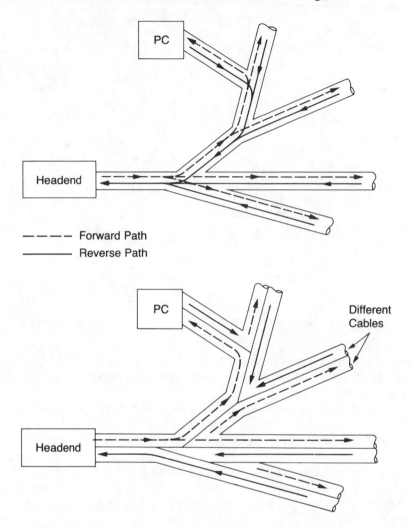

Figure 3-24 Single-cable versus dual-cable network

messages. Also, frequency signals may not require translation, only reampli-fication. However, there are twice as many network drops, provisions for adapter connectors, connectors, and cables as in the single-cable network. All of these must be attached to the correct network. And during installation, the directional components must be carefully placed in the proper direction (oriented) on not one but two networks.

Dual-cable networks are more expensive than single-cable systems. This is because of duplication of hardware, increased potential for installation errors, and the larger number of components.

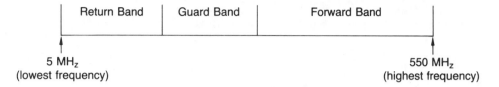

Figure 3-25 Division of frequencies on a single-cable broadband network

SINGLE-CABLE FREQUENCY BANDS

A single-cable network provides for bidirectional traffic by partitioning its cable's bandwidth into independent frequency ranges. As an analogy, consider how interstate highways are divided by medians into traffic directions (such as northbound and southbound), and into independent traffic lanes within the same travel direction. Note that one travel direction may have more lanes than the other and some lanes may be used for special traffic, such as trucks.

The partitioning on a network is done by dividing the bandwidth into three frequency ranges. The lowest frequency range is the return or reverse band, which transmits messages from the nodes to the headend in the return direction. The highest range is the forward band, which transmits messages from the headend to the nodes in the forward direction. The middle range is the guard band. It acts as a safety zone (a median strip) to separate signals on the return and forward bands. As Figure 3-25 illustrates, the return band has a narrower frequency range, hence fewer channels, than does the forward band.

The forward and reverse bands are then further subdivided into independent, 6-MHz transmission channels. Six MHz is the bandwidth of television signals.

Partitioning of the bandwidth in this manner, called *frequency division multiplexing,* allows a single cable to carry several simultaneous signals. Each signal maintains its individual identity by staying within its allotted frequency range (electronic "traffic lane") within its frequency band (direction of travel) as it travels on the cable.

STANDARD INDUSTRY FREQUENCY ARRANGEMENTS

Currently there are three standard ways of allocating frequency bands—*subsplit, midsplit,* and *high-split.* The placement of the guard band differentiates the three types; Table 3-3 summarizes them.

Cable TV (CATV) systems commonly are branching-tree networks. LANs that use these components can carry television as well as data signals. To do this requires the allocation of a 6-MHz channel within the medium's frequency range. So if a LAN has only 25 MHz of bandwidth on the return band, as in a subsplit

	Return Band Freq.	Guard Band Freq.	Forward Band Freq.	Number of Channel Pairs
Subsplit	5 MHz to 30 MHz	30 MHz to 54 MHz	54 MHz to 550 MHx	4
Midsplit	5 MHz to 116 MHz	116 MHz to 168 MHz	168 MHz to 550 MHz	17
Highsplit	5 MHz to 186 MHz	186 MHz to 222 MHz	222 MHz to 550 MHz	30

Table 3-3 Frequency Ranges for the Three Types of Broadband Standards.

system, only four television channels are possible before the return band is completely used.

Early CATV amplifiers could not handle frequencies above 200 MHz, so it made sense to limit the number of return bands to allow more CATV subscriber channels on the forward band. Over time, amplifier quality and range improved and the inequality of the frequency allocation between forward and returnbands grew commensurately. To rectify the situation, the guard band was moved up in frequency. Moving the guard band to a higher frequency makes more return channels possible.

However, the disparity between forward and return band frequency allocations was not nearly as severe in the past as it is now. The IEEE's effort to establish a high-split frequency standard reflects the continuing evolution of broadband networks.

SINGLE-CABLE FREQUENCY TRANSLATORS

Dual-cable networks do not require guard bands, because the entire bandwidth of each cable is completely available to transmitters. When the signals arrive at the headend, they only require amplification before redistribution, typically at the original frequency. This approach is not possible in single-cable networks, because single-cable systems must perform translation.

SINGLE-CABLE VERSUS DUAL-CABLE

Dual-cable networks provide the most bandwidth and potentially the cleanest signals, because every node can be balanced. If done automatically, however, balancing is very expensive. Yet errors can occur if it is done manually. With manual balancing, nodes that are moved must often be rebalanced, involving continuing maintenance costs and central coordination.

In the final analysis, both single-cable and dual-cable have advantages. However, most single-cable LANs use less than 33 percent of their total bandwidth. So the higher bandwidth of a dual-cable system is usually unnecessary. In addition, single-cable networks require substantially less network management. But they do require balancing during installation, and this can be tricky. Finally, single-cable systems have proven to be as much as twice as reliable as dual-cable systems, because single-cable networks have fewer components.

ACCESS METHODS

The LAN access method is how a node gains the right to transmit a signal on a network. Access control may be centralized or distributed. In either case, if access is granted when the node demands it, the LAN has a *demand access* method. The alternative is a controlled access method.

Because the nodes share a common broadcast channel, the network must coordinate accessing. This time-sharing of a single transmission channel by multiple nodes is called *time division multiplexing,* or TDMPX.

Access to the network

Star—nodes polled to see if they want access, or when it senses the network is free

Ring—node can transmit through central control, at a reserved time, at any time, or when it senses the network is free

Bus—nodes can be polled, sense when the network is free, or monitor the system to find out if it is free

---

Star Networks

In an active star network, the central controller periodically queries, or polls, the nodes to determine whether they have anything to transmit. With demand control, a node gains access by signaling the central node rather than by waiting to be polled. Circuit-switch networks, such as telephone switching systems, and networks of dumb terminals attached to minicomputers or mainframes, use demand control.

Ring Networks

A centrally controlled ring is usually called a *loop* (Fig. 3-26). Access is controlled by a *master node*. There are three popular approaches to distributed control:

- The slotted-ring, in which nodes can transmit messages only at specific, reserved time intervals
- The insertion-ring, in which nodes can transmit at any time but must be able to receive and store messages that arrive while a node is transmitting
- The token-ring, which allows a node to detect when it can transmit a message

In the slotted-ring approach, a selected number of fixed-length messages called *slots* continually circulate on the ring. The slots can be empty or full, respectively designating whether or not the slot is currently carrying data to the node on the ring.

When a node is waiting to transmit data and receives an empty slot, it marks the slot as full and places its data in the passing slot. The transmitting node is prohibited from transmitting another message until the slot returns.

When the slot eventually returns, it is marked empty by the node, allowing the slot to be subsequently used by another node or another message. The first node is then free to transmit another message when another empty slot arrives.

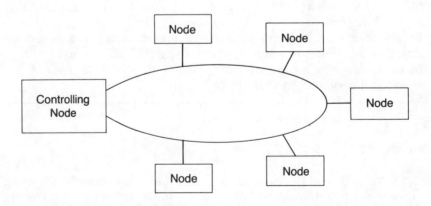

Figure 3-26 Loop network

In the insertion-ring, or register-insertion-ring, approach, each node has a storage area that can hold the largest permissible ring message. Nodes that are actively transmitting data can simultaneously accumulate an independently arriving message in the storage area. After transmission is completed, the accumulated message is then transmitted on the ring.

In the token-ring method, a node uses what is called token-passing to sense when the medium is idle. A circulating message, called a *token,* confirms to a node that the medium is available. If the node wants to transmit, it "grabs" the token, temporarily removing it from the network and gaining exclusive access to the medium.

When the node has finished, it restores the token signal to the network, which allows another node to "grab" the token and gain access. This method is like passing a microphone around during a question-and-answer period. One person takes the microphone, uses it for a while, and then puts it back in circulation. A ring topology naturally favors a token-passing scheme, because there is always a clearly defined "next" node.

One important advantage of token-passing is that it allows messages to be classified by importance. Higher-priority activities can thus gain access before those of lower priority. In addition, a token-ring makes it easy to calculate the maximum and minimum time normally required for a node to gain access. This allows heavily loaded networks to exhibit more predictable behavior during periods of heavy competition for media access.

BUS NETWORKS

Bus networks can use a variety of access methods:

- Central polling
- The token-passing bus access method, also known as token-bus
- A distributed control demand access method known as Carrier Sense Multiple Access with Collision Detect (CSMA/CD)

Central Polling

In this access mode, a master node controls the transmission of other nodes by periodically querying them and authorizing them to transmit as appropriate.

Token-Bus

A token-bus uses token-passing, as does the token-ring. In this case, the procedure is like a panel discussion, in which each person has a microphone.

As in a token-ring, each token-bus node must pass the token. Because there is no natural "next node," each must know where to pass it. This is usually achieved through memory tables in each node. These tables require some effort to maintain in dynamic networks that may undergo constant changes. Nodes such as portable equipment, test sets, or outside connections may come and go or move around.

With a bus topology, messages need not be regenerated by each node, though it needs more channel capacity for token-passing than does a token-ring. Token-buses are a trade-off between the predictability of a token passing access method and the decreased wiring costs of a bus topology.

CSMA/CD

One of the most popular ways to access a bus network is the demand distributed method called Carrier Sense Multiple Access with Collision Detect (CSMA/CD). Here all nodes monitor the network to see if it is idle (carrier sense). If so, any node can begin transmission (multiple access).

When two or more nodes transmit simultaneously, their messages collide and interfere with each other. This means the nodes must be able to detect the collision (collision detect) and wait for an appropriate interval, different for each node, before attempting to retransmit.

CSMA/CD is like a household telephone line with several extensions. A person lifts the receiver and learns if anyone is already using the phone (carrier sense). If the line is idle, anyone can use it (multiple access). If two people attempt to talk at the same time, however, they hear their messages collide (collision detect), and they must try again, one at a time.

The amount of time a node waits before retransmitting can vary widely, depending on the network's design. In general, CSMA/CD is well suited for the bursts of communication found in many distributed applications. However, under extremely heavy use, the network can theoretically become unstable, statistically "clogging" with collisions and retransmissions. You can compare it to a single telephone line with several active teenagers.

In practice, the fear of clogging, or electronic gridlock, is usually a bigger problem than clogging itself. Proper message pacing techniques reduce the probability of clogging to about the statistical probability of automobile gridlock in North Bend, Nebraska (pop. 1,361).

Network gridlock can be avoided in small networks by a CSMA variant known as Carrier Sense Multiple Access with Collision Avoidance (CSMA/CA). In this case, each node has a "reservation" that guarantees its right to transmit. If a node does not use its opportunity, others can sense this, and advance their "reservations" a corresponding amount of time.

Despite CSMA/CD's poor image in some data communication circles, it has become and will remain a popular access method. Partly because of its efficiency in many environments, IBM uses it in two of its LAN offerings.

Signaling techniques
Baseband—transmits one signal at a time, using entire medium
Broadband—transmits concurrent signals on the same medium

SIGNALING TECHNIQUES

There are two types of signaling techniques for a LAN—*baseband* and *broadband*.

Baseband Signaling

A baseband signal uses the entire cable, preventing simultaneous transmission of another signal. When used on twisted-pair and shielded twisted-pair wire and coaxial cable, the signal is typically provided as a varying voltage level. For example, ETHERNET networks use fluctuations between 0.0 volts and −1.2 volts to signal data transmission. There can be only one signal on the cable at a time since there can be only one voltage on the cable at a time.

Fiber-optic cables signal with light. Some techniques allow more than one pair of laser transmitters and receivers to exchange data simultaneously. But this medium can be considered baseband because of its connector and tapping problems.

With the exception of fiber optic lasers, baseband signaling techniques are usually limited to a maximum transmission rate of 100 million bits per second (100 Mb). The amplification of a baseband signal requires its complete reconstruction, which causes delays. TDMPX techniques are traditionally used in broadband networks because only one signal can be present at any given time.

The lone signal on the line must be receivable by all devices. This means that the network's transmission speed is determined by the slowest receiver. (Technically, a ring is an exception because it can have different speeds between nodes.) If the transmission speed of one device increases, the speed of all devices must usually increase, as well. This transition to the new speed can disrupt an entire network.

For example, suppose one node on a network can receive only 10 characters per second. Perhaps its user simply refuses to retire a beloved teletypewriter, is hesitant to buy new equipment, or can use only low-speed gear certified for industrial or military environments. Then the network can transmit only at 10 characters per second, even though everyone else can handle higher speeds. Otherwise, the low-speed user would not be able to receive any messages.

Finally, baseband techniques are extremely susceptible to noise and to an electrical phenomenon known as a *ground loop,* so baseband networks must be grounded very carefully. This can be complicated by local electrical codes.

Broadband Signaling

Broadband signaling allows multiple signals of different types to be present on the medium concurrently—data, voice, and video. It also allows the transmission of different signals at different speeds.

Broadband signaling divides the cable bandwidth into multiple frequency ranges called channels, each usually 6 MHz wide, and assigns each of their transmission signals to a channel within the medium's bandwidth. The presence of multiple channels on a single cable is what allows transmission of different signals concurrently, each potentially independent in function and use.

Each channel has a special signal called a *carrier.* A transmitting node varies the carrier's characteristics to send information. The variable characteristics are frequency (within the channel's frequency range), arrival pattern (phase), and signal strength (amplitude).

Modulation is the process of modifying the carrier to transmit data. *Demodulation* is translating the signals to receive data. All broadband nodes have modems that perform both functions. Some modems can switch frequencies on command from their node and are called *frequency agile* modems.

Broadband LANs are not required to follow the cable TV practice of dividing the frequency spectrum into 6-MHz channels. But many do, since it is less expensive to use existing CATV equipment.

Because the access to the medium is first controlled by frequency, broadband uses frequency division multiplexing (FDM). Once a signal is assigned to a channel, it can transfer data using token-bus access polling, CSMA/CD, or some other technique. Networks on different channels can also operate at different data rates, each in its own frequency channel.

Broadband networks are immune to ground loop problems. They are also largely immune to noise that could devastate a baseband network. This is because the frequency of such noise is well below the frequencies broadband networks use.

Coaxial Cable and Frequency Modulation Synergism

A modem can vary its carrier's amplitude or frequency. Amplitude modulation (AM) is more susceptible to noise interference than is frequency modulation (FM). AM and FM are the methods used for radio transmission, as well.

Thunderstorm-induced static on AM radio is evidence of its susceptibility to environmental noise. FM transmissions are relatively noise-immune.

Frequency modulation is also called frequency shift key modulation (FSK). Like AM, FSK is a general way of transmitting information that cannot be applied directly to the media as a baseband signal for a variety of reasons, including medium sharing. In FSK, the frequency of a carrier is varied precisely around a specific frequency called the *center frequency* in the channel's frequency spectrum.

Unlike AM, FSK has excellent immunity to distortion and external noise, which is why FM radio reception remains clear during a thunderstorm. Even if a signal is slightly distorted, its frequency remains intact and needs amplification at the headend only. So there is virtually no delay to repair most damage. In contrast, damaged baseband signals must be completely received and regenerated, potentially introducing substantial delay, or worse, complete loss of information. In this case, the message must be retransmitted.

In summary, the excellent immunity to noise of coaxial cable and the robust nature of FM can combine to give broadband systems superior transmission quality. As an added benefit, amplifiers for FSK networks are simpler to design than those for AM.

Signal-Encoding Techniques

After you select the modulation scheme, you must determine how to encode information on the channel. For example, you must have some way of distinguishing a transmission from a failed circuit. A technique called *Non Return to Zero (NRZ)* addresses this problem. It uses negative and positive voltages for actual signals. A zero voltage then indicates impaired transmission.

This still leaves transmitters and receivers with the problem of synchronization. How does the receiver know when the signal starts and ends? We need some kind of indicator, such as the starter's gun that marks the beginning of a race. Furthermore, we may need to resynchronize to avoid drift.

In baseband signaling, a popular way of avoiding drift is called *Manchester encoding*. The transmission of each data bit contains subtle voltage shifts, which the receiver detects. This allows the nodes to stay synchronized. Even if the signal is slightly impaired, the receiver can often deduce the data. It does this in much the same way that military radio operators can understand garbled messages if the senders use distinct sounds, such as "alpha," "bravo," and "charlie," rather than just words or letters.

The PC Network uses a third type of encoding called *Non Return to Zero Inverted (NRZI)*. In this technique, the transmitter detects zero bits. When a zero bit is transmitted, the signal meanings for binary one and binary zero are reversed. This new interpretation of the bit signals continues until another zero is detected, when the meanings of the data signals revert to their original values.

Long transmissions of binary zero bits result in a constantly flip-flopping synchronized signal that the receiver deciphers correctly, assisted by the many signal changes caused by the flip-flopping.

LAYERED ARCHITECTURE

Operating a LAN requires a significant amount of software. Because of this, several groups have formed to try to standardize LAN protocols, or procedures for transferring information. Such standards allow interchange of devices within LANs, giving establishments a greater return on their investments.

The ISO OSI Layered Model

The International Standards Organization (ISO) has divided the task of moving data reliably from one communication node to another into seven separate functions, or layers. These layers comprise the ISO Open Systems Interconnection (OSI) architecture (Table 3-4).

A message originates at the top (or application) layer and descends within the node to the bottom (or physical) layer. There it is sent onto the medium and finally removed at the bottom layer of the receiving node. The message then rises like a bubble to the top layer of the receiving node, where an application finally accepts it. You may compare this approach to sending mail through a hierarchy of local, city, state, national, and international services. Each level has its own rules, access methods, and protocols.

Layer	Function
Application	Provides the user a function
Presentation	Performs character translation, encryption, message compression, and so on
Session	Determines the rules of dialogue (message exchange)
Transport	Performs a uniform end-to-end transmission service independent of the network
Network	Routes, assembles, and disassembles messages into and from data packets
Data Link	Sends, receives, and frames data packets, provides error-free adjacent channel
Physical	Sends and receives encoded signals

Table 3-4 The ISO Open System Interconnection seven-layer model.

Each layer of the transmitting node attaches routing information, similar to the routing information attached to an outgoing letter or package, to the message as it descends. The corresponding layer in the receiving node interprets and removes this information. Such capability allows exchange of data with high integrity for long periods, in what are known as *communication sessions*. They provide end-to-end connections using virtual circuits, which create the illusion of point-to-point connections. Obviously, this is how telephone networks work, as well.

Having such capability is expensive. If your node does not have a powerful microprocessor such as an INTEL 80286 or INTEL 80386, it may be to your advantage to select a LAN that minimizes the impact procedures have on the nodes. One way is to dedicate a second processor to communication activities, like having a dedicated shipping department within an organization. The communications coprocessor would perform its duties independent of the main node's coprocessor.

As a final note, the computational power required to implement existing layered protocols is forcing many people to revisit their "heavyweight" designs. Often, it is discovered that the protocols are optimized for slow-transmission, high error rate environments. Because LANS typically provide high-transmissions rates with few errors, use of existing layered protocols is somewhat questionable, especially within high-performance networks such as FDDI. Thus, new protocols generally referred to as "lightweight" protocols are emerging that may be more suitable to high-performance LAN environments. Examples of lightweight protocols include the French Government's GAM-T-103 and Protocol Engine Inc.'s Express Transfer Protocol (XTP).

IEEE 802 Standards Groups

Three committees of the Institute of Electrical and Electronics Engineers, Inc. (IEEE) have published standards:

- IEEE 802.2—Logical Link Control
- IEEE 802.3—CSMA/CD
- IEEE 802.4—Token-Passing Bus
- IEEE 802.5—Token-Ring

The standards are available from: Secretary, IEEE Standards Board, 345 E. 47th Street, New York, NY 10017, USA.

Chapter 4

An Introduction to IBM's LAN Offerings

IBM currently markets four LAN systems:

- The IBM Token-Ring
- The IBM PC Network Broadband
- The IBM PC Network Baseband
- The IBM Industrial LAN

The IBM Industrial LAN is a 10-megabit broadband token-bus LAN. Its adapters are manufactured for IBM by Ungermann-Bass, a wholly owned subsidiary of Tandem Computers of Santa Clara, California. The IBM Industrial LAN is mentioned here only for completeness and will not be discussed further.

Each of the remaining three LAN systems contains a variety of workstation adapters. Each LAN's features, designs, supporting components, and significant strengths are discussed in the next three sections.

PC AND PS/2 SYSTEM CONNECTIVITY

Via the IBM LAN Support Program, IBM Token-Ring, PC Network Broadband, and PC Network Baseband adapters present similar industry standard application programming interfaces. This allows applications to run virtually unchanged on all adapters.

Using the IBM Token-Ring/PC Network Interconnect Program, PC Network NetBIOS applications can communicate with NetBIOS applications on Token-Rings. Independent Token-Ring Networks interconnect using the IBM Token-Ring Bridge Program to create even larger enterprise networks.

Because of its strategic importance and high system connectivity with the other two IBM LANs and IBM central processors, it is appropriate to focus on the flexibility of the IBM Token-Ring within the IBM product line.

THE IBM TOKEN-RING CONNECTIVITY OVERVIEW

The IBM Token Ring can attach to the following IBM processors:

- The IBM PC and PS/2 family with the exception of the PC Junior and the IBM PC Convertible
- The IBM System 370 family, operating under both VM and MVS control, via channel-attached IBM 3725, 3745, 3174, and the remarkable, little-known IBM 8232 control units

- The IBM 9370 family via integrated Token-Ring adapters or a channel-attached IBM 8232 control unit
- The IBM System/36 family via integrated adapters
- The IBM System/38 family via integrated adapters
- The IBM PC/RT family via integrated adapters

PC and PS/2 application packages available from IBM provide a variety of terminal emulators, network server, and distributed application support. By adhering to programming interfaces such NetBIOS and IBM's APPC/PC, custom applications can communicate peer to peer with mainframe hosts and exploit both their processing speed and multigigabyte storage devices. This is possible because IBM's OS/2 Extended Edition preserves these LAN programming interfaces.

From a wiring perspective, central processor connectivity can use standard IBM Cabling System wiring facilities which have been designed to preserve your establishment installation investment. A complete discussion of these connectivity possibilities is well beyond the scope of this book (and you probably would not be able to lift such a book to buy it anyway), so the remainder of this book focuses on PC and PS/2 LAN essential offering topics. Master this material and you likely have half of the IBM LAN communication learning curve behind you, putting you well ahead of the pack.

In conclusion, while IBM LAN systems provide PC and PS/2 workstations a significant opportunity to function in isolation to centralized service, the spectrum of IBM components available for those central computing facilities provides a strong likelihood that they can support satellite PC and PS/2 as the occasion arises.

Section 3
IBM Token-Ring Hardware

Chapter 5

IBM Token-Ring

THE IBM TOKEN-RING AND THE IBM CABLING SYSTEM

Announced October 15, 1985, the IBM Token-Ring uses a subset of wiring and connection components from the IBM Cabling System announced by IBM in May 1984. In some instances a Token-Ring can use telephone wiring for node drop cables. While a complete discussion of the IBM Cabling System is beyond the scope and subject of this book, the various types of IBM Cabling System cables used in IBM Token-Rings are summarized in Appendix L.

TOKEN-RING OVERVIEW

The IBM Token-Ring is IBM's strategic LAN for data communication. It operates on cables containing two sets of twisted pair. Network connections typically use a special IBM Cabling System plug called a *data connector*.

The IBM Cabling System data connector is hermaphroditic; two data connectors can connect with themselves (see Fig. 5-1). In addition, the data connector is self-shorting. Shorted data connectors are said to be *wrapped*. This allows unused data connectors to automatically reroute inbound signals back to the network, bypassing unused or inoperative connections. Data connectors have a 15-year life design that includes 1,000 insertions and removals.

The IBM Token-Ring provides a 4-megabit instantaneous transmission data rate using a token-passing access method within a logical ring topology. The physical topology is a star-wired topology because IBM Token-Rings require nodes to attach to concentrators called IBM 8228 Multistation Access Units.

Token-Ring Wiring Considerations

Nodes attach to 8228 concentrators with drop cables called *lobes*. Lobe cables can be IBM Cabling System cables such as Type 3 media telephone wiring. Workstation adapters connect to work-area data connectors using 6-foot adapter cables. The lobes then stretch from the work-area data connectors to 8228 concentrators located in establishment wiring closets. (For planning purposes, stand-alone 8228 concentrators are considered wiring closets.)

For convenience, lobe cables may be organized within wiring closets by connecting them to industry-standard patch panels, called *distribution panels*.

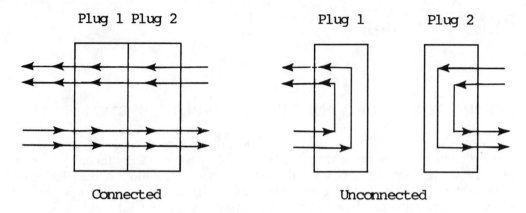

Figure 5-1 The IBM data connector self-shorting capability

Distribution panels typically provide 64 connections that each intervene between one lobe wiring-closet data connector and its 8228 concentrator connection.

Both a lobe's distribution panel and 8228 concentrator are typically mounted in industry-standard racks (Fig. 5-2). The racks have optional strain reliefs that help a lobe's cable weight from interfering with connecting the lobe's data connectors to the rear of the distribution panel. Racks can hold multiple distribution panels and 8228 concentrators. A lobe's 8228 concentrator is usually mounted in the same rack as the lobe's distribution panel. Cables of various lengths, called *patch cables,* complete the lobe connections by connecting front distribution panel connectors to 8228 concentrators.

8228 concentrators within the same or different wiring closets connect with each other to create a larger Token-Ring network. These interwiring closet connections must use IBM Cabling System cable which includes patch cables. Where possible, however, connections between 8228 concentrators located in different wiring closets should use permanently installed IBM Cabling System cables (versus patch cables), for maximum-size networks. Even so, interwiring closet connections may require repeaters to boost signal strength.

Though it is permissible to use patch panels to connect wiring closets in small networks, telephone twisted pairs are never allowed to connect 8228 concentrators in the same or different wiring closets. Consult the IBM Token-Ring Introduction and Planning Guide for restrictions on patch cable networks.

Maximum Number of Nodes

A variety of considerations determines the number of nodes a Token-Ring can support. These include:

- The type of lobe cable used (data grade or telephone twisted pair)

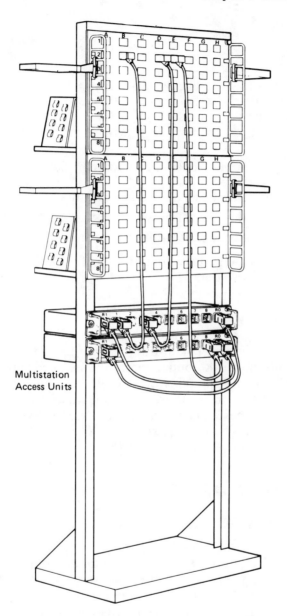

Figure 5-2 Distribution panel with IBM 8228 MAUs installed (Diagram courtesy of International Business Machines Corporation)

Type of Cable Used	Maximum Network Nodes	Maximum Network 8228s
Permanently Installed IBM Cabling System Cables	260	33
IBM Cabling System Patch Cables	96	12
Telephone Twisted Pair	72	9

Table 5-1 Maximum Network Nodes as a Function of Cabling Type.

- The number of network 8228 concentrators
- The length of the longest network path
- The number of repeaters in the network

Table 5-1 has a summary, and the IBM Token-Ring Introduction and Planning Guide has more detail.

Token-Ring Bridging

Finally, two or more Token-Ring networks can join to form a larger network. Each internetwork connection requires a dedicated Token-Ring node running the IBM Token-Ring Network Bridge Program. If more than one path exists from one network to another, the connections must insure that copies of special network messages, called *limited-broadcast messages,* appear only once on any single network. The IBM Token-Ring Network Bridge Program provides this support and is discussed in Chapter 15.

IBM TOKEN-RING ADAPTERS

IBM provides five different Token-Ring adapters for PC and PS/2 work-stations. They are:

- The IBM Token-Ring Network Adapter connects members of the original PC family as well as the PS/2 Models 25 and 30. This adapter has 8K of on-board memory for network activities.
- The IBM Token-Ring Network Adapter II connects members of the original PC family as well as the PS/2 Models 25 and 30. This adapter has higher performance than the IBM Token-Ring Network Adapter and is recommended as the adapter of choice for the IBM Token-Ring Network Bridge Program. The higher performance comes from an additional 8K (for a total of 16K) of memory for network activities, which permit the

adapter to transmit larger network packets (which is more efficient for the adapter).

- The IBM Token-Ring Network Adapter/A connects members of the PS/2 family with the exception of the Models 25 and 30. This adapter has 16K of on-board memory for network activities.

- The IBM Token-Ring Network Trace and Performance Adapter II connects members of the original PC family as well as the PS/2 Models 25 and 30. This adapter can operate with the IBM Token-Ring Network Trace and Performance Program as well as function as a normal network adapter.

- The IBM Token-Ring Network Trace and Performance Adapter/A connects members of the PS/2 family with the exception of the Models 25 and 30. This adapter can operate with the IBM Token-Ring Network Trace and Performance Program as well as function as a normal network adapter.

Adapters other than the IBM Token-Ring Network Trace and Performance Adapter II and the IBM Token-Ring Network Trace and Performance Adapter/A have an empty socket for an Initial Remote Program Load (RPL) feature that allows medialess workstations to boot from network RPL servers.

Token-Ring adapters that connect to Type 3 media lobes require a special adapter cable. This special cable has a built-in filter housed in a 9-pin connector at the workstation end and a 6-pin standard modular telephone jack at the lobe end. The cable's filtering helps keep signal radiation levels from the twisted pair within FCC regulation specifications. This cable is not available from IBM but can be purchased from independent media vendors.

THE IBM 8228 MULTISTATION ACCESS UNIT CONCENTRATOR

IBM Token-Ring network workstations require IBM 8228 Multistation Access Unit concentrators to connect to network. Because 8228 concentrators can be sensitive to shocks and excessive vibration, they should be installed in racks with distribution panels or in permanently wall-mounted Component Housings. They do not require a power source.

An 8228 concentrator provides eight receptacles, each of which allows one workstation attachment. In addition, there are two receptacles labeled RI and RO, respectively (see Fig. 5-3).

The RI receptacle on the left side of the 8228 front is the Ring In receptacle; the RO receptacle on the right side of the 8228 front is the Ring Out receptacle. Under normal operation, the RI receptacle receives inbound signals and the RO receptacle passes the signals to the next downstream 8288.

Both the RI and RO receptacles arrive covered by dust covers which should

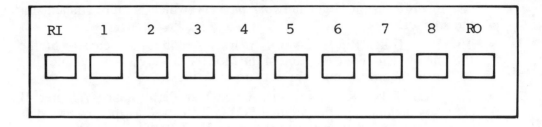

Figure 5-3 The front of an IBM 8228 Multistation access unit

remain intact until a cable is installed. The RI and RO receptacles should be used only to connect 8228 concentrators to one another, as illustrated in Figures 5-4 and 5-5. Additionally, 8228-to-8228 connections must use the RI and RO receptacles and not the lobe receptacles.

If no cable is present in an RO receptacle, arriving signals wrap onto the alternate ring and continue to travel on it until they encounter a wrapped RI receptacle. At that point, the signals wrap onto the main ring, as illustrated in Figure 5-6. This allows a single 8228 to operate without a cable between its RI and RO receptacle.

RING LENGTHS

The Main Ring Path Length

The cables that connect a ring's 8228 concentrators and wiring closets comprise a ring's *main ring path*. While the main ring path cabling contains two twisted pair, only one pair, variously referred to as the the *forward, primary,* or *main* ring or path, is normally used to transmit data. The other pair, variously referred to as the *alternate* or *backup* ring or path, is used in error situations or during diagnostic procedures.

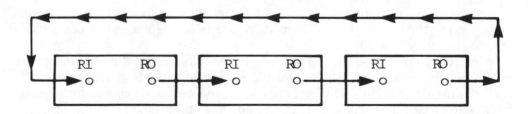

Figure 5-4 Horizontally connecting 8228 concentrators

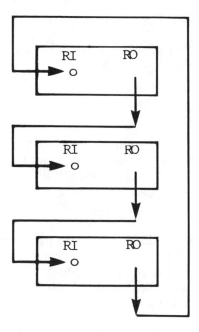

Figure 5-5 Connecting vertical 8228 concentrators

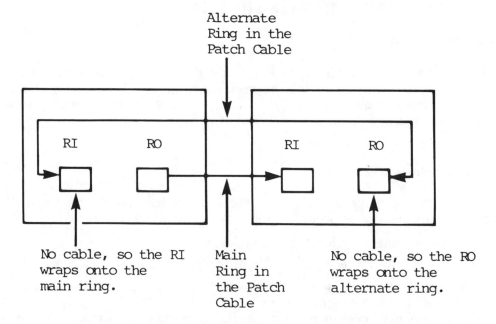

Figure 5-6 How RI and RO wrapping preserves ring operation

The Adjusted Ring Length

A ring's adjusted ring length is the main ring path length minus the length of the shortest cable in the main ring path.

The Active Path Length

A ring's *active length* is the length of the main ring path plus twice the length of each attached (active) lobe. Lobe length doubling is required because data flows to nodes and back to the node concentrators as it traverses the ring. A primary difference between a lobe and the main ring path is that the main ring path needs only one twisted pair to transport data, while a lobe requires two twisted pair.

Lobes dynamically attach and detach from rings, varying the ring's active path length. This changes the distance signals travel before they are regenerated by another adapter. Network designers must plan networks that not only accommodate these changes but continue to operate with the worst-case (longest) path lengths that may occur during normal operation and error situations.

WORST-CASE SIGNAL STRENGTH SCENARIOS

Normal Operation

The worst-case signal strength scenario during normal operation occurs when the node on the longest lobe begins transmitting to itself on a ring that has no other attached (active) nodes. The signals must traverse the entire ring active path unassisted by other adapters (Fig. 5-7).

Error Situations

The worst-case error-situation signal strength scenario occurs when the node on the longest lobe begins transmitting to itself on a ring that:

- has no other attached (active) nodes, and
- whose shortest main path cable has failed

In this situation, the node's signals must traverse the adjusted ring length twice as well as the lobe length twice (see Fig. 5-8).

Networks need designs that tolerate this type of failure scenario. Surviva-

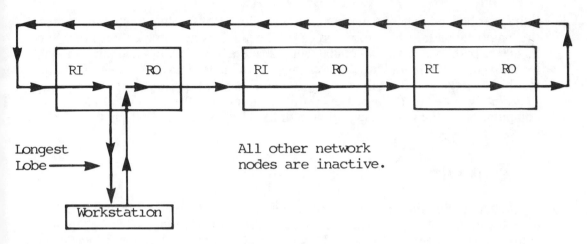

Longest
Lobe —→

All other network
nodes are inactive.

Workstation

Figure 5-7 Worst-case signal strength during normal operation

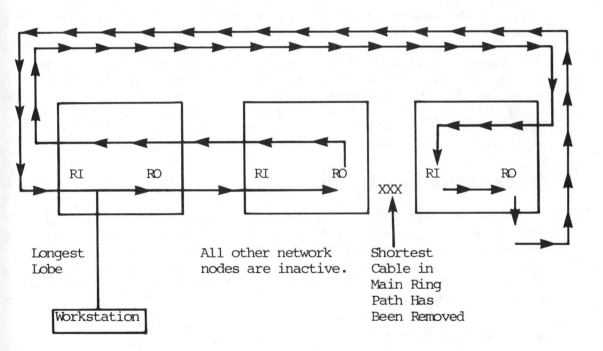

Longest
Lobe

All other network
nodes are inactive.

XXX

Shortest
Cable in
Main Ring
Path Has
Been Removed

Workstation

Figure 5-8 Worst-case signal strength during error situation

bility is enhanced by using permanently installed IBM Cabling System cables on the main ring path instead of patch cables because using patch cables limits the main ring path to a maximum of 400 feet (120 meters) and allows a maximum lobe length of only 150 feet (45m). This means patch cable rings are either small and reliable or large and unusable during network problem periods.

Finally, note that the presence of repeaters (see the following) alters the computation of the main-ring path length for worst-case signal strength calculations.

ATTACHMENT

When a workstation powers off or its lobe is disconnected from its 8228's receptacle, a special insertion circuit in the workstation's 8228 receptacle automatically closes and wraps. This disconnects the workstation's lobe from the ring so data signals completely bypass the entire lobe. If all workstations attached to an 8228 are powered off, the ring signals pass directly through the concentrator.

When a workstation powers on, the Token-Ring adapter-open sends a special mild voltage "phantom" data signal to the 8228 receptacle. After a short period, an internal special insertion circuit opens in the lobe's 8228 receptacle, causing a quiet click as the receptacle reinserts the lobe into the ring.

This process is called *attachment* and requires the special insertion circuits to be in an operational state before it can function properly. Note that the RI and RO receptacles do not have these special insertion circuits, so workstations cannot operate if they are connected to them.

Finally, having the workstation supply the power to open the special insertion circuit allows 8228s to avoid supplying their own power. This allows networks to have 8228 concentrators in areas without convenient power outlets.

8228 RECEPTACLE WARNING

The RI and RO receptacles do not have special insertion circuits. Thus, workstations cannot attach to an 8228 using these receptacles. Moreover, any patch cable or main ring path cable that connects to an RI or RO receptacle must connect to another ring RO and RI receptacle and provide an operational circuit. If it does not provide an operational circuit, the ring fails because the RI and RO receptacles cannot self-wrap if a connector is inserted in the receptacle.

THE IBM 8228 SETUP AID

Shocks and vibrations, such as those encountered in shipping, can leave 8228 concentrator receptacle special insertion circuits in unusable states. In this situation, the special insertion circuits must be set back to an operational state before they can be used. This is done using a small hand-held device called the IBM 8228 Setup Aid.

The IBM 8228 Setup Aid is used to prepare 8228 concentrators for operation after an 8228 concentrator is installed but before cables are connected to it. The Setup Aid resets receptacle special insertion circuits with a gentle battery current. You insert it in each 8228 receptacle and leave it in for 4 seconds after its small indicator light shuts off. The Setup Aid should not be used in 8228 concentrators that are active on a network.

THE IBM 8218 COPPER AND 8219 OPTICAL FIBER REPEATERS

IBM 8218 Copper and 8219 Optical Fiber Repeaters are IBM Token-Ring devices that receive and amplify Token-Ring signals on data-grade and optical cable respectively (Fig. 5-9).

IBM 8218 Copper Repeater

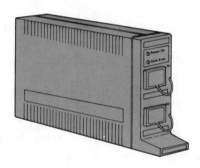

IBM 8219 Optical Fiber Repeater

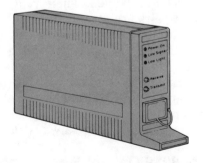

Figure 5-9 The IBM 8218 copper and 8219 optical fiber repeaters (Diagrams courtesy of International Business Machines Corporation)

The 8218 Copper Repeater transmits a maximum distance of 2,460 feet (750 meters), and the 8219 transmits a maximum distance of 1.24 miles (2.0 kilometers). Because these units regenerate received signals, any section of the ring located between any two repeaters is considered an independent ring for worst-case planning scenarios.

Because these units are similar in design and size, they can be mounted in the same IBM Cabling System IBM Rack Mounting Assembly and use the same type IBM Cabling System Surface Mounting Bracket to attach to surfaces such as walls.

Using an IBM Cabling System Surface Mounting Bracket to mount an IBM 8218 Copper or 8219 Optical Fiber Repeater to a surface requires the repeater be plugged into a nearby power source. Alternately, mounting the unit in an IBM Rack Mounting Assembly allows the IBM Rack Mounting Assembly to provide power to multiple repeaters.

Warning: Do not power off an IBM Rack Mounting Assembly during problem determination or network maintenance activities. Your network will stop.

Finally, each 8218 and 8219 is packaged with a test connector that tests whether the unit is operating correctly. If not, a low-signal indicator light on the front of the repeater illuminates.

The IBM 8218 Copper Repeater

Like all amplifiers, IBM 8218 Copper Repeaters amplify signals in only one direction. This means they must be installed in pairs so rings can use the alternate ring to continue operation in the event of network problems or network maintenance procedures. One repeater amplifies the main ring while the other amplifies the normally idle alternate ring.

This requires careful cabling because 8218 Copper Repeaters are identical and there is no switch to select which ring's signals (main ring path or alternate ring) it should amplify. The solution requires two IBM Cabling System Yellow Cross-Over Patch cables. Their yellow color indicates the main and alternate ring twisted pairs are switched inside the cable. Even with the visual warning, these cables must be precisely installed.

Each IBM 8218 Copper Repeater has a Ring In and Ring Out port labeled "RI" and "RO" respectively. These are analogous to the RI and RO ports on 8228 concentrators. Figure 5-10 illustrates how to properly cable a pair of repeaters, and Figure 5-11 illustrates why the wiring arrangement works. Yellow cross-over patch cables connecting the RO ports of repeater pairs are 8 feet long, so copper repeater pairs are always close to each other and usually side by side.

The IBM 8219 Optical Fiber Repeater

Like IBM 8218 Copper Repeaters, IBM 8219 Optical Fiber Repeaters operate as pairs. However, unlike their copper counterparts, IBM 8219 Optical

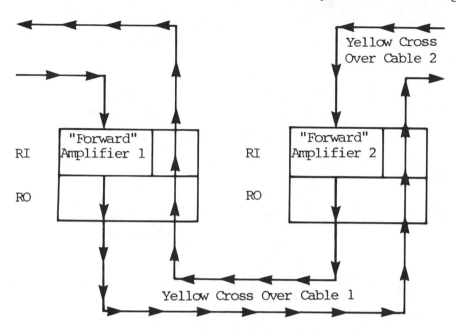

Figure 5-10 Wiring two IBM 8218 copper repeaters

Fiber Repeaters are installed on opposite sides of an optical fiber cable—up to 2 kilometers apart—and each unit handles both the main and alternate rings.

The IBM Token-Ring Network Installation Guide has more detail on the design, installation, and accessories of the IBM 8219 Optical Fiber Repeater.

USING TELEPHONE TWISTED PAIR FOR LOBES

In some instances, IBM Token-Rings can use existing building telephone twisted pair wiring. The wiring must conform to IBM Cabling System Type 3 Media Specifications and, if used, it can be used only for lobe cables; using Type 3 media on the main ring path is not supported.

Moreover, if any one lobe uses telephone twisted pair (voice-grade) lobes, all ring lobes must use it; IBM does not support mixing data-grade and voice-grade lobes on the same ring. The only exception to this rule is for the IBM 3725 and 3745, which require a Data-Grade Media-to-Type 3 Media Filter for ring attachment.

Finally, if lobes are bundled with voice-application twisted pairs, the lobes and voice circuits must be separated before routing the voice circuits to telephone switching equipment and the lobes to their distribution panels or concentrators. Devices called Type 66 connecting blocks facilitate this separation and are discussed in the PC Network Baseband material in Section 5.

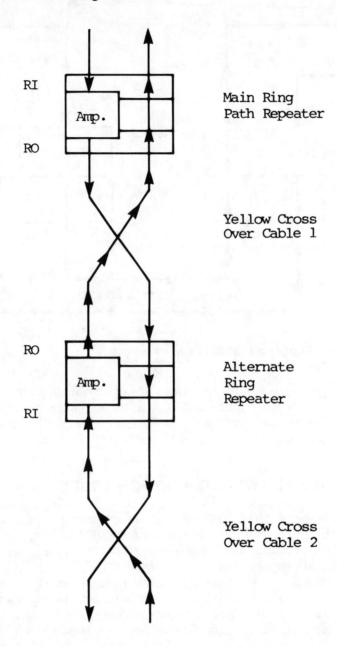

RI

Main Ring
Path Repeater

Amp.

RO

Yellow Cross
Over Cable 1

RO

Alternate
Ring
Repeater

Amp.

RI

Yellow Cross
Over Cable 2

Figure 5-11 Another view of wiring two IBM 8218 copper repeaters

The Data-Grade Media-to-Type 3 Media Filter Cable

The Data-Grade Media-to-Type 3 Media Filter Cable consists of a cable terminated by two IBM Cabling System data connectors that contain low-pass filtering components. The cable's filtering helps keep signal radiation levels from the twisted pair within FCC regulation specifications.

The cable is white with a green stripe at one end. The cable is always oriented so the end without the stripe connects to the 8228 concentrator. This cable is not available from IBM but can be purchased from independent media vendors.

In addition to 3725 and 3745 connection applications, the Data-Grade Media-to-Type 3 Media Filter is required to support lobe connections to the main ring path for rings that use lobe voice-grade media.

Length Restrictions

Maximum lobe lengths in rings that use voice-grade lobe cables are less than in rings that use data-grade lobe cables because signals attenuate three times faster on voice-grade media than on data-grade media. Moreover, unshielded voice-grade media is more susceptible to external interference than shielded data-grade media.

Unlike IBM Cabling System cables, telephone twisted pair cables terminate in work areas with standard 6- or 8-pin modular plugs. This requires a special adapter cable that has a built-in filter housed in a 9-pin connector at the workstation end and a 6-pin standard modular telephone jack at the lobe end.

Configuration Considerations

Rings that use voice-grade lobes and do not use repeaters must:

- use one wiring closet with all lobes shorter than 330 feet (100 meters) or
- use two wiring closets that are within 390 feet (120 meters) of each other

Otherwise, repeaters must be used to strengthen signal strength. The number of repeaters a ring requires depends on the number of network wiring closets and the distance between them. The IBM Token-Ring Network Telephone Twisted-Pair Media Guide has the details.

CONCLUSION

The IBM Token-Ring is IBM's strategic Local Area Network. It provides unrivaled connectivity within the IBM product line and is well documented by numerous IBM publications. These publications are listed in the bibliography and are available from your IBM representative.

Section 4

PC Network Broadband Hardware

Chapter 6

The PC Network Broadband LAN and the PC

Announced August 14, 1984, the PC Network Broadband is a LAN for IBM personal computers that operates on single-cable broadband cable within two 6-MHz channels. As a peer-to-peer network, it does not require centralized control. The PC Network Broadband transmits data at an instantaneous transmission rate of 2 million bits per second, using the internationally adopted IEEE 802.3 CSMA/CD standard as its access method.

As in all broadband networks, PC Network Broadband nodes transmit signals on one channel, called the *reverse* or *return path*. These signals travel to a central control point, called the *headend*. There, a frequency translator electronically cleans the signals, amplifies them, and rebroadcasts them to all network nodes on a second, higher-frequency channel, called the *forward channel*. Like all broadband networks, the PC Network Broadband is balanced. That is, the received signal strength is within the same strength range, regardless of the network distance between the transmitter and the receiver.

There are three families of PC Network Adapters, and they are distinguished from one another by the frequency pairs they use. Though adapters from the three families can coexist on the same broadband network, network bridges are required for adapters in one family to communicate with adapters in another family. If bridges are used on a midsplit broadband network, up to 3,000 nodes can be connected to the network.

Low-cost components are available in kit form to facilitate installation of small networks. However, designing a custom network that can be properly balanced after installation and withstand inevitable expansion requires experience (see Section 7).

PC NETWORK BROADBAND ADVANTAGES

The PC Network Broadband offers all the general advantages of broadband networks:

- **Long useful life.** Using the same durable and reliable components as in cable TV systems, the PC Network Broadband is extremely cost-competitive and can be expected to have a long useful life.

- **Ease of installation.** Broadband network cable is easily installed and expanded by semiskilled labor, using inexpensive, widely available components.

- **Isolation.** The natural isolation resulting from a broadband network's branching-tree topology makes it easy to find and repair problems, while the remainder of the network continues or resumes productive work.

- **Versatility.** Custom cabling and translators allow the PC Network Broadband to coexist on the same cable with voice, video, and other services.

- **Immunity from environmental interference.** PC Network Broadband combines a robust frequency modulation signaling technique with coaxial cable's exceptional immunity. It is insensitive to external interference found in hostile environments. In addition, its CSMA/CD access method is well suited to the bursty communication patterns found in many environments.

- **Layered architecture.** The PC Network Broadband uses and enjoys all the advantages of an open and well-documented layered architecture. This allows the PC to do productive work, while the adapter handles many of the communications functions.

WHAT DEVICES DOES THE PC NETWORK BROADBAND SUPPORT?

With the exception of the PC Jr and PC Convertible, the PC Network Broadband supports the PS/2 and the entire IBM personal computer family. This limitation may seem to contradict the requirement for a LAN to support a variety of devices, but the limitation is only superficial. The PC's open and well-documented architecture allows attachment of cards from a variety of vendors, expanding the availability of devices on the network.

For example, given the proper adapters and programming, the PC can appear to be virtually any desired communications device with the proper hardware and software. This allows a single PC to connect to different systems, assuming different "personalities" to do so:

- Asynchronous terminals, such as ASCII terminals or an IBM 3101 terminal in any of its many models

- Bisynchronous devices, such as a remote job entry workstation

- A 3270 terminal, a 3276/8 terminal attached to a 3270 controller, or a 3276 SNA/SDLC terminal

Apart from communications, the PC can support a wide variety of data storage devices, such as optical disks, diskettes, and fixed disk drives. It can gather information from light pens, bar-code scanners, digitizing pads, touch screens, keypads, and infrared data devices. In addition, the PC can present information on displays ranging from inexpensive black-and-white monitors to high-resolution multicolor units.

Chapter 7

The PC Network Broadband Adapters

OVERVIEW

There are three families of PC Network Adapters. Table 7-1 summarizes them and Figure 7-1 illustrates them.

The first family has a frequency offset of 168.25 and the other two have frequency offsets of 192.25, which allows them to coexist with MAP broadband networks as well as operate in both midsplit and high-split networks.

IBM PC Network Broadband adapters are the heart of the PC Network. Each workstation must contain one to communicate on a network. The adapter identifies the PC by name to other network nodes, reports its status, sends and receives data, and executes diagnostic routines when the PC is rebooted. Depending on the adapter, it can relieve the PC of much of the network communications processing.

The PC communicates with the adapter card and, hence, the network either through a NetBIOS (Network BIOS) ROM located on the adapter or through support provided by the IBM LAN Support Program or the PC Network Protocol Driver. These adapter support procedures are the fundamental mechanism for control of the adapter. Their implementation allows programmers to write applications without worrying about the precise mechanics of network protocols.

INSTALLING THE ADAPTER

For a PC Network Broadband using the IBM PC Network Broadband cabling system, the adapter is attached to one tap of an eight-way splitter. This splitter must be part of a distance kit (described in detail in Chapter 8) or the connection hardware that comes with each IBM PC Network Broadband Translator Unit. An adapter cannot be directly attached to a base expander.

To facilitate network connection, each adapter is packaged with a flexible 3-meter RG-59 coaxial attachment cable. This cable attaches directly to the adapter and either directly to the eight-way splitter or to an RG-11 coaxial cable that, in turn, is attached to the splitter. The RG-11 cable can be up to 200 feet long and cannot be composed of more than three cables joined together, because each connection erodes the strength of passing signals.

WHAT THE ADAPTER DOES

A PC Network Broadband adapter transmits and receives data on two fixed-frequency ranges. These frequencies cannot be varied; the adapter is not

Adapter	Supported Workstation Family	Reverse Path Frequency	Forward Path Frequency	Split Type
PC Network Adapter	PC	47.75 MHz	216 Mhz	
PC Network Adapter II	PC	to	to	Mid-split
PC Network Adapter II/A	PS/2	53.75 MHz	222 MHz	
(Frequency 2)		53.75 MHz	246 Mhz	Mid-split and
PC Network Adapter II	PC	to	to	
PC Network Adapter II/A	PS/2	59.75 MHz	252 MHz	High-split
(Frequency 3)		59.75 MHz	252 Mhz	Mid-split and
PC Network Adapter II	PC	to	to	
PC Network Adapter II/A	PS/2	65.75 MHz	258 MHz	High-split

Table 7-1 The Three Families of PC Network Broadband Adapters.

frequency-agile. The adapter unit must be connected to an operating PC Network to pass its power-on diagnostic tests. Unlike adapters for other networks, a PC Network Broadband adapter cannot be used in isolation for diagnostic testing.

NetBIOS

NetBIOS is an application programming interface that first appeared with the original PC Network adapter (LANA card) manufactured for IBM by Sytek, Inc., of Mountain View, California. It provides applications access to network services and status information such as transmission error counts.

The LANA card provides NetBIOS services with an adapter ROM. All other IBM LAN adapters require the IBM LAN Support Program to provide a NetBIOS application programming interface. NetBIOS is described in greater detail in Chapter 15.

Protocol ROM

The protocol ROM provides LANA cards with the programmed protocols they use in their network communication activities. PC Network Adapter II and

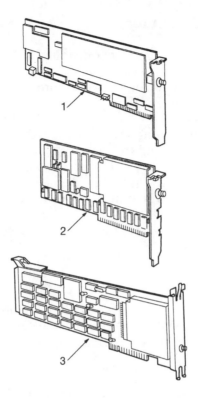

Figure 7-1 The IBM PC network hardware adapters. (*1*) PC network LANA adapter (*2*) PC network II adapter (*3*) PC network II/A adapter. (Drawing courtesy of International Business Machines Corporation)

II/A adapters must use the PC Network protocol Driver Program in lieu of the IBM LAN Support Program if they need to use these protocols.

ATTACHING PCs TO THE PC NETWORK BROADBAND

A PC Network Broadband adapter card or a PC Network Broadband II adapter card inserted into a non-PS/2 workstation links the workstation to a broadband PC Network. However, for a PC Network Broadband adapter card to communicate with a PC Network Broadband II adapter (and vice versa), both nodes must use the same type adapter software. That is, either the node with the PC Network Broadband II adapter must use the IBM PC Network Protocol Driver program or both nodes must run the IBM LAN Support Program.

As the installation instructions for a specific model of PC accompany each adapter, we will not repeat them here but will only mention items that may be overlooked.

The IBM Personal Computer

A standard PC can accommodate only one PC Network Broadband adapter card. It must go in the main (system) unit, not in an expansion unit. Some PCs need modifications to handle the network card. The PC Network Broadband does not operate with early BIOS ROMs.

The original ROMs lacked what we call the "optional BIOS consideration." This is necessary for supporting the IBM PC Network Broadband Adapter, as well as the XT's fixed disk, and the IBM Extended Graphic Adapter and other adapter cards. (This dependency is discussed in detail in Appendix D.)

Fortunately, the remedy for this deficiency is simple. First, run the following BASIC program, which displays your PC's date of manufacture:

```
10 DEFINT V:DEF SEG=&HFFFF
20 FOR V=5 TO 15
30 PRINT CHR$(PEEK(V));
40 NEXT
```

Then, if your PC was manufactured before October 27, 1982, you must buy an upgraded ROM module kit from your IBM dealer or IBM representative. Call for details and prices. Or if you prefer, take the system unit to a dealer for upgrading.

PC XT and PC AT

An IBM PC XT or PC AT can house two adapters in its system unit. An adapter cannot be installed in a PC XT's expansion unit.

If two adapters are installed on a single PC XT or PC AT, each appears as a separate node on a PC Network. Moreover, each of the adapters can be connected to a different network, if required. This allows a single PC XT or PC AT to communicate with nodes on two independent networks. This is how two networks can be "bridged."

Finally, any PC XT with a fixed disk and 320 KB memory or an enhanced PC AT can function as a PC Local Area Network Program file or print server.

Portable PC

Like the IBM Personal Computer, a standard configuration IBM Portable PC can use one PC Network Broadband adapter. It must go in the first of the two long expansion slots. You may have to move the Color Graphics Monitor Adapter from slot 1 into slot 2.

ATTACHING PS/2s TO THE PC NETWORK BROADBAND

With the exception of the PS/2 models 25 and 30, all PS/2 models connect to a PC Network broadband network using a PC Network II/A adapter. PS/2 Models 25 and 30 use the same adapters as the PC family.

Chapter 8

The Frequency Translator

WHAT IS A FREQUENCY TRANSLATOR?

PC Network Broadband nodes cannot directly receive each other's signals. Transmitted signals must first travel on a return (reverse) path to a central location. There they are filtered, amplified, and retransmitted at a higher frequency by a frequency translator on the forward path for receipt by all network nodes. This chapter discusses the anatomy of a frequency translator and its use in passive networks.

Frequency translation does not affect the signal's content. It is like changing the key or octave in which a tune is being played. The amount a signal's frequency changes is called its *frequency offset*.

The equipment that converts the signal frequency is the frequency translator unit or translator, for short. Another name for it is the headend, an ambiguous term that sometimes refers to the actual central location of the frequency translator.

THE PC NETWORK BROADBAND TRANSLATOR UNIT

The PC Network Broadband Translator Unit is a low-cost, data-only frequency translator for a passive midsplit broadband network dedicated for use as a PC Network (Fig. 8-1). The nodes must use a return frequency of 47.75 MHz to 53.75 MHz and a forward frequency of 216 Mhz to 222 MHz. (Frequency 2 and 3 PC Network broadband networks must use custom translators.)

A "passive network" means no signal amplifiers other than the one in the frequency translator are allowed on the network. In this situation, the PC Network Broadband can have a maximum radius of 1,000 feet, with 256 nodes or less.

Because this LAN is dedicated to the PC Network, it does not support coexisting television or other signal transmission. In some instances, a PC Network Broadband Translator Unit functions on an active broadband network. But IBM neither recommends nor supports this application. It should be considered only as a last-resort emergency attempt to make a network operational.

The PC Network Broadband Translator Unit is accompanied by a power transformer and several other necessary components. The unit, which is 6 by 3 by 2 inches, should be located near a reliable power outlet and at the "center" of the physical network.

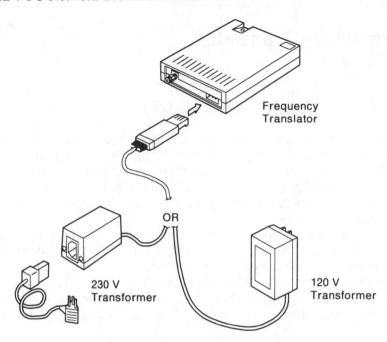

Figure 8-1 The PC network broadband translator unit (Drawing courtesy of International Business Machines Corporation)

THE PC NETWORK BROADBAND TRANSFORMER

The translator gets its electrical power from the PC Network Broadband Transformer. A transformer is included with every translator but boxed separately. The transformer's built-in cord plugs into a regular 60-Hz, 120-volt electrical wall outlet (50 Hz and 230 volts elsewhere). If you are using the 50-Hz, 230-volt power supply, you need a separate PC power cord to provide connection to the wall outlet.

NOTE: The transformer is the translator's only power source. It should always be connected to a highly reliable power outlet and insulated from power surges and voltage spikes. This type of outlet is typically found in computer machine rooms. If you do not have a special room for computers, plug the transformer into an outlet far from those used for equipment that uses power intermittently, such as compressors.

THE FREQUENCY TRANSLATOR CONNECTION HARDWARE

Several other PC Network Broadband components, collectively called the *frequency translator connection hardware,* allow the translator to be attached to up to eight PC Network Broadband nodes within a radius of 200 feet (Fig. 8-2).

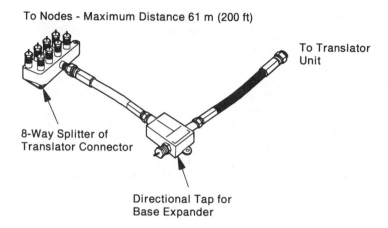

To Nodes - Maximum Distance 61 m (200 ft)

To Translator
Unit

8-Way Splitter of
Translator Connector

Directional Tap for
Base Expander

Figure 8-2 The PC network frequency translator connection hardware (Drawing courtesy of International Business Machines Corporation)

The translator connection hardware, which is preassembled and boxed with the translator unit, consists of an expansion tap with an attached terminator, two cables, a directional coupler, and an eight-way splitter with attached terminators.

Terminators

A terminator prevents network problems by discarding unwanted signals traveling on a forward path, converting their strength to gentle heat. Terminators perform three important functions. It is their job to:

- minimize the emission (signal egress) of network transmissions from unused connector taps
- prevent the creation of potentially disruptive signal reflections within the network through unused network taps
- prevent unwanted signals from entering a network (signal ingress)

A terminator should be attached to any unused network tap. So be sure to save spare terminators for future use.

Eight-Way Splitters

A splitter receives a signal traveling on the forward path (from the headend) and divides it into multiple signals of equal strength. These normally continue traveling on the forward path by separate cables, although terminators on the eight-way splitter may discard some of them.

A splitter also receives multiple signals traveling on the reverse path (toward the headend), combines them into a single signal, and passes it forward to the headend. The directionality of a broadband network mandates that a reverse path signal arriving on one of a splitter's cables cannot leak onto another cable also carrying signals to the headend.

An eight-way splitter produces eight signals from a single signal traveling on the forward path. Or it combines up to eight signals traveling on the reverse path. Note that if two signals are transmitted on the same channel at the same time, they eventually combine and are detected as a collision. However, if the signals are on different channels, collisions on the return path do not occur.

The eight-way splitter provided in the translator hardware permits connection to the translator of eight PC Network Broadband nodes, located up to 200 feet away.

Directional Couplers

A directional coupler links a smaller network branch to a larger one, in a way that produces a directional flow of signals.

The signal that emerges from the IBM PC Network Broadband Translator Unit travels on the forward path of the network's trunk cable. The directional coupler, located at the opposite end of the cable from the translator, connects the trunk cable to the 1-foot cable. The coupler takes the signal strength supplied by the translator and diverts a small, fixed amount of it to the 1-foot cable. The diverted portion is now at the correct strength for the eight-way splitter. The remaining signal passes through the directional coupler to its expansion tap where it may be consumed by a terminator or passed onto a base expander (see Chapter 9).

Conversely, when a node attached to the cable's eight-way splitter transmits a signal, the directional coupler routes it from the 1-foot cable to the trunk cable. In addition, the directional coupler prevents the signal from reaching its expansion tap.

The directional coupler has three connectors, one for each cable and one for use with the optional base expander that is initially terminated. These connectors must be oriented correctly to produce the desired signal directivity. Otherwise, the directional coupler prevents signals from passing through it, because it is improperly oriented.

TRANSLATORS FOR LARGER NETWORKS

The PC Network Broadband Translator Unit can be replaced with a commercial translator, which when combined with custom cabling can create a network of 1,000 nodes within a 30-square-mile area. Such a LAN can provide a multitude of network services, in addition to the PC Network Broadband. Thus, any network constraints introduced by IBM's low-cost translator unit are not permanent or insurmountable. Also, note that commercial translators are required for Frequency 2 and 3 PC Networks.

Chapter 9

The IBM PC Network Broadband Cabling Components

This chapter will help you gain an understanding of the cable kits available for small PC Networks—their advantages and disadvantages.

NETWORK BALANCING CONSIDERATION

Like all broadband networks, the PC Network operates as a balanced network. That is, the received signal strength is within a specified range, regardless of how far apart a transmitter and receiver are. However, achieving this is a bit tricky, since a broadband network must be balanced in both the forward and reverse directions. As we discuss in Section 7, signal strength loss depends on network cable characteristics. But it also depends on the forward and reverse signals' frequencies, the temperature of the cable, and the number of taps. Add the fact that signals travel varying distances, and the problem can easily (and usually does) become too difficult for a neophyte network designer. In the final analysis, the design of a large network requires special expertise.

But what about small networks? Are they also hard to configure? The answer: no. Partially assembled IBM Cabling Components are available for various sizes of PC Networks. They provide conveniently matched components for an entry-level network installation.

Keep in mind that while these components are adequate for small networks, they are not mandatory. Any PC Network, even a small one, can use custom cabling.

WHAT ARE THE CABLING COMPONENTS?

The IBM PC Network Broadband Cabling Components are a low-cost way to provide reliable cabling for small PC Networks (72 nodes or less). The following components are available:

- The PC Network Broadband Translator Unit connection hardware, which is discussed in Chapter 8
- IBM Coaxial Cable, which is available in premeasured lengths of 25, 50, 100, and 200 feet, with connectors already attached at both ends
- The Base Expander, which allows the attachment of up to eight distance kits to the network
- The Short Distance Kit, which allows the attachment of up to eight PC Network nodes, each located as far as 200 feet from the translator

- The Medium Distance Kit, which allows the attachment of up to eight PC Network nodes, each located as far as 600 feet from the translator
- The Long Distance Kit, which allows the attachment of up to eight PC Network nodes, each located as far as 1,000 feet from the translator

COMPONENT ADVANTAGES

The IBM PC Network Broadband Cabling Components provide an expedient way to install a PC Network Broadband, without concern for the complexities of network balancing. You can think of them as premeasured ingredients for a variety of network "cabling recipes."

With them, you can easily install a network of as many as 72 nodes within a radius of up to 1,000 feet from the translator. Because the cables are of specific length, they can be mass manufactured and sold at low cost. In addition, they can be pretested for high reliability. For example, the cables are manufactured and sold with connectors already attached.

IBM COAXIAL CABLE

IBM Coaxial Cable is the standard 75-ohm cable used for television. IBM uses three of the many varieties in its cabling components:

- RG-59—the 3-meter attachment cable packaged with each PC Network Broadband adapter
- RG-6—the cables packaged with each IBM PC Network Broadband Translator's connection hardware components
- RG-11—the beige cables used as drop and distribution cables. They have standard connectors attached during manufacturing, and come in 25, 50, 100, and 200-foot lengths (Fig. 9-1)

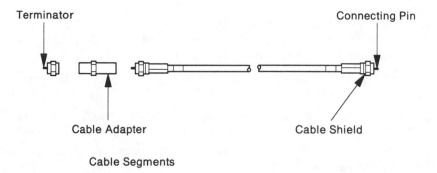

Figure 9-1 IBM coaxial cable (Drawings courtesy of International Business Machines Corporation)

These cables are all high quality, premeasured, preassembled, and pretested. They should never be cut, trimmed, or punctured. If you have excess cable, coil it in a ceiling or other convenient location.

In addition, since quality deteriorates each time a signal passes through a cable connector, never use more than three cables to connect an adapter's RG-59 cable and its eight-way splitter tap. For instance, you can construct a 200-foot cable from a single 200-foot section, or from two 100-foot sections, or from two 50-foot sections and a 100-foot section, but not by connecting eight 25-foot sections together! The specific rule is, "Never use more than seven cable sections between a PC Network Broadband adapter and the PC Network Broadband Translator Unit."

A WORD ON CABLE INSTALLATION

It is always a good idea to test a cable before installing it in an inaccessible area, such as a ceiling or wall. Simply lay it out on the floor, connect it to a PC and a translator, and see if the PC can operate as a network node when it is powered up. This testing can usually be performed without unrolling the cables. In addition, be sure to label a cable's ends for identification during subsequent repair or maintenance. Tags and labeling instructions are included with each IBM PC Network Broadband Translator Unit. Finally, be sure to keep a log of each cable's length, routing, and end-point locations for future reference.

WHAT IS A BASE EXPANDER?

A Base Expander is an eight-way splitter attached to the directional coupler packaged with every PC Network Broadband Translator Unit (Fig. 9-2). Unlike the eight-way splitter supplied in the connection hardware, you cannot attach a PC Network Broadband node directly to a Base Expander. The expander exists

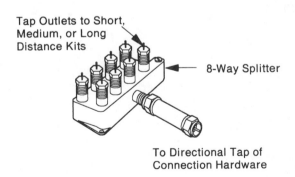

Figure 9-2 The PC network base expander (Drawing courtesy of International Business Machines Corporation)

only to provide connection taps for up to eight Short, Medium, or Long Distance Kits that connect to its taps in any combination.

For installation, first remove the terminator from the directional coupler expansion tap and then replace it with the Base Expander. Keep the terminator for future installation on unused Base Expander taps.

WHAT ARE THE IBM DISTANCE KITS?

The IBM Short, Medium, and Long Distance Kits provide a means of attaching more than the eight nodes available with the Translator Unit hardware. Each type of distance kit consists of an eight-way splitter, to which the network nodes attach their drop cables, and other components, called *attenuators,* that compensate for variations in network signal strength. These variations are due to the different distances between the nodes and the translator and to signal strength loss (attenuation) that can occur as the signal travels down the cable. The unit of signal strength is the decibel (dB).

Depending on the specific distance kit used, the nodes may be up to 1,000 feet from the headend. Since the connection hardware allows nodes to be up to only a maximum of 200 feet from the translator, you must use a distance kit for any node beyond this distance.

Each type of kit allows attachment to its eight-way splitter of up to eight nodes that can be located any distance up to 200 feet from the distance kit. A distance kit is attached to a PC Network by a coaxial cable. This cable, in turn, is attached to a Base Expander tap at the other end.

Since a Base Expander has eight taps, a maximum of 72 nodes can be attached to the network using only Cabling Components (that is, eight nodes on the connection hardware and eight nodes on each of the eight distance kits).

The Short Distance Kit

Short Distance Kits connect to a Base Expander tap using a 1-foot RG-6 coaxial cable (Fig. 9-3).

Because the nodes may actually be only a few feet from the translator, their signals must be significantly "throttled down" to avoid overpowering the translator's receiver. This is done with a strong 20-decibel attenuator.

The Medium Distance Kit

Medium Distance Kits attach to a Base Expander tap using a 400-foot RG-11 coaxial cable (Fig. 9-4). The 400-foot connection can consist of a combination of

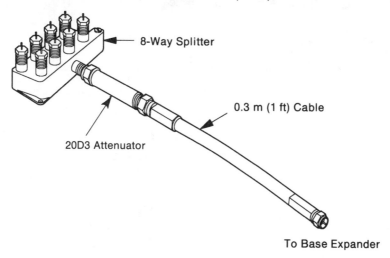

To Nodes - Maximum Distance 61 m (200 ft)

8-Way Splitter

0.3 m (1 ft) Cable

20D3 Attenuator

To Base Expander

Figure 9-3 The PC network short distance kit (Drawing courtesy of International Business Machines Corporation)

three RG-11 coaxial cables. However, since signal quality deteriorates each time a signal passes through a connector, as few cables as possible should be connected. Preferably, you should use two 200-foot cables. In any event, the final cable should be exactly 400 feet long.

Because the nodes may be up to 600 feet from the translator, their signals must be "throttled down" somewhat to avoid overpowering the translator's receiver. This is done with an 8-decibel attenuator. To compensate for the uneven signal loss from unequal forward and return frequencies, a 10-decibel tilt attenuator is also included with a Medium Distance Kit. The tilt attenuator throttles down the different send and receive frequencies by a calibrated amount to compensate for their uneven attenuation on the cable.

The Long Distance Kit

Long Distance Kits attach to a Base Expander tap using an 800-foot RG-11 coaxial cable connection (Fig. 9-5). The 800-foot connection should consist of a combination of four 200-foot RG-11 coaxial cables. However, since signal quality deteriorates each time a signal passes through a connector, preferably you should use four 200-foot cables. In any event, the final cable should be exactly 800 feet long.

Because the nodes may be up to 1,000 feet from the translator, their signals do not have to be "throttled down" to avoid overpowering the translator's

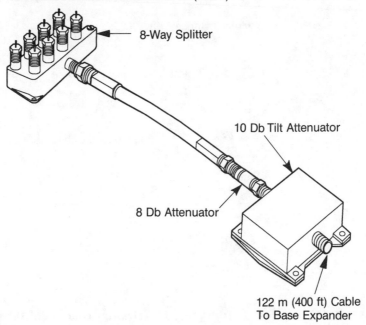

Figure 9-4 The PC network medium distance kit (Drawing courtesy of International Business Machines Corporation)

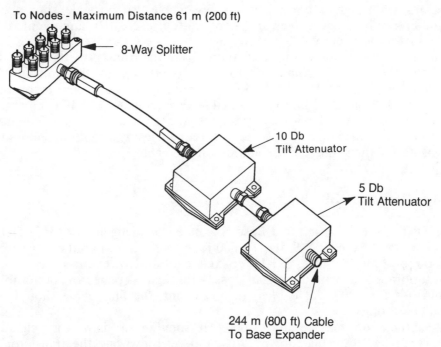

Figure 9-5 The PC network long distance kit (Drawing courtesy of International Business Machines Corporation)

receiver. So a Long Distance Kit has no attenuator. However, two tilt attenuators—one 10-decibel and one 5-decibel—are required to compensate for the significant uneven signal loss that occurs on the 800-foot cable due to the equal frequencies between the forward and return paths.

Further discussion in Section 7 shows how to expand the utility of cable kit networks by integrating several installed cable kit networks, and easily extending a cable kit's radius to 2,000 feet.

You can then use cable kits as an entry-level network facility, while still allowing for later growth and new interconnection requirements.

Section 5

IBM PC Network
Baseband
Hardware

Chapter 10

The IBM PC Network Baseband and the PC

Announced April 4, 1987, the Baseband IBM PC Network is a LAN for IBM personal computers that operates on data-grade wiring containing two sets of twisted pairs (four wires). There are two IBM PC network baseband adapters—they are illustrated in Figure 10-1. Network connections can use either IBM Cabling System Type 3 cables with industry-standard telephone jacks or IBM Cabling System PC Network Baseband Cables if IBM Cabling System wiring is used. See Figure 10-2 for an example of an appropriate IBM PC Network baseband telephone jack connector.

Small networks of IBM PC Network Baseband workstations can use a serial daisy-chain connection approach. To create a larger hybrid-star network, an IBM PC Network Baseband Extender can interconnect these smaller networks, possibly by using existing telephone wiring.

As a peer-to-peer network, a baseband IBM PC Network does not require centralized control. The PC Network Baseband transmits data at an instantaneous transmission rate of 2 million bits per second, using the internationally adopted IEEE 802.3 CSMA/CD standard as its access method.

The IBM PC Network Baseband Adapter family has two members. They are the PC Network Baseband Adapter and the PC Network Baseband Adapter II/A. The PC Network Baseband Adapter supports the original IBM PC family models as well as the PS/2 models 25 and 30. The PC Network Baseband Adapter II/A supports the remaining PS/2 family models.

The PC Network Baseband Adapter and the PC Network Baseband Adapter II/A are virtually identical to the IBM PC Network Broadband Adapter II and the IBM PC Network Broadband Adapter II/A, respectively. They differ only in the modem used to transmit and receive network signals. Hence these adapters share many of the same installation and design features of their broadband adapter counterparts.

IBM PC NETWORK BASEBAND ATTACHMENT STRATEGIES

The Wrap and Terminator Plugs

Each PC Network Baseband Adapter and Adapter II/A has two industry-standard telephone connector–type ports on its rear face plate. When a card is manufactured, each port is plugged using one of two special plugs. One plug is manufactured using clear plastic and has the letter "T" engraved on it. The other plug is manufactured using black plastic and has the letter "W" engraved in it; see Figure 10–3 for details.

The clear plug with the letter "T" is a Terminator Plug and the black plug

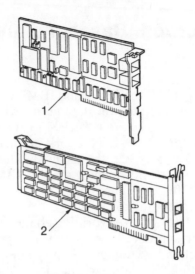

Figure 10-1 The IBM PC network baseband adapters. (*1*) PC network baseband adapter (*2*) PC network baseband/A adapter (Drawings courtesy of International Business Machines Corporation.)

with the letter "W" is a Wrap Plug. They serve radically different purposes. Warning: Confusing the two types of plugs is a virtual guarantee of major network problems.

Removing the two plugs allows a PC Network Baseband adapter to attach to a network. It does this by connecting to two other adapters that are each logically located to one side of the attaching node, as illustrated in Figure 10-4.

Figure 10-2 IBM PC network baseband telephone jack connector (Photograph courtesy of Brand Rex.)

Figure 10-3 PC network baseband wrap and terminator plugs (Courtesy of Virginia Plastics Company.)

Which port is used to connect to an adjacent node is unimportant; either will do because the ports function identically. But do not lose the plugs as they may be needed in the future.

Also, note the connection wiring must have data-grade quality with correct electrical impedance, attenuation, and crosstalk characteristics, such as:

- IBM Cabling System Type 3 cables or
- the 25-foot IBM PC Network Baseband Adapter Cable (sometimes referred to as the IBM baseband PC Network telephone twisted pair cable)

This restriction eliminates many inexpensive cables sold as telephone extension cords (which often have correct connectors but wiring that does not meet PC Network Baseband media requirements).

Appendix G lists data-grade wiring vendors. An IBM representative can

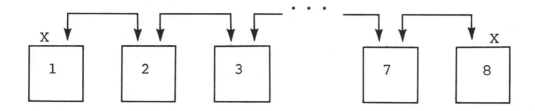

Figure 10-4 PC Network Baseband Daisy Chaining with probable hazardous behavior because of missing (X) wrap and terminator plugs.

provide the names of other suppliers offering cables meeting IBM Cabling System Type 3 specifications.

Serial Daisy Chaining

An IBM-suggested maximum of eight nodes can be networked using the daisy-chain approach described previously. However, two nodes remain that are each logically at an "end" of the network. In Figure 10-4, these workstation adapters are numbered 1 and 8. Each of these adapters connects only to one other network adapter—numbered 2 and 7 respectively. This leaves one empty port in each of adapters 1 and 8. Because of this, the network wiring is seriously incomplete and virtually guarantees failure.

To allow the network to function properly, one of the open ports must be plugged with a wrap plug and the other must be plugged with a terminator plug, as illustrated in Figure 10-5. It does not matter which port is plugged with what plug, but it is essential that only one of each type plug be used.

Warning: Incorrectly installing wrap and terminator plugs virtually guarantees memorable network problems.

Wiring Explanations

A baseband PC Network requires wrap and terminator plugs to complete the network wiring because it uses two sets of twisted pair wires in different ways. It

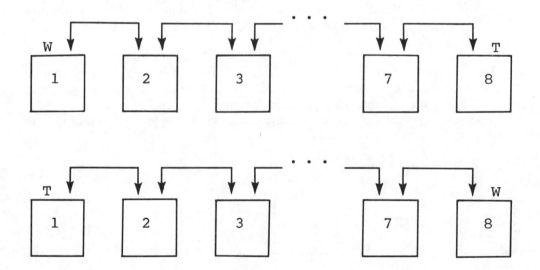

Figure 10-5 PC Network Baseband Daisy Chains that are correctly configured with wrap (W) and terminator (T) plugs

uses one pair (the black wire and the orange wire in IBM Cabling System wiring) to transmit data. It uses the other pair (the red wire and the green wire in IBM Cabling System wiring) to receive data.

The wrap plug connects the data-transmit pair to the data-receive pair, forming a single bus from the two independent sets of twisted pair wires. This connection allows transmitted data on the transmit-wire pair to eventually appear on the receive-wire pair. See Figure 10-6.

However, transmitted data flows bidirectionally on the media—both to-wards and away from the wrap plug connection. This means signal reflections may occur on the data-transmit pair if the bus is not terminated at the network end point not having the wrap plug (point B in the illustration).

Similarly, signal reflections may occur on the data-receive pair if the bus is not terminated at the network end point not having the wrap plug (point B in the illustration). Installing the terminator plug prevents both potential reflections by absorbing the network signals at the bus end points.

Daisy Chain Distance Restrictions

Looking at Figure 10-6, note that the adapter with the network terminator plug is in a unique situation. This adapter transmits data that travels the daisy chain's entire length. There it encounters the wrap plug and begins its return trip on the receive-data wire pair. The data travels the entire length of the daisy chain again and eventually arrives at the originating adapter, which receives the message, checks for collisions, etc. as the arriving signal disappears into the terminator plug.

Most baseband networks, including the IBM Token-Ring and IBM PC Network Baseband, use voltage fluctuations to encode data. These signals naturally attenuate as they travel along media. However, unlike IBM Token-Ring adapters that each rebuild, hence reamplify, data signals before passing them onto the next workstation, PC Network Baseband adapters attenuate data signals as they pass through because PC Network Baseband adapters consume signal strength during data reception. Thus, the maximum span of a daisy-chained baseband IBM PC Network is a function of both the number of adapters in the network and the length of the wiring.

IBM suggests the restrictions in Table 10-1 for daisy-chained configurations: Two points are clear:

- A workstation adapter attenuates the signal about as much as 25 feet of cable. So if, say, ten workstations are close together, it is possible they might all operate a single daisy chain if the wiring is, say, less than 150 feet; the only way to know is to try and monitor the results with the diagnostic programs provided with the IBM PC Network Hardware Maintenance and Service Manual.

- Recalling the wrap and terminator plug discussion, the table indicates that a signal can travel at least 600 feet (two 300-foot trips) if there are two nodes in the network. This observation will come in handy shortly.

The PC Network Baseband Extender

Some PC Network Baseband networks need to span more than 300 feet or contain many more than eight nodes. To address these networks, IBM provides the PC Network Baseband Extender (Figure 10-7).

This device allows a maximum of ten daisy chains to connect to it, each connecting to an extender port that is labeled "IN." Because each daisy chain can have a suggested maximum length of 300 feet or eight attached workstations, it follows that the PC Network Baseband Extender can support up to 80 workstations within a suggested maximum 600-foot radius circle.

Using the PC Network Baseband Extender

PC Network Baseband daisy chains connect to a PC Network Baseband Extender IN port at one end of the daisy chain. The adapter at the other end of each attaching daisy chain must have a clear terminator plug in one of its ports.

Warning: Forgetting to install a daisy chain's required terminator or inadvertently installing a wrap plug in its place virtually guarantees significant network problems.

Clearly, the PC Network Baseband Extender must somehow provide the same function to each daisy chain as a wrap plug. A PC Network Baseband Extender does this by receiving data from its daisy chains, retiming the data in 32-bit buffers, and rebroadcasting the data to each daisy chain. However, it does not check for network collisions; that work is left to the adapters.

Number of Network Nodes	Maximum Cable Length
2	300 ft. (91.4 m)
3	275 ft. (83.8 m)
4	250 ft. (76.0 m)
5	225 ft. (68.5 m)
6	225 ft. (68.5 m)
7	200 ft. (61.0 m)
8	200 ft. (61.0 m)

Table 10-1 IBM-recommended PC Network Baseband maximum distances, assuming data-grade wiring.

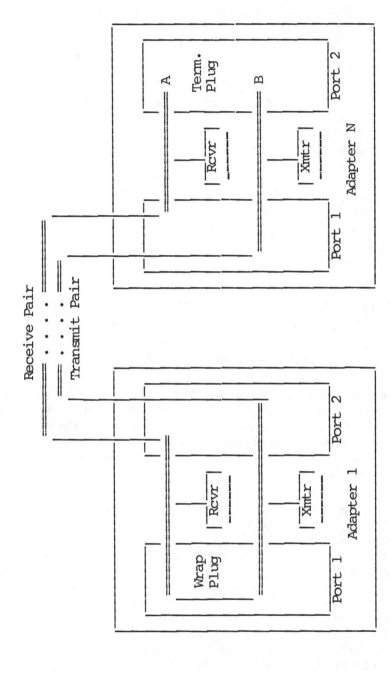

Figure 10-6 The wrap plug connects the two twisted pairs, creating a single bus. The terminator plug eliminates signal reflections at both bus ends.

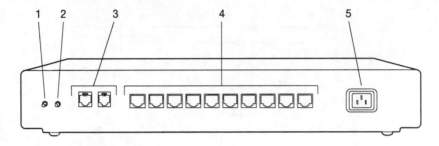

1. Test Button
2. Dual LED (red or green)
3. **OUT** Ports (can be used interchangeably)
4. **IN** Ports
5. Power Cord Connector

Figure 10-7 The IBM PC network baseband extender (Drawing courtesy of International Business Machines Corporation.)

The PC Network Baseband Extender OUT Ports

In addition to ten IN ports that connect PC Network Baseband daisy chains, the PC Network Baseband Extender has two other ports labeled "OUT". These ports are plugged with a terminator and wrap plug respectively. The PC Network Hardware and Maintenance Manual explains the purpose of these extender plugs in the General Information PC Network Baseband section. The material discussing the wrap plug reads:

The wrap plug is also used in an OUT port of the highest level of extender in the network.
Note: In any network configuration there must be only one black wrap plug installed.

The possibility of "levels of extenders" in a network is solidified with material from the PC Network Baseband Extender Technical Reference Manual, which provides the information in Table 10-2 regarding Packet Propagation Delay due to an extender's 32-bit buffer retiming activities.

Since the manual indicates retiming is done for upstream and downstream

Number of Retimings	Delay (Microseconds)
1	16
2	32
3	48
4	64
5	80
6	96

Table 10-2 PC Network Baseband propagation delays due to extender retimings.

(inbound and outbound) data, having an extender in a network packet's path results in a 32-microsecond delay.

Three points are now important to note:

- The broadband IBM PC Network LANA card has a 100-microsecond transmission delay tolerance.
- With appropriate software, the broadband IBM PC Network Adapter II operates on a PC Network interchangeably with broadband IBM PC Network LANA cards.
- The broadband IBM PC Network Adapter II and IBM PC Network Baseband Adapter use the same mother card design.

It follows that an IBM PC Network Baseband Adapter also has a 100-microsecond delay tolerance.

Extending Baseband PC Networks

The preceding discussion establishes the following observations:

1. Only one wrap plug is allowed in any baseband PC Network.
2. If an extender is used, the wrap plug must be used in an extender.
3. If more than one level of extender is present, the wrap plug must be used in the highest level of extender.
4. If a data packet passes through an extender, a 32-microsecond delay occurs due to retimings.
5. A PC Network Baseband Adapter can tolerate a 100-microsecond delay.

It follows a packet can pass through three levels of extenders successfully if line propagation delays are less than 4 microseconds. Now the only problem is to figure out how to connect the various levels of extenders.

Assume there are only two levels of extenders in a network, as illustrated in Figure 10-8. It seems the only extender ports in level 1 that would generally be available are OUT ports and the only extender ports in level 2 that would generally be available are IN ports.

Assuming these connections would work, the question now becomes: what is the span of such a network? That answer is easy. Remembering that

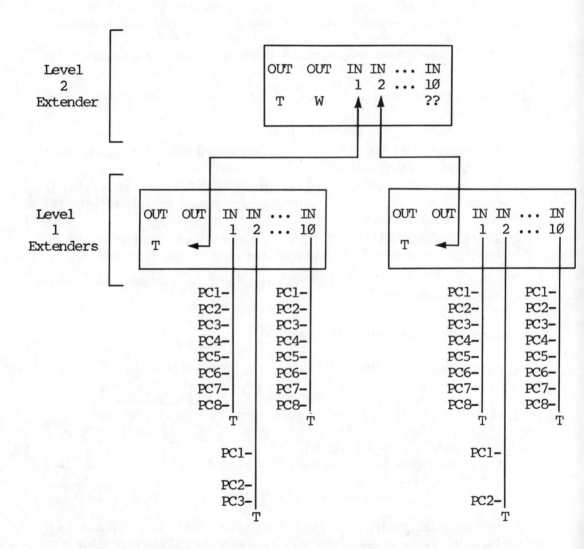

Figure 10-8 PC Network Baseband hierarchical configuration as implied by PC Network Baseband technical reference manuals

1. a signal travels up to twice the media's length on daisy-chain networks without extenders, and
2. noting that extender-to-extender data transmissions need to travel only one length of the connecting media before they hit a receiving extender which completely rebuilds the data signal,

it seems likely links between levels could be up to 600 feet long.

Using similar reasoning, it would seem the length of any level-1 daisy chain could be significantly increased beyond the suggested 400 foot maximum— perhaps beyond 600 feet if only one node were attached.

Thus, IBM's PC Network Baseband Technical Reference Manual implies using a two-level baseband PC Network appears to provide a network with up to 800 nodes with a maximum network radius of 1,000 feet (400 plus 600).

Likewise, a three-level network would appear to support 8,000 nodes within a maximum 1,600-foot radius. Assuming the signals travel about two-thirds the speed of light, the remaining 4 microseconds left after the signal retimings before the adapter times out allows a network radius of over 2,618 feet. (See Appendix B for a discussion on network radius computations.)

However, like the IBM cable kit extensions discussed in the Custom Broadband Network section, any configuration involving more than one level of extender is not supported by IBM. As the IBM PC Network Baseband Planning Guide states:

Network operations with non-specified media, jacks, plugs, connector blocks or cable distances may not be adequate and are not recommended.

Caveat emptor.

PC NETWORK BASEBAND WIRING-CLOSET CONSIDERATIONS

In some environments, PC Network Baseband can use existing building wiring to attach serial daisy chains to facilities located in central wiring closets. If the wiring conforms to IBM Cabling System Type 1, 2, 3, 6, 8, or 9 Cable specifications, PC Network Baseband daisy chains can connect directly to an IBM Cabling System data-connector wall jack or a data-connector distribution panel outlet using a 25-foot IBM Cabling System PC Network Baseband Cable. In this instance, the main thing to observe is that total cable lengths do not exceed the IBM suggested maximums.

Alternately, PC Network Baseband cables exist to connect adapters to both nonmodular and modular telephone connectors. In this situation, the wiring must:

- be solid copper
- be well insulated
- be in good condition
- have at least two pairs
- have a minimum of two twists per foot
- be #22 or #24 American Wire Gauge (AWG)
- be free of splices, stubs, and bridge taps
- have the correct electrical characteristics
- be far enough from electrical lines, fluorescent lights, and other interference
- meet one of the following industry specifications: REA PE-71, Bell Systems 48007, or ANSI/ICEA S-80-576-1983

These and other considerations are discussed in IBM's PC Network Baseband Planning Guide (S68X-2269). Note that a primary obstacle to using wiring closets is that they are often controlled by other departments. So, getting access to a suitable wiring closet as well as permission to use building wiring may be the first challenge a network installer faces. In other words, using existing building wiring can prove very difficult for many reasons as well as require technical consultants.

Assuming you are allowed access to a wiring closet, you can mount PC Network Baseband Extenders in a Token-Ring distribution rack in the closet. Or you can set extenders in a convenient place near where the cables enter the wiring closet.

Using Non-IBM Cabling Wiring

Daisy chains connect to standard modular or nonmodular wall jacks using IBM PC Network Baseband Cable and IBM PC Network Baseband General Purpose Cable, respectively. In all likelihood, the two data-grade twisted pairs will be bundled with at least one other telephone-communications (voice) twisted pair.

The data-grade twisted pairs are later separated from the voice twisted pairs using a standard telephone equipment item called a *connecting block*. (See Figure 10-9.) Connecting blocks facilitate the effort of separating or connecting bundles of different wires. The IBM PC Network Baseband Planning Guide (S68X-2269) suggests the Siemon Company's S66M2-3 connecting block or equivalent is an appropriate selection for this task. This type connecting block can handle 25 twisted pairs (50 wires).

From the connecting block, telephone wires are routed to telephone switching equipment. The data pairs can be joined into one 50-wire (25 twisted pair, not all of which must be used) IBM Cabling System Type 3 cable. This

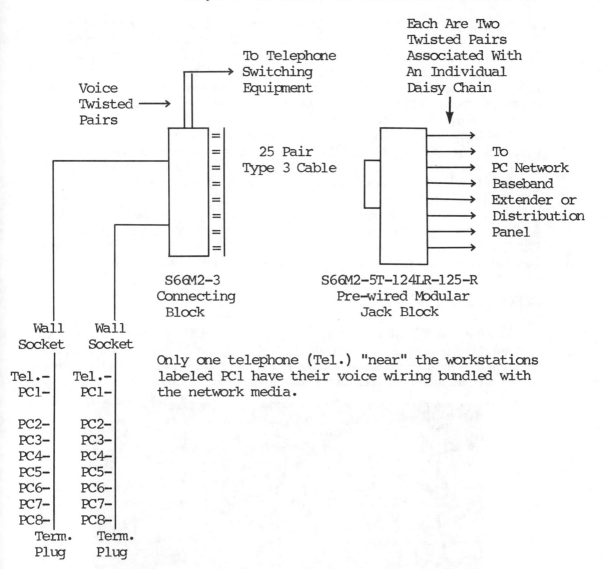

Figure 10-9 Conceptual view of using building wiring in a baseband PC network. Voice circuits are separated from network media at the S66M2-3 connecting block. The remaining (data) twisted pairs are connected to a 25-Pair Type 3 Cable which connects with a 50-pin connector to a S66M2-5T-124LR-125-R prewired modular jack block. S66M2-5T-124LR-125-R prewired modular jack block recombines the twisted pairs associated with each daisy-chain network at its industry-standard telephone outlets. Cables connect these outlets to a PC Network Baseband Extender or to a Data-Connector Distribution Panel for eventual connection to a PC Network Baseband Extender.

larger cable is routed to another device called a *prewired modular jack block.* This prewired modular jack block should be physically located near the PC Network Baseband extender or its optional data-connector distribution panel.

The 50-wire cable attaches to the prewired modular jack block using a 50-pin connector. The prewired modular jack block's circuitry combines the correct twisted pair sets and internally attaches them to standard telephone jack outlets exposed on the sides of the block.

The IBM PC Network Baseband Planning Guide suggests that the Siemon Company's S66M2-5T-124LR-125-R block or equivalent is an appropriate selection for a prewired modular jack block. Figure 10-10 illustrates this block, which provides 12 telephone jacks, each having two twisted pair attached to it (leaving one unused twisted pair).

Cables are then run from the prewired modular jack block telephone jack outlets either to a data-connector distribution panel outlet using a 25-foot IBM Cabling System PC Network Baseband Cable or directly to a PC Network Baseband Extender using IBM PC Network Baseband Adapter Cables.

CONCLUSION

The baseband IBM PC Network is a powerful IBM LAN that is easy to configure, install, and expand. Its competitive cost, flexibility, performance, and adherence to industry standards make it a remarkable value. Its wide applicability warrants increased attention within a spectrum of environments.

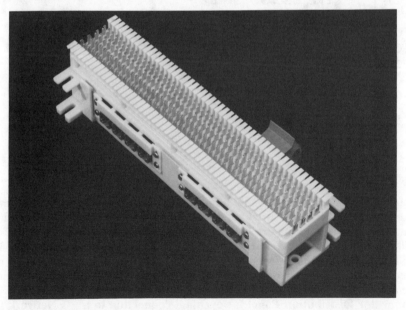

Figure 10-10 The Siemon Company's S66M2-5T-124LR-125-R prewired modular jack block (Photo courtesy of the Siemon Company.)

Section 6
IBM LAN Software

Chapter 11

Introduction to the PC Local Area Network Program

The IBM PC Local Area Network Program is a low-cost product that allows users of IBM LANs providing NetBIOS services and other NetBIOS-compatible networks to exchange messages and share devices. This chapter explains the program, its command menus, sharing and using devices, and network names.

The IBM PC Local Area Network Program, called NET, requires DOS 3.1 or later. To execute NET, simply enter its name with appropriate parameters. In most cases, you use NET either with menus or with direct commands.

After inspecting the optional specification parameters for validity, NET begins operation and seems to disappear from your system by returning control to DOS. However, it remains in your workstation's memory awaiting new commands. (Technically, NET is a DOS terminate-and-stay-resident application.)

To provide its services, NET relies on DOS commands, such as ATTRIB and SHARE for file sharing. Under some conditions, NET can be immediately invoked by simultaneously pressing Ctrl-Alt-Break (the "network request keys") to acquire a NET menu.

The diskette containing NET also has the following:

- A new version of the DOS MODE command
- Two new DOS extensions, REDIR and PSPRINT, which are discussed later in this chapter
- Three new DOS commands, APPEND, PERMIT, and FASTOPEN, discussed in Chapter 13, "Using the NET Commands"
- An updated NetBIOS.COM module, which may replace the PC Network LANA adapter's NetBIOS ROM support

IBM PC LOCAL AREA NETWORK PROGRAM SERVICES

NET Initialization, Machine Names, and Additional Names

When you first execute ("initialize") NET in a network workstation, you must give the workstation a unique name on the network, called a network or machine name. To change this name, you must reset the workstation (turn it off and back on or press Ctrl-Alt-Del twice) and re-execute NET using the new name.

You can request that your machine be known on the network by additional names, as described in Chapter 15's discussion of NetBIOS.

Message Exchange

NET allows you to send a message to other workstations on your network either by specifying the recipient's machine or additional name, or by broadcasting it to all machines. To receive messages, the machine must have initialized NET using the appropriate name or subsequently specified the additional name to NET.

The recipients of network messages can either look at them immediately or place them in a data file for later review, a process called *logging*. In some cases, messages can be forwarded to other machines.

Sharing

By using DOS, REDIR, and PSPRINT, NET allows applications running in one workstation to use network devices on other machines connected to the network. Such applications require no change to use these network devices and invoke normal DOS services, as if the network devices were directly attached to the client machine.

NET CONFIGURATIONS

What a workstation can do on a network depends on how NET was initialized. There are four possible configurations (see Fig. 11-1 and Table 11-1):

- Server (abbreviated SRV), which allows all network functions
- Messenger (MSG), which provides all functions except sharing (SHARE) of disks, directories, and printers
- Receiver (RCV), which receives, saves, and sends messages, and uses network disks, directories, and printers
- Redirector (RDR, not to be confused with the REDIR.EXE module), which sends messages and uses network disks, directories, and printers. RDR contains two components, a Print Redirector (PRDR) for print operations, and a Disk Redirector (DRDR) for disk sharing

NET CONFIGURATION HARDWARE REQUIREMENTS

Table 11-1 illustrates NET services, their configurations, and suggested workstation memory requirements. The memory requirement allows only for NET's requirements, assuming that the default parameters were selected when NET was initialized. (We discuss the parameters and their defaults later in excruciating detail.) Finally, all configurations require a double-sided diskette

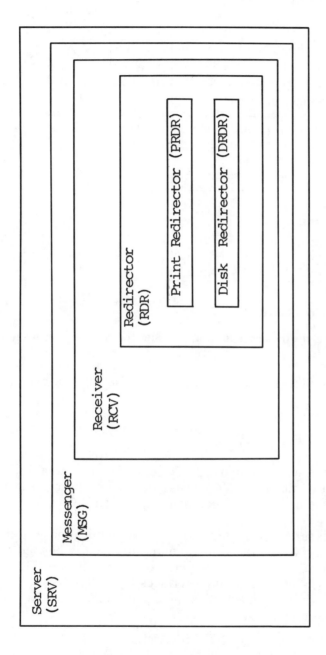

Figure 11-1 The IBM PC local area network program's functional layers

Functions	Configuration (Suggested Memory)			
	SRV (350K)	MSG (160K)	RCV (68K)	RDR (50K)
Share disks, directories, and printers	Y	*	*	*
Use network request keys (Ctrl-Alt-Break)	Y	Y	*	*
Receive messages for other names	Y	Y	*	*
Transfer messages to other computers	Y	Y	*	*
Receive messages	Y	Y	Y	*
Save (log) messages	Y	Y	Y	*
Send messages	Y	Y	Y	Y
Use disks, directories, or printers	Y	Y	Y	Y

Table 11-1 Services by Configuration.

Explanation: Y indicates the configuration provides the service,* means it does not.

drive; the server configuration requires a fixed disk as well, even if it is only a print server.

INVOKING NET SERVICES

There are three ways to invoke NET services after initialization: program calls, menus, and commands. We discuss the menu approach in Chapter 12, "Using the NET Menus," and the command approach in Chapter 13, "Using the NET Commands."

Program calls are a way for workstation applications to invoke NET services directly; however, the programming involved is beyond the scope of this book. For information, refer to the PC Local Area Network Program User's Guide, Appendix C, "Programming Interfaces."

The following discussion assumes the use of commands. In a nutshell, the command to share a device is

NET SHARE

and a device is used by a network machine with the command

NET USE

PRELIMINARY NET CONCEPTS AND DEFINITIONS

Device Owners

A device's owner is the machine to which a device (such as a printer) is directly attached. That is, the device is local to the owner.

Device Network Names

Because it is easier to remember symbolic names than device hardware addresses, DOS has designated names for several of the more commonly used devices. These special device names cannot be used as file names, because they are reserved by DOS for exclusive use with associated devices.

DOS reserves the following device names (use of a colon after a reserved name is optional and the names may also be specified in lowercase letters):

1. CON—console keyboard or screen
2. COM1 or AUX—first serial adapter port
3. COM2—second serial adapter port
4. COM3—third serial adapter port (PS/2 only)
5. COM4—fourth serial adapter port (PS/2 only)
6. LPT1 or PRN—first parallel printer port
7. LPT2—second parallel printer port
8. LPT3—third parallel printer port
9. NUL—dummy (nonexistent) device

DOS also uses single alphabetic (such as A, B, C, D) letters to distinguish various storage devices. However, you can use these as file names, although it is better to avoid them for clarity.

Shared Printer Network Names

For a shared printer, deriving the network name is easy. A printer can be uniquely identified by its owner's machine name and DOS reserved device name. For example, if owner BABS wants to share its LPT2 printer, the explicit network name for the device is

$$\backslash\backslash BABS\backslash LPT2,$$

but the owner can still call it LPT2. This procedure is much like the use of first names and last names.

Note the two back slashes in front of the machine name and the single back slash in front of the printer's name. Machines that want to use this printer must know that its network name is\\BABS\LPT2. However, for a shared subdirectory, arriving at the network name is not quite so easy.

Shared Subdirectory Network Names

Each fixed disk or diskette subdirectory has an associated path, such as \GREGORY\ STEVEN or \MELISSA\ ANN. (If you need to brush up on this, see Appendix A, "Subdirectory Concepts.") Since DOS requires directories with the same path name to reside on different disk or diskette drives, a drive can also be used to identify a shared subdirectory.

It is not generally advisable to share a diskette drive subdirectory. For a discussion, consult the NET User's Guide chapter, "Managing the Server Computer," in the "Sharing Diskette Drives" section.

Suppose now that an owner named BABS shares its \GOODY subdirectory on its current drive. The explicit network name for this subdirectory is

\\BABS GOODY

The owner, of course, can still call the subdirectory \GOODY.

If SHOES were a subdirectory of TWO, which, in turn, were a subdirectory of GOODY, its explicit network name would be

\\BABS\GOODY\TWO\SHOES

Here, \GOODY\TWO\SHOES is the path name for the shared subdirectory. It is important to note that the subdirectory's drive specifier (for instance, C:) is not part of its path name.

Shortnames

Since hierarchical path names can be very long, NET provides a way of assigning short "nicknames," called *shortnames*. A shortname is an eight-character name assigned to a network device when it is shared with the network. For example, an owner might assign GTS as a shortname for \GOODY\ TWO\SHOES. Then the network name becomes

\\BABS\GTS

In practice, a subdirectory can have up to 150 shortnames. An alternative name may be easier for particular users to remember, avoid conflicts with local names, or fit in procedures or programs.

Finally, we can also assign a shortname to a printer. For example, we could call the LPT2 printer on the BABS machine CURSIVE. Its network name is then

$$\backslash\backslash BABS\backslash CURSIVE$$

Note that the printer is not known on the network by its explicit name if it is not shared that way.

Advantages of Shortnames

It is a good practice to use shortnames wherever feasible. They allow easy changeover to new or emergency backup devices. Suppose BABS has two printers, LPT1 and LPT2, and that it shares LPT1, using PRINTER as a shortname. If LPT1 fails, it could be removed from network service. LPT2 can then be shared on the network, using PRINTER as a shortname. Network users can access it without having to change any of their NET commands.

A subdirectory can also be shared with a shortname. If a new subdirectory file or program becomes available, it can be loaded into a new subdirectory and and shared with the network using the same shortname, after the first subdirectory is removed from service.

This easy renaming of network devices allows the uniform use of new levels of hardware, data, and programs, without affecting existing network procedures. Also, if trouble develops with the new device, it can be removed from service. Another device, perhaps the old one (gone but not forgotten), can be reshared on the network under the same shortname. Furthermore, devices that are shared using the NET menus always take a shortname.

Dedicated Server

An owner can optionally dedicate its entire resources for use by other network users, becoming a dedicated server. If a server is not dedicated, it can also be used as a normal workstation and can even access another server as a network user.

Foreground versus Background

The services of a nondedicated server are provided to other network users largely by background tasks performing background processing. That is, the services are obtained from the server as unobtrusively as possible and are not always visible to the server's user. By the same token, a nondedicated server processes applications by foreground tasks (foreground processing), without appearing to be a server.

"No Free Network Lunch"

Here, this old saying means that an owner forfeits some convenience by sharing a device. For example, an owner cannot use a shared printer with DOS PRINT. Instead, the owner must issue a

NET PRINT (parameters)

command with appropriate parameters. In addition, servers that share any subdirectory with a diskette drive or fixed disk cannot execute the DOS commands CHKDSK, DISKCOMP, DISKCOPY, FDISK, FORMAT, JOIN, LABEL, RECOVER, SUBST, SYS, and VERIFY for the shared drive(s).

Finally, background processing may delay foreground processing. Naturally, there are ways to control the delay—via a process called *tuning*. Tuning is discussed in Chapter 13, "Using the NET Commands," and Chapter 14, "PC Local Area Network Program System Perspectives."

NET SHARE PRIMER

Any network machine can be a server if it meets the hardware requirements. Owners become servers when they initialize NET in the server configuration and make a device(s) available to other network machines by executing a

NET SHARE explicit-device-name (parameters)

command. This command shares the device under the conditions indicated by the parameters.

A server can simultaneously share up to 150 devices on the network with a maximum of 29 different machines; the precise number in each case is specified in the NET initialization command. If one user stops using the server, another can take its place.

A NET server provides two types of services: file service (a "file server") and print service (a "print server"). A server can be either a file server, a print server, or both. It can even use devices on other servers.

Regardless of its type, the server should be maintained to insure its availability. For more information on server maintenance, consult the NET Users' Guide chapter "Managing the Server Computer."

File Servers

A file server shares a local subdirectory(ies) on either fixed disk or diskette drive. Network users can then access all files in the shared subdirectory and in all subdirectories hierarchically beneath it. Technically we call this *sharing at the subdirectory level*.

To share a single file, you must copy it to an empty subdirectory and share the subdirectory. If the root directory of a drive is shared, the entire contents of the drive's active partition are available on the network. While this is clearly a special case of subdirectory sharing, it is discussed explicitly in the NET User's Guide chapter "Disk Sharing."

Users may want to share files but keep others from deleting or modifying them. To do this, you must specify the way a subdirectory can be used (its "access rights") when it is shared. If different users require different access rights, the subdirectory can be shared many times using different names. Once specified, the subdirectory access rights apply to every file when accessed by the corresponding network name (shortname or explicit name).

The access rights and their corresponding parameters are:

- Read/Write/Create/Delete (/RWC)—Allows network users to create new files as well as to modify, read, and delete existing files. This parameter is the default for access rights. (It is called Read/Write/Create access rights in the Net User's Guide.)

- Read-Only (/R)—Allows network users only to read the files in the subdirectory. They cannot modify or delete existing files or create new files.

- Write-Only (/W)—Allows network users only to modify existing files in the subdirectory. They cannot read or delete existing files or create new ones. However, they can append information in a file or modify a specifically designated section of one.

- Read/Write (/RW)—Allows network users to read and modify existing files, but not to delete them or create new files.

- Write/Create/Delete (/WC): Network users can create new files, as well as delete and modify existing files. However, they cannot read files. This parameter is called Write/Create access rights in the NET User's Guide.

When a user program requests access to a file in a shared subdirectory, the program indicates the file's "sharing mode" (the way it can be accessed and the degree of exclusive use). The access rights specified in the request must not conflict with those the subdirectory was shared with. For example, a user machine may attempt to open a file in a subdirectory shared as read-only, in a manner that would allow it to write, change, or delete the file. In this case, the server denies the user access to the file and issues a "sharing violation" error. This message notifies the user that the open process has failed.

You can provide the same type of restriction or "file attribute" for the owner with the DOS ATTRIB command. An owner would then receive a sharing violation error if it attempted to open a read-only file in any other mode.

In summary, successful access of a file by an owner depends on its access rights and sharing mode, as well as the file's attribute in the subdirectory, and the sharing mode specified when the file is opened by potential users.

In addition, successful access of a file by network users depends on which access rights and sharing mode are specified in the file's open request, as well as the file's attribute in the subdirectory, the access rights specified for users when the subdirectory was shared, and the sharing mode specified when the file is opened by potential users.

For example, if a file's attribute is read-only or if its subdirectory was shared as read-only, multiple users may open the file in read-only mode. If a file's attribute is not read-only and its subdirectory is not shared as read-only, then file access is granted on the basis of the access rights and the sharing mode specified in the file's open request. In this case, the granting of access rights incorporates both the access rights and sharing modes specified in the open request and currently in effect at the time for other users. Appendix I discusses file access rights and sharing modes for multiple users.

In some cases, you can provide different network users with different access rights by sharing the subdirectory multiple times, specifying different short-names. However, doing so allows network users to simultaneously update the same file(s) and can cause problems in many applications.

For example, consider a manufacturing application that automatically orders more parts when quantities get low. Suppose there are 10,000 units of a particular item and two users simultaneously request the current inventory count and to reserve 9,999 and 10 parts, respectively. If the first transaction is completed before the second, the system appears to have 9,990 parts in stock after the second transaction is done. This is because each user thought there were 10,000 parts available. In fact, the inventory is actually overcommitted, because the users jointly expect to obtain 10,009 units.

Temporary File Servers

The PERMIT command allows a workstation connected to the network to act temporarily as a dedicated file server for a single network machine. The temporary server need not have initialized NET to use this command. The PERMIT command is explained in detail in the NET User's Guide chapter, "DOS Commands for PC Local Area Network Program."

PC Local Area Network Program Installation Aid

The PC Local Area Network Program Installation Aid is an automated program installation facility for network file servers. It is intended to simplify access to server devices by network users, and to facilitate maintenance of server files for IBM program products. It creates private subdirectories for network users and also an APPS subdirectory, whose individual files are marked read-only for the owner. In addition, it creates a NETPATH.BAT batch file and puts it in the user's private directory. The Installation Aid also provides HELP.BAT and documents NET procedures for users.

How well the PC Local Area Network Program Installation Aid meets its goals varies with each network and user environment. For more information, consult the NET User's Guide chapter, "Managing the Server Computer" in the "Organizing the Server's Fixed Disk" section.

Print Server

A print server can share up to three printers simultaneously. It requires a fixed disk, even if the server is only sharing its printer(s). The fixed disk holds files temporarily while they are waiting to be printed, a process called *spooling*. A print server must finish printing one file before it can begin another. So if a print server shares multiple printers, only one of them can be printing at a time.

Once a printer is shared with the network, it is controlled by the DOS PSPRINT extension. It can no longer be used by the DOS PRINT command, although the owner's user can access the printer as a network device. If a parallel printer is shared by the NET menus, this access is automated for the owner's user. However, the owner can use the printer only with NET PRINT, unless it is first removed from network service.

Remote Program Load Server

IBM LAN adapters allows workstations—for example, one without disks— to boot off of the network. NET does not provide such a service, and it is mentioned here only for completeness. Note that IBM Token-Ring adapters require a Remote Program Load feature to perform this activity.

NET USE PRIMER

NET allows you to use network devices that have been made previously available to network users by their owners. To access a shared device, you simply execute a

NET USE device-name (parameters)

command, with appropriate device name and parameters. The sequence is important; a device cannot be used before it is shared. NET USE allows you to simultaneously access 32 devices that can be owned by up to 31 different machines.

The device name is the same one specified in the owner's NET share command. If a device was shared with a shortname, it must be used with a shortname. If, for example, BABS shared a directory with a path name of \GOODY\TWO\SHOES, the NET USE command would be

NET USE \\BABS\GOODY\TWO\SHOES (parameters)

This would allow you to enter the DOS command

TYPE \\BABS\GOODY\TWO\SHOES\NORDSTRM.$$$

This displays the NORDSTRM.$$$ file in the specified directory.

Network Virtual (Imaginary) Drives

Since the novelty of typing a network name such as \\BABS\
GOODY\TWO\SHOES would soon wear off, NET allows you to assign a
virtual drive specifier (an "imaginary drive specifier"; see Appendix A) to the
subdirectory in the NET USE command. In this case, the command could be

NET USE E: \\BABS\GOODY\TWO\SHOES (parameters)

This would allow you to enter the DOS command

TYPE E:NORDSTRM.$$$

Curiously, the command

DIR E:

executes correctly with the second form of the NET USE command, while the
command

DIR \\BABS\GOODY\TWO\SHOES

fails with the first form of the NET USE command. This is a characteristic of
DOS, not of NET. So it is a good idea to assign virtual drive specifiers for
network subdirectories.

Finally, note that you cannot use F: through Z: as virtual drives, unless you
specify a LASTDRIVE command in your workstation's CONFIG.SYS file.
Consult the NET User's Guide's "LASTDRIVE Command" discussion and the
material in this book titled "CONFIG.SYS Considerations" in Chapter 13.

Licensing Considerations

A file server allows applications to be centrally accessed by users on a
network. However, the applications must be licensed for the network user
machines that execute them. Note that sharing licensed programs on a network
may result in a copyright violation, unless specifically allowed by the license.

Chapter 12

Using the NET Menus

NET MENU OVERVIEW—WHY MENUS?

The PC Local Area Network Program (NET) menus make NET services easy to use. Among other things, they let you send messages, access network devices, and share your devices with other network users. Each network service or device access requires a separate request.

The menus also let you save your requests. This lets you obtain the same services automatically when you next turn on your machine. You need not use the menus again unless you want to add a new service or discontinue one.

You do not have to use menus. With time, you may become proficient enough to enter NET commands directly at the DOS prompt. In this instance, the menus can still prove extremely useful, because some services can be accessed only from the menus. Also, the menus provide a way to enter DOS commands directly, without having to end the current application.

NET FAST-PATH COMMANDS

If your machine functions in a Server or Messenger configuration, you can immediately obtain a NET menu by simultaneously pressing the Ctrl, Alt, and Break keys. Then, pressing the F2 key provides a command input line. You do not have to leave your application to obtain the DOS prompt. This approach is called the *fast-path* for NET commands, because it lets you quickly enter a NET request without going through the menus. Later, you can return to your application by holding down Esc and pressing Enter.

But don't worry about the mechanics. The menus are very clear. If you do get confused, you can always press the F1 key to obtain a help screen.

NET MENU PRIMER

NET Adaptive Hierarchical Menus

NET menus form an adaptive hierarchy. To understand this, consider an analogy. Suppose you run a restaurant that caters to customers with widely varying budgets. That is, you serve big spenders as well as thrift minded customers. To determine what someone wants, you always ask, in a cultivated French accent, "What'll ya have?"

```
┌─────────────────────────────────────────────────┐
│                                                 │
│               What'll Ya Have?                  │
│                                                 │
│                                                 │
│           1. Something Inexpensive              │
│           2. Something Amusing                  │
│                                                 │
│           Your Selection ──▶ __                 │
│                                                 │
│     Please Select Your Entry and Press Enter    │
│                                                 │
└─────────────────────────────────────────────────┘
```

Figure 12-1 Customer qualification menu

If the customer replies, "What's cheap?", you whip out the thrift mimeographed menu. Alternately, if the customer replies "Amuse me," you present the elegantly printed big-spender menu with appropriate grace and dignity.

As you might suspect, the menus (and prices) are different. Only the food is the same. The big-spender menu offers everything the thrift menu does, as well as many more high-priced selections. The set of menus is adaptive to your customer's desires (and pocketbook).

The thrift menu has several categories—soup, salad, sandwiches, and

```
┌─────────────────────────────────────────────────┐
│                                                 │
│                 Amusing Menu                    │
│                                                 │
│                                                 │
│            1. Soups                             │
│            2. Salads                            │
│            3. Sandwiches                        │
│            4. Beverages                         │
│            5. Kangaroo Entrees                  │
│            6. Jack-Rabbit Entrees               │
│                                                 │
│            Your Selection ──▶ __                │
│                                                 │
│     Please Select Your Entry and Press Enter    │
│                                                 │
└─────────────────────────────────────────────────┘
```

Figure 12-2 Amusing menu

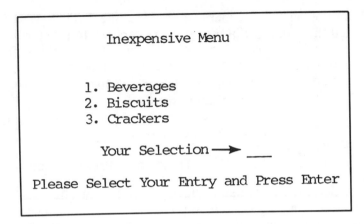

Figure 12-3 Inexpensive menu

beverages, with several selections under each category. As you might suspect, we can easily computerize this approach to service.

The computerized restaurant works as follows. When a customer sits down, the computer at his or her table shows the display illustrated in Figure 12-1.

The menu's aim is to determine the customer's needs. Suppose the customer selects No. 2 (Something Amusing). Your computer then displays the menu in Figure 12-2.

Alternately, the Inexpensive Menu would appear as indicated in Figure 12-3.

In this situation, we say the succession of menus is hierarchical, because you can represent them as illustrated in Figure 12-4.

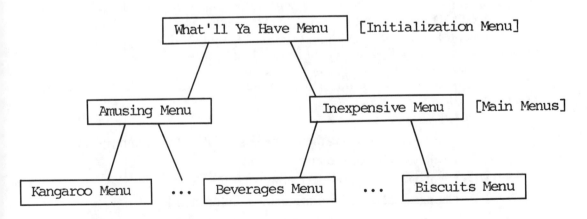

Figure 12-4 Hierarchical menus

In the same sense, NET's menus are hierarchical. The "What'll Ya Have Menu" is called the *initialization menu*. The response to it determines whether the Amusing or the Inexpensive menu is presented. Note that the process is not reversible: Customers never see the initialization menu once they have selected from it. The next menu, either the Amusing or the Inexpensive Menu, is called the customer's *main* or *first menu*.

Significance of the Menu Structure

With the NET menus, the selections vary with your configuration. If your machine is a Server, your menus have different selections than if it is a Redirector. In fact, some Server selections appear more than once. For example, two selections on the main menu (Disk or Directory Tasks and Network Status Tasks) display the devices that you are using.

This chapter discusses the menus as they appear for a Server, because they include all selections available to the other configurations. However, the menu structure is different for each configuration. We are assuming NET version 1.21 here.

MECHANICS OF USING THE NET MENUS

Figure 12-5 shows a typical NET menu, one for a Server to initiate sharing a disk or subdirectory.

As with most NET menus, the responses are straightforward. You simply fill in the blanks or *field(s)*. Press Tab to move to the next field, and press Enter when you are done. Here, there are three fields at the top: the DOS name for the disk or directory, its network name, and the password for access. You might enter "\GOODY\TWO\SHOES," "GTS," and "$$$."

A fourth field, access rights, offers selection 5, "Read/Write/Create/ Delete," as its default value. Your request appears on line 23. If an error occurred, the reason for it precedes the message.

The keys used to move through each menu are listed at the bottom. The complete set includes:

Special keys:

- Esc—Returns to previous menu or exits NET if at the main (first) menu
- F1—Displays help for the current screen
- F2—Displays a fast-path NET command line
- F3—Changes colors (if you are using a color monitor)
- Ctrl-Home—Returns to main (first) menu
- Ctrl-Break + Enter—Exits the NET menus

```
                                              PC LAN PROGRAM

       Start Sharing Your Disk or Directory


DOS name for disk or directory


Network name for your disk or directory


Password for disk or directory (Optional)


Other users can                    4. Write/Create/Delete
1. Read only                       5. Read/Write/Create/Delete
2. Read/Write
3. Write only

5 Choice


   Tab - Cursor to next field       F1 - Help
   Enter - Continue                 Ctrl-Home - Return to
   Esc - Previous Menu                          main menu
```

Figure 12-5 Typical net menu

Editing keys:

- Cursor right—Moves the cursor to the right one position
- Cursor left—Moves the cursor to the left one position
- Tab—Moves to the next field
- Home—Moves the cursor to the beginning of a field
- End—Moves the cursor to the end of a field
- Ins—Allows character insertion at the current cursor position
- Del—Deletes the character immediately above the cursor
- Ctrl-End—Erases all characters to the right of the cursor to the field end
- Backspace—Moves the cursor one position to the left and erases the character

Accessing the NET Menus

With the Server or Messenger configuration, you can leave an application and access the NET menus by pressing Ctrl-Alt-Break. Otherwise, you must have access to the network subdirectory first, and then enter NET at the DOS prompt.

If NET begins executing without having been initialized, it presents a logo screen. To continue, press Enter. If NET has been initialized, you see the main NET menu. Otherwise, you are queried for information that allows NET to initialize.

Initializing NET from the Menus

Specifying the Computer Name from the Menus

The first item you must supply to initialize NET from the menus is the network name (also called computer name or machine name in other PC Network documentation) for your machine.

The name may not be more than 15 characters long. It cannot start with an asterisk or contain any embedded spaces. Lowercase letters are the same as uppercase letters. Punctuation marks are permitted. When you have entered your computer name, press Enter and proceed to the configuration selection stage.

Specifying the Configuration from the Menus

NET now asks which functions you expect to use, not if you want your machine to be a Server, Messenger, Receiver, or Redirector. This step is equivalent to the "What'll Ya Have?" process in the analogy. The first question is

N Share your printer? disks? directories?

The default answer is N (no). If you change it to Y (Yes), NET concludes your machine must operate as a Server. Otherwise, NET provides the following query:

Y Add usernames, forward messages, and use the network request key?

Here, usernames means additional names, and the default is Y (yes). If you accept the default by pressing Enter, NET concludes that your machine must operate as a Messenger. Otherwise, NET provides the following query:

Y Receive and save messages?

Here again the default is yes. If you accept it, NET concludes that your machine must operate as a Receiver. Otherwise, NET concludes your machine must be a Redirector since it is not any of the other three options.

This process selects the configuration for your machine's operation. It also determines the menu selections, which vary with the configuration.

CHANGING STARTING DEFAULTS FROM THE MENUS

At this point, NET has determined your machine's configuration. It now must obtain operating parameters by asking:

N Changing defaults for starting?

The default here is no. If you change it to yes, you are presented with the list of parameter defaults shown in Figure 12-6.

The exact list presented varies with the tentative configuration. The values in parentheses following each prompt indicate the range of valid specifications. The START parameters being specified are indicated in brackets immediately under the corresponding prompt and are not present on the actual menu. The significance of each parameter follows:

- /ASG: applies to all configurations. It specifies how many disks, directories, printers, and diskettes located on other network machines your machine uses. Each device is considered separately, even if it is located on the same machine as another device being used, or even if it is the same as a device shared with a different shortname.

- /MBI: applies to the Server and Messenger configurations. Server and Messenger configurations can receive messages and hold them in a temporary storage area in memory for later viewing. NET alerts you to stored messages by a beep or message. The parameter specifies the size of the message storage area in characters or in kilobytes (for example, 8K). The 1,600- byte default provides room for about nine short

5 Number of devices to be used? (1-32)
[/ASG]

1600 Size of buffer for messages waiting? (256-60000 characters)
[/MBI]

1 Number of additional names that will be receiving messages? (0-12)
[/USN]

10 Number of devices to be shared? (1-150)
[/SHR]

512 Size of buffer for printing? (512-16384 characters)
[/PRB]

10 Number of network computers that will be using your devices? (1-25)
[/RDR]

Figure 12-6 NET menu initialization defaults

Y   Do you want to do these tasks?

	[Applicable Configuration]
Send messages to other computers	[SRV, MSG, RCV, RDR]
Use network disks, directories, and printers	[SRV, MSG, RCV, RDR]
Receive messages from other computers	[SRV, MSG, RCV]
Allow saving of messages on a save file	[SRV, MSG, RCV]
Use the network request key	[SRV, MSG]
Receive messages for other computers	[SRV, MSG]
Transfer messages to other computers	[SRV, MSG]
Share your disks, directories, and printers	[SRV]

Figure 12-7 The NET Menu confirmation query

messages. When the area fills, no more messages can be received until some space has been reclaimed by viewing the stored messages.

- /USN: applies to the Server and Messenger configurations. Your machine is known on the network by its machine name and by as many as 12 other aliases (NET uses four of the original 16 on the adapter). These aliases could be additional names or could be the result of other machines forwarding their messages to your machine. In that case, your machine automatically assumes their machine's name until the forwarding is stopped. That is, every message destined for the other forwarding machine name stops at this device.

- /SHR: applies to the Server configuration. It specifies how many disks, directories, printers, and diskettes you plan to share with the network. Note that multiple network users can simultaneously use the same device. If the same device is shared using different shortnames, each request counts as a separate shared device.

- /PRB: specifies the size of the buffer for a shared printer Server. PSPRINT controls this buffer. The larger it is, the better the printer's performance. Like the /MBI: parameter, you can specify the value in kilobytes (for example, 8K).

- /RDR: specifies the number of machines anticipated to use your machine when operating as a Server. A given machine can access multiple devices on a Server but is counted only once in the Server's calculation of this parameter. It limits the number of redirectors that can access a Server simultaneously. An additional machine can access the Server only if one of the existing machines ceases accessing it.

Once NET has initialized, you cannot change these values unless you turn off your machine. Chapter 11 describes the memory requirements for each parameter, in the discussion of NET START.

CONFIRMING YOUR SELECTIONS

At this point, NET has determined your machine's configuration and operating parameters. It then asks you to confirm your choices by making sure that the list of functions is consistent with your requirements (Fig. 12-7).

The values bracketed in Figure 12-7 do not appear on the actual prompt. Because a configuration cannot be respecified once initialized, it is important to understand the implications of the save file and network request keys.

If your machine is a Server, Messenger, or Receiver, you have the option to choose to log all messages your machine receives. Otherwise, unlogged messages immediately appear on your screen, interfering with what is already there. The prior screen contents may not be recoverable, depending on your application.

If you reply to the NET Menu Confirmation Query with a Y (yes), NET attempts to initialize. Otherwise, you are reprompted for configuration information. Nothing entered is permanent until NET actually initializes. So at any time during specification, you can press Esc and return to an earlier screen. After NET initializes, you are presented with the NET main menu (Task Selection menu).

MAIN MENU (TASK SELECTION MENU)

The NET main menu provides the hierarchical menus that allow you to invoke NET services. Figure 12-8 shows the various selections in a Server's main menu, each of which we'll discuss presently.

There are three things to remember about menus. First, whenever you are in a menu, pressing Ctrl-Home always restores the main menu. In addition, all network names that you specify on menus are actually shortnames, the preferred way of naming network devices. Finally, for security reasons passwords cannot be specified as an asterisk as they can in NET commands.

Message Tasks

Message tasks are the NET requests that allow you to send and view received messages, start and stop message logging, add and delete name aliases,

---

Main Menu Task Selection

    1. Message Tasks

    2. Printer Tasks

    3. Disk or directory tasks

    4. Print queue tasks

    5. Network status tasks

    6. Pause and continue tasks

    7. Save or cancel the network setup

Figure 12-8 The Server Configuration Main Menu

and stop receiving or forwarding messages for or to another network name. The selections on the Message Task Menu, with the NET commands (if any) in brackets, can be defined as follows:

1. Send messages [NET SEND]—Messages can be sent to a specific network name or as a general broadcast.
2. View received messages—Messages stored in memory are deleted after they are viewed. This service must be accessed from the menus, because there is no comparable NET command.
3. Start or stop saving messages [NET LOG]—Messages can be logged on a local or network disk.
4. Start or stop receiving messages for another name [NET NAME].
5. Start or stop forwarding messages [NET FORWARD].
6. Display names that can receive messages at your computer [NET NAME].

Printer Tasks

Printer tasks are the NET requests that allow you to control the activities or use of a print server. The types of activities you can control depend on whether your machine is the actual print server or whether you are using another machine configured to operate as a print server.

1. Start or stop sharing your printer [NET SHARE].
2. Start or stop using a network printer [NET USE]—If you USE a network printer, your applications must transmit a special close-file message to the print server. This occurs automatically when an application closes the device (for example LPT1, LPT2, or LPT3) or changes the way it is requesting DOS print services. If it does not occur automatically, you can force it by simultaneously pressing Ctrl-Alt-PrtSc. However, do not do this prematurely. If you do, your print file is be split into two and you have to press Ctrl-Alt-PrtSc again to print the second half.
3. Print a file [NET PRINT]—If you are sharing a printer, you cannot control it with the DOS PRINT command. You must use the network service.
4. Change the print size on a network printer [DOS MODE command]—The new setting is used only with your machine's files. Other machines use their own printer MODE setting.
5. Display devices you are sharing [NET SHARE]—This selection also displays shared subdirectories.
6. Display network devices you are using [NET USE]—This selection also displays used subdirectories.

Disk or Directory Tasks

Disk or directory tasks are the NET requests that allow you to control the activities or use of a disk server. The types of activities you can control depend on whether your machine is the actual disk server or whether you are using another machine that is configured to operate as a disk server.

1. Start or stop sharing your disk or directory [NET SHARE]—Sharing a disk amounts to sharing the disk's root directory.
2. Start or stop using a network disk or directory [NET USE]
3. Display devices you are sharing [NET SHARE]—This selection also displays shared printers.
4. Display devices you are using [NET USE]—This selection also displays used printers.

Print Queue Tasks

Print Queue tasks are NET requests that involve a shared printer on a Server configuration.

1. Check or change print queue on your computer—You must use the menus for this service, since there is no NET command for this activity. This selection only applies to a Server that owns a shared printer. It allows the owner's user to

   a. update the PRINT queue
   b. hold a print file for later printing
   c. release a print file that was previously held or experienced an error while it was being printed
   d. cancel a print file that is printing or is waiting to print
   e. immediately print a file, even if one is currently printing
   f. print a file immediately after the current file completes printing

2. Check print queue on another computer [NET PRINT]—This selection allows you to check the status of your files that have been spooled to a network machine. You can only view information regarding your files, unless you use the network remote control to operate the print server. A print file can be in one of eight possible states:

   a. Canceled (by the Print Server operator)
   b. Held—(that is, the printing cannot occur until the print request is released for printing)
   c. Paused

    d. Print File Error—The print file could not be found.

    e. Printer Error

    f. Printing

    g. Spooling (That is, the file has not yet been completely received at the printer. It is considered received when the special close-file message is received.)

    h. Waiting—The file is waiting to be printed.

For more information on Printer sharing and using, see the material in the NET User's Guide, ''Managing Shared Printers.'' It is in the chapter titled ''Managing the Server Computer.''

    3. Start or stop printing a separator page [NET SEPARATOR]—This selection allows a print Server to specify whether to put a separator page between print files. This page can show information about the file's origin and perhaps a logo for the next file. (Also see Appendix G.)

Network Status Tasks

Network status tasks are the net requests that allow you to monitor the status of various network services, such as print queues, that you are using or providing to the network users. Some of these tasks must be requested from the NET Menus because they have no NET Command equivalent. Here are some network status tasks:

    1. Check or change print queue on your computer. You must use the menus for this service, because there is no comparable NET command.

    2. Check print queue on another computer—[NET PRINT].

    3. Display names that can receive messages at your computer—This is also a Message task.

    4. Display devices that you are sharing—[NET SHARE].

    5. Display network devices that you are using—[NET USE].

Note that items 1 and 2 are also Print Queue tasks and that items 4 and 5 are also Disk or Directory Tasks.

Pause and Continue Tasks

This menu allows you to select a NET service that you want to suspend (to allow the owner direct access to devices) or resume (to reinstate sharing). Sharing a subdirectory may keep an owner from using it.

1. Pause or continue using network disks and directories—[NET PAUSE and NET CONTINUE].
2. Pause or continue using network printers—[NET PAUSE and NET CONTINUE].
3. Pause or continue receiving messages—[NET PAUSE and NET CONTINUE].
4. Pause or continue sharing your devices—[NET PAUSE and NET CONTINUE].
5. Pause or continue printing files—[NET PAUSE and NET CONTINUE]. This selection allows you to pause or continue printing on all printers or on an individual printer.

Save or Cancel the Network Setup

This selection allows you to save or cancel your NET configuration and currently selected services. There is no comparable NET command.

If you save your network setup, you should make special note of the fact that your machine's AUTOEXEC.BAT file is renamed AUTOUSER.BAT. (The file is not destroyed, only replaced.) Then the configuration and service information can be saved as NET commands in a new AUTOEXEC.BAT file. The AUTOEXEC.BAT executes an AUTOUSER command as its last statement. This allows your machine to restart normally after NET has completed initialization.

When your system is subsequently reset, the new AUTOEXEC.BAT asks whether you want to start NET and use it the way it was last saved. Doing so allows you to automatically restore your NET services every time you restart your system. While you can always change your current NET services, the changes do not appear in your saved configuration, unless you save them.

Note that this process may not work completely as intended, because your original AUTOEXEC.BAT may contain PATH statements that the new AUTO-EXEC.BAT tries to override. The details of the process are in the NET User's Guide, Chapter 4, "Setting Up and Using the PC LAN Program," under "Saving Your Network Setup." Also note that a special user area is provided in the new AUTOEXEC.BAT. Statements placed in this area are copied intact to any new AUTOEXEC.BAT file that NET creates.

If you cancel your current network setup, NET replaces AUTOEXEC.BAT with a skeleton replacement that has no NET configuration or service information. But it preserves the commands within the user area.

Chapter 13

Using the NET Commands

This chapter presents an overview of the NET commands. It is not meant to replace the detailed discussion in the NET User's Guide.

The commands, discussed in the order you will be likely to use, are:

- NET—accesses the menus
- NET START—allows use of network services
- NET SEND—transmits a message
- NET PRINT—accesses or monitors printer services
- NET PAUSE—temporarily suspends a function
- NET CONTINUE—resumes a paused function
- NET NAME—allows a device to display its name(s)
- NET FORWARD—starts or stops the forwarding of messages
- NET LOG—starts or stops the logging of messages
- NET SHARE—shares a device
- NET ERROR—displays errors
- NET SEPARATOR—separates sections of printing
- NET FILE—allows detection of locked files

You can see an example of these commands by typing out an AUTOEXEC-.BAT file after saving your network configuration via the menus.

NET commands can be entered either at the DOS prompt or by pressing F2 in a NET menu to obtain a NET command line (fast-path).

NET

Function: Start NET

NET command, which can be entered only at the DOS prompt, allows access to the NET menus. If your workstation is a Server or a Messenger, the menus are also obtainable via the network request keys.

If NET has not been initialized, you see the NET initialization menus before getting the main menu.

Applicable NET Configurations: SRV, MSG, RCV, and RDR
Command Syntax Summary:
To start the NET menus:

NET

NET START

Function: Initialize NET

This command starts NET via a DOS prompt command. Once successfully executed, NET START cannot be reexecuted until your machine is reset. You must execute NET START before using NET services.

The NET START command has many optional parameters. They cannot all be specified in one command that starts a Server configuration. The next chapter describes the parameters and their relationships in detail.

Applicable NET Configurations: SRV, MSG, RCV, and RDR

Command Syntax Summary:

To start NET:

NET START configuration computername [/parameter1] [/parameter2] [...]

where the configuration is SRV, MSG, RCV, or RDR; computername is your machine name (specified without two leading back slashes), and parameters are specifications related to the configuration.

NET START PARAMETER OVERVIEW

What follows is only an introduction to NET START parameters (Chapter 14 discusses them in more detail). Since not all parameters apply all the time, we have grouped them by configuration(s) and summarized them in Table 13-1.

We specify the value of a parameter as:

/PRM

where/PRM is the name and n the value. For example, to assign the/SRV parameter a value of 18, specify:

NET START RDR BABS/SRV:18 . . .

Parameters That Apply to All Configurations

/ASG:n (Server Devices Simultaneously Used)

/ASG specifies the maximum number of shared network devices your machine simultaneously uses. Note that this parameter refers to the number of devices (not machines) your machine accesses. Its value can range from 1 to 32. The default value is 5.

/ASG reserves an amount of memory equal to approximately 90 times the value specified.

/SRV:n (Server Computers Simultaneously USEd)

/SRV specifies the maximum number of computers with shared network devices your machine simultaneously uses. This parameter's value can range

NET START Command Parameter	RDR RCV	MSG	SRV	RANGE	DEFAULT	NOTES
/SRV - # of computers via USE	Y	Y	Y	1–31	2/3	2
/ASG - # of network devices	Y	Y	Y	1–32	5	
/SES - # of NetBIOS sessions	Y	Y	Y	2–254	varies	3
/CMD - # of NetBIOS commands	Y	Y	Y	2–254	varies	3
/NBC - # of network buffers	Y	Y	Y	1–64	4/2	4
/NBS - network buffer size	Y	Y	Y	512B–32K	4K	1, 4
/PBx - print buffer size	Y	Y	Y	80B–16K	1K/512B	5
/MBI - message buffer size		Y	Y	512B–60K	1750B	6
/TSI - time slice int. fgd/bgd		Y	Y	00–99	54	
/USN - # of extra names		Y	Y	0–12	1	
/REQ - # of Server msg receives			Y	1–3	2	7

Table 13-1 Summary of the NET START parameters.

NET START Command Parameter	RDR RCV	MSG	SRV	RANGE	DEFAULT	NOTES
/RQB - buffer sizes for /REQ's			Y	512B–32K	8K	7
/CAC - Server Disk Cache Size			Y	varies	112K	8
/EXM - Disk Cache Location			Y	N/A		
/SHB - buffer size locks/blocks			Y	512B–60K	2K	
/SHL - # of locked file ranges			Y	20–1,000	20	
/PRB - print buffer size			Y	512B–16K	2K	
/PRP - bkg. print priority			Y	1–3	3	
/SHR - # of shareable devices			Y	1–999	5	
/RDR - # of RDRs accessing Server			Y	1–251	10	

Table 13-1 Summary of the NET START parameters. (*Continued*).
Notes:

1. B corresponds to bytes, K to 1,024 bytes.
2. /SRV defaults to 3 for Servers and to 2 for other configurations.
3. The values of /SES and /CMD can be determined by the configuration and other parameter values.

from 1 to 31. The default value is 3 or 2, depending on whether your workstation is a Server (3) or another configuration (2).

/SRV reserves an amount of memory equal to approximately 70 times the value specified.

/NBC:n (Network Buffer Count)

/NBC specifies the number of network input/output buffers your machine has available for using shared subdirectories on network Server machines. Your machine uses these buffers to transfer data to and from the network disk.

This parameter's value can range from 1 to 64, and defaults to 3 for configurations other than a Server, in which case the default is 2. It should be greater than the maximum number of network Server files simultaneously open. (Also see Chapter 14.)

/NBS:n (Network Buffer Size)

/NBS specifies the size of each network input/output buffer available for using shared subdirectories on network Server machines.

The value of /NBS is specified in bytes and can range from 512K to 32K. The default value is 4K bytes. It should be as large as the Server's /RQB value, if possible.

/NBC and /NBS together reserve an amount of memory equal to the product of their specified values. Their product cannot exceed 32K.

Table 13-1 notes (*Continued*).

---

4. The maximum settings of /NBC and /NBS are constrained by the relationship:

    (/NBC */NBS) ← 32K

5. /PBI defaults to 512 bytes for computers with less than 128K memory. For all others, it defaults to 1K bytes. /PB2 and /PB3 always default to 128 bytes.
6. /MBI has 2 default values: 1,600 if the PC Local Area Network Program is started from the menus, and 1,750 if the PC Local Area Network Program is started with a NET START command.
7. The maximum settings of the /REQ and the /RQB parameters are constrained by the relationship:

    (/REQ */RQB) ← 32K.

8. /CAC varies from 128 to 15,232 if /EXM is present, and from 16 to 360 otherwise. (The value denotes K bytes.)

/PBx:n (Network Print-File Transmission Buffer Size)

/PBx specifies the size of the buffer used to transfer files to a printer. Here, the x can be 1, 2, or 3 for print files redirected from LPT1 (PRN), LPT2, and LPT3, respectively, to network printers.

/PBx is to a used printer what/NBS is to a used file, and partially replaces it in a print-file transfer. Just as each file has one /NBS-size buffer, each used printer has one /PBx-size buffer.

Note: /PB1 defaults to 1,024 bytes; /PB2 and /PB3 default to 128 bytes.

Each network printer that your machine accesses has its own network print buffer. In any event, no more than a total of 16K can be reserved for Print-File Transfer Buffers.

The value of /PBx can range from 80 to 16K bytes. It defaults to 1,024 bytes for /PB1 and 128 bytes for all other cases. It should be specified as large as the Server's /RQB value if possible.

/PBx reserves an amount of memory equal to the total of the memory requested on all /PB1, /PB2, and /PB3 specifications.

/SES:n (Concurrent NetBIOS Sessions)

/SES specifies the maximum number of network NetBIOS sessions your machine can conduct simultaneously. This includes NET sessions as well as any other sessions other software may conduct simultaneously.

The value of /SES can range from 1 to 254 and apply only to NET operations. For other software packages, add their requirements to the NET values. The default varies with the configuration:

1. For a Redirector: 9
2. For a Receiver: 9
3. For a Messenger: The greater of 9 or /SRV + /USN + 2
4. For a Server: The greater of 16 or /SRV + /USN + /RDR + 2

/USN applies only to Servers and Messengers, and /RDR applies only to Servers. They are discussed subsequently under those headings.

If /RDR, /USN/, and /SRV are not specified, /SES defaults to 16. The /SES parameter does not require reserved memory but affects performance. (Also see Chapter 14.)

/CMD:n (Simultaneous NetBIOS Commands Presented)

/CMD specifies the maximum number of network NetBIOS commands your network adapter can have simultaneously pending. This includes NET commands as well as commands from other software.

The value of /CMD can range from 1 to 254. The default varies with the configuration and has a value of 12 if /USN and /REQ default. Otherwise the default is:

For a Redirector: 8 (must be at least 2)
For a Receiver: 8 (must be at least 4)
For a Messenger: The greater of 8 or /USN + 4 (must be at least /USN + 4)
For a Server: The greater of 8 or /USN + /REQ + 5 (must be at least /USN /REQ + 5)

The /USN and /REQ parameters are discussed later.
/CMD does not require reserved memory but affects performance.

Server and Messenger-Only Parameters:

/MBI:n (Network Message Buffer Size)

/MBI specifies the size of the buffer used to temporarily store arriving network messages (see Chapter 10) when your machine is not logging them to a file. NET regards the storing of these messages as a background task.
The value of /MBI can range from 512 bytes to approximately 60K bytes. It defaults to 1,750 bytes.
/MBI reserves the amount of memory specified in the request.

/USN:n (Extra Name Count)

/USN specifies the maximum number of additional names (network aliases you request) and forwarded names your machine can be known by. These extra names can be used only to receive messages, not to send them.
The value of /USN can range from zero to 12. The default value is 1.
The/USN parameter reserves an amount of memory 600 times the value specified in the request. It affects the /SES and /CMD parameters.

/TSI:fb (Time Slice Interval Specification)

/TSI determines the ratio of time that is available to satisfy background and foreground processing requirements. In a Server, background tasks consist of the activities required to service machines accessing local network devices. For both Servers and Messengers, the receiving and logging of messages are also background tasks.
Alternately, in a Server, print Server activity (PSPRINT activity) is both a foreground and a background task. In both the Server and Messenger configurations, the user's applications are foreground tasks.
The value of /TSI is specified as two one-digit numbers that both vary from 0 to 9; the first digit applies to the foreground, the second to the background. The default value is 54.
The value of the individual digits indirectly specifies how long the foreground or background processing has before it must relinquish control to the other. The time allotment corresponding to each digit is listed in Table 13-2. Note that a /TSI setting of 00 disables time slicing and allows network users to obtain

Digit Value	Timer Ticks	Allotted Time
0	1	.055 Second
1	2	.110 Second
2	3	.165 Second
3	5	.275 Second
4	7	.385 Second
5	11	.604 Second
6	15	.824 Second
7	21	1.154 Seconds
8	28	1.538 Seconds
9	36	1.978 Seconds

Note: One timer tick corresponds to about .055 second.

Table 13-2 /TSI Digit Time Allotments

the best response by permitting the foreground to execute only when there is nothing to do in the background. Selecting a /TSI value of 00 is not advised if a machine is sharing a printer, since printing is considered a foreground activity.

If either the foreground or background completes processing, it relinquishes control to the other for its allotted time. However, if activity warrants, each time slice is completely used by the foreground or background before it relinquishes control. Restated, foreground or background activity continues to run until it is preempted.

This means if the values are set high (for instance, 99), there are noticeable periods of processing discontinuity between foreground and background activity, causing both network-using machines and the Server's applications to behave erratically. For example, application activity may be "jerky" because of lulls in sharing or other Server background activities.

Alternately, if the values are set too low, processing is less erratic but is degraded by constant switches between foreground and background activities.

In summary, the effect of the /TSI parameter varies with the system load, as well as with the services provided to other network machines. The value of /TSI for a dedicated Server would certainly be different from the value for a Server that is only lightly used by other machines. You must experiment with this parameter to determine what is best for your needs.

Server-Only Parameters

/CAC:n (Server Disk Data Cache Buffer Size)

/CAC specifies the number of K-bytes to be used for caching disk data. If the IBMCACHE.SYS device driver is being used, a value of zero should be specified to avoid unpredictable results.

The value of /CAC can range from 128 to 15,232 if /EXM is specified; otherwise, it can range from 16 to 360. The default is 112.

/CAC reserves an amount of memory 1,024 times the specified value. The location of the reserved memory depends on the /EXM parameter.

/EXM (Server Disk Data Cache Location)

/EXM specifies whether the server's disk data cache buffer should reside in the workstation's standard 640K real-memory address space or in its extended memory (protected memory located above the first memory megabyte).

If /EXM is specified, the server's disk data cache buffer is placed in extended memory; otherwise, the parameter is absent and standard memory is used for the buffer.

/EXM consumes no memory.

/REQ:n (Server Receiver-of-Messages Buffer Count)

/REQ specifies the maximum number of message receives a Server can simultaneously have outstanding to service user machine requests (for shared devices).

The value of /REQ can range from 1 to 6. It defaults to 6, and affects /CMD.

/REQ and /RQB together reserve an amount of memory equal to the product of their specified values, which cannot exceed 48K.

/RQB:n (Server Receiver-of-Messages Buffer Size)

/REQ specifies the buffer size for each message a Server can simultaneously have outstanding to service user-machine requests (for shared devices).

The value of /RQB is specified in bytes. It can range from 512 to 32K and defaults to 8K.

/REQ and /RQB together reserve an amount of memory equal to the product of their specified values, which cannot exceed 48K.

/SHB:n (Sharing Buffer Size)

/SHB specifies the size of the buffer a Server uses to keep track of file sharing and block locking activity on shared subdirectories and disks.

The value of /SHB can range from 512 to 60K bytes. It defaults to 2K bytes.

/SHB reserves an amount of memory equal to the specified request.

/SHL:n (Sharing Lock Count)

/SHL specifies the size of the index buffer a Server uses to keep track of activity in the buffer controlled by /SHB. Thus, /SHL affects /SHB.

The value of /SHL is specified as a count equaling an amount of memory 90 times its size. The count can range from 20 to 1,000; it defaults to 20.

/PRB:n (Print Buffer Size)

/PRB specifies the size of the buffer used by PSPRINT for printer sharing services. Because NET can print only one file at a time, the same buffer on a given print server is used for printing all files, regardless of the printer used. If a print server has two files to print (one on LPT1 and another on LPT2), it must complete one before starting the other.

The value of /PRB is specified in bytes. It can range from 512 to 16K and defaults to 2,048.

/PRB reserves an amount of memory equal to the specified request.

/PCx:n (Printer Character Count)

/PCx:n specifies the maximum number of characters PSPRINT can send to a shared printer in one PSPRINT transmission burst. The value of x specifies the printer and the value of n specifies the number of characters.

x	Printer
1	LPT1 or PRN
2	LPT2
3	LPT3

This parameter is very useful when PSPRINT is used with a high-speed printer, such as IBM's 3812 Page Printer.

Since PSPRINT operates as both a foreground and background task, the /PCx:n parameter can help control the amount of processing PSPRINT consumes. The larger the value of n, the faster the printing occurs on high-speed printers. With such printers, n should equal approximately 150. Otherwise, the default (/PRB) should be adequate. In any event, $1 < n < $ /PRB

/PRP:n (Print Priority)

/PRP specifies the priority of PSPRINT (printer sharing) activities with respect to other foreground (application execution) activity.

The value of /PRP is specified as 1, 2, or 3 for low, medium, or high priority. The default is 3.

/PRP consumes no memory.

/SHR:n (Sharing Count)

/SHR specifies the maximum number of devices you can concurrently share. If a device is shared with several shortnames, each counts as a different device.

The value of /SHR is a count equal to an amount of memory (350 + /SES) times its size. It can range from 1 to 999 and defaults to 5.

/RDR:n (Redirector Count)

/RDR specifies the maximum number of different machines that can simultaneously use network devices on a given Server. If a machine stops using a Server, another can take its place.

The value of /RDR is specified as a count ranging from 1 to 251. Its default is 10, and it affects /SES.

/RDR consumes no memory.

Table 13-1 summarizes the NET START command parameters.

NET USE

Function: Establish a connection to network devices

NET USE allows your workstation to access network devices that have been previously shared. A device that was shared with a shortname must be used with it.

Applicable NET Configurations: SRV, MSG, RCV, and RDR

Command Syntax Summary:

- To use a remote disk or directory as a local drive:
  NET USE d: \\computername\ path | shortname password | *
- To stop using a remote disk or directory as a local drive:
  NET USE d: /D
- To use a remote root directory as a local drive:
  NET USE [d:] \\computername [password | *]
- To gain access to a remote directory but not to use it as a local drive:
  NET USE \\computername\ path | shortname [password | *]
- To stop using a remote directory not being used like a local drive:
  NET USE \\computername\ path | shortname /D
- To use a network printer:
  NET USE printname \\computername\ shortname | printdevice [password | *]
- To stop using a network printer:
  NET USE printname /D
- To display devices you are using:
  NET USE

NET SEND

Function: Send a message to another machine

The recipient is specified as a network name that must be known on the network for NET SEND to successfully execute. The name may be a machine name, an additional name, or a forwarded name.

Alternately, the name may be specified as an asterisk, indicating a broadcast message. In any event, the message can be only about 100 characters. To send larger messages, you must use the menus.

Applicable NET Configurations: SRV, MSG, RCV, and RDR

Command Syntax Summary:

NET SEND computername | addname | * message

NET PRINT

The Net Print command controls the printing of data on network print-server machines. It also allows users to monitor the status of their print requests.

Functions: Access or Monitor Network Printer Services

This includes:

1. Printing a file on a network printer that your machine is using
2. Displaying the status of your print files on a network print queue
3. Displaying status of a local shared print queue

A Server uses this instead of DOS PRINT command with a printer that it has previously shared. Unlike DOS PRINT, NET PRINT does not allow you to use the ? and * "wildcard" characters in the file specifications.

Applicable NET Configurations: SRV, MSG, RCV, and RDR

Command Syntax Summary:

- To transmit a file to a network printer:
  NET PRINT [d: \\computername1]\[path]filename [.ext] printdevice
- To display the status of a remote print queue:
  NET PRINT \\computername2
- To display the status of a local shared print queue:
  NET PRINT

NET PAUSE

Function: Temporarily suspend a workstation network program service

NET PAUSE resets redirected devices to local devices and allows reclaiming of shared resources or a specific printer for private use. The paused function remains in memory but is suspended until it is possibly reactivated by a subsequent NET CONTINUE command. Otherwise it is the same as a permanent suspension. A NET PAUSE command can pause more than one service.

The functions that can be redirected are:

- SERVER—abbreviated SRV
- MESSENGER—abbreviated MSG
- RECEIVER—abbreviated RCV
- Redirector services consisting of

  Disk redirector—abbreviated DRDR
  Print redirector—abbreviated PRDR

Applicable NET Configurations: SRV, MSG, RCV, and RDR
Command Syntax Summary:

- To pause a NET function:
  NET PAUSE [DRDR] [PRDR] [RCV | RECEIVER]
  [MSG | MESSENGER] [SRV | Server]
- To pause a printer:
  NET PAUSE PRT|PRINT [=printdevice]

NET CONTINUE

Function: Resume a paused service
NET Continue is used to resume a service after NET PAUSE has suspended it. A NET Continue command can resume more than one service.

Applicable NET Configurations: SRV, MSG, RCV, and RDR
Command Syntax Summary:

- To continue a NET function:
  NET CONT[INUE] [DRDR] [PRDR] [RCV | RECEIVER]
  [MSG | MESSENGER] [SRV | Server]
- To continue a printer:
  NET CONT[INUE] [PRINT | PRT] [=printname]

NET NAME

Function: Provide additional network name services
NET NAME allows any machine to display its network machine name. In

the case of Servers and Messengers, NET NAME also displays any additional names being used for message receipt and any names used for forwarding. Additional and forwarded names cannot send messages, only receive them. This is why messages can be forwarded only once.

Servers and Messengers can delete additional and forwarded names, terminating message receiving on behalf of those names. However, machine names can never be deleted.

The number of names that a Server or Messenger can add or for which it assumes message forwarding is limited by the /USN parameter on the NET START command.

Applicable NET Configurations: SRV, MSG, RCV, and RDR
Command Syntax Summary:

- To add an additional name for message receipt:
  NET NAME addname
- To delete an additional or forwarded name from message receipt:
  NET NAME name /D
- To display all computer/additional/forwarded names:
  NET NAME

NET FORWARD

Function: Start or stop forwarding of your messages
NET FORWARD allows your machine to forward messages addressed to your machine name or an additional name to another machine. It also terminates the forwarding of messages. Messages are forwarded only once, and the target must be a Server or Messenger. Your forwarded name is added to those of the target machine, so it must be accounted for in the /USN parameter on its NET START command.

Applicable NET Configurations: SRV, MSG
Command Syntax Summary:

- To start message forwarding:
  NET FOR[WARD] yourname1 | username1 othername2 | username2
- To stop message forwarding:
  NET FOR[WARD] yourname1 | username1/D

NET LOG

Function: Use or Monitor NET Logging Services
NET LOG allows you to start or stop using a message log and monitor the

logging. The log can be a file, printer, or the console (CON). The messages are appended to any existing log file.

Applicable NET Configurations: SRV, MSG, RCV

Command Syntax Summary:

- To start logging to a file:
  NET LOG [d:│\\computername] [path] filename [.ext]
- To log to a device (for example, printer or CON):
  NET LOG printdevice│CON
- To turn on or turn off previous logging:
  NET LOG/ON]│OFF
- To display logging status:
  NET LOG

NET SHARE

Function: Share a device on the network

NET SHARE allows your machine to start or stop sharing devices on the network and to monitor the status of devices it is sharing. A NET SHARE must execute for a device before a network machine can use it. NET SHARE can optionally specify access rights to the device and a shortname. Devices shared or used via the menus automatically use shortnames. The number of devices a Server can share is determined by the /SHR parameter on the NET START command.

A Server can share printers, disk subdirectories, and disks. Disk sharing consists of sharing a disk's root directory. If you share a PRN, LPT1, LPT2, or LPT3 printer, NET executes a NET USE command automatically. For AUX, COM1, and COM2 printers, on the other hand, you must explicitly issue a NET USE command.

In any event, you can no longer use the DOS PRINT command for a printer you are sharing. If you use printers you share with the network, you must increase the NET START /RDR parameter by 1 for each shared printer you use.

Applicable NET Configurations: SRV

Disk-Sharing Command Syntax Summary

- To start sharing a disk requires a shortname:
  NET SHARE shortname=d:[\] [password│*] [access rights]
- To stop sharing a disk requires a shortname:
  NET SHARE shortname /D

Directory-Sharing Command Syntax Summary

- To start sharing a directory using a shortname:
  NET SHARE shortname=[d:]path [password | *] [access rights]
- To stop sharing a directory shared by using shortname:
  NET SHARE shortname /D
- To start sharing a directory without shortname:
  NET SHARE [d:] path [password | *] [access rights]
- To stop sharing a directory shared without a shortname:
  NET SHARE path [access rights] /D

Printer Sharing Command Syntax Summary

- To start sharing a printer without a shortname:
  NET SHARE printdevice [password | *]
- To stop sharing a printer shared without a shortname:
  NET SHARE printdevice /D
- To start sharing a printer with a shortname:
  NET SHARE shortname=printdevice [password | *]
- To stop sharing a printer shared with a shortname:
  NET SHARE shortname=printdevice /D
- To display sharing status:
  NET SHARE

NET ERROR

Function: Display network errors

The NET ERROR command displays the most recently occurring network errors that can be stored in NET's error log.

Some errors that can occur are:

- Access errors (unavailable resources)
- NetBIOS errors
- Print queue errors
- Invalid requests to a Server

Applicable NET Configurations: SRV and MSG
Command Syntax Summary:

- To display the error log:
  NET ERROR

- To display the error log and then delete it:
  NET ERROR/D

NET SEPARATOR

Function: Start or stop using a separator page

NET SEPARATOR controls whether a *separator page* is printed on a shared printer. A separator page is a special page that appears between print files. NET SEPARATOR can optionally set the printer MODE (number of lines per page and character size) for every new print file. A separator page definition must be less than 512 bytes in size or an error occurs.

The PQ.SEP file that comes with NET is the default separator page definition file for the IBM Color Printer. It is described in Chapter 10 of the NET User's Manual. A better choice is PQ.OEM, which also comes with NET.

The default NET separator page specifications can be changed. They are in a file named PQ.SEP that comes with the NET program. For an example of specifying a separator page, refer to the discussion in Chapter 10 of the NET User's Guide. Appendix G of this book contains an extensive separator page definition suitable for an IBM Proprinter.

Applicable NET Configurations: SRV, MSG, RCV, and RDR

Command Syntax Summary:

- To obtain the separator page specification file name for all printers you are sharing:
  NET SEP[ARATOR]
- To specify PQ.SEP (default separator page) as the separator page file name for a printer you are sharing:
  NET SEP[ARATOR] printdevice
- To specify a separator page specifications file name for a printer you are sharing:
  NET SEP[ARATOR] printdevice [d:] [path] filename [.ext]
- To stop using separator pages for printer you are sharing:
  NET SEP[ARATOR] printdevice /D

NET FILE

Function: Monitor and control locking activity

NET FILE allows you to detect locks currently in existence for files on devices you have shared, and the names of the users that own the locks. It provides a mechanism that allows you to selectively close open files that are locked, so other machines can access them.

Applicable NET Configurations: SRV
Command Syntax Summary:

- To display the status of all open files:
  NET FILE
- To display the status of a specific file:
  NET FILE [d:] [path] filename [.ext]
- To close a specific file:
  NET FILE [d:] [path] filename [.ext] /C

PC-DOS PC LOCAL AREA NETWORK COMMANDS

Four new PC-DOS commands—APPEND, FASTOPEN, MODE, and PERMIT—appeared with the PC Local Area Network Program. Consult the NET User's Guide for a more detailed discussion of them.

APPEND

APPEND is similar to the DOS PATH command. However, it locates data files in designated directories instead of program files and batch files.

FASTOPEN

FASTOPEN provides PC-DOS with a high-performance directory information caching capability. This can significantly accelerate directory location and searching activities.

MODE

MODE is modified to function with printers provided by network Print Servers. It has the same effect as changing the print mode of a printer from the NET menus. It precedes every print file your machine transmits to a Print Server machine, with the current MODE setting selected by the MODE command or by the NET menus. This helps insure that your file prints in the correct font and spacing.

PERMIT

PERMIT allows any workstation, even one that is not running NET, to become a temporary dedicated file Server to a specific user. The file sharing continues either until the user machines stops using the selected directory or until Ctrl-Break is pressed.

CONFIG.SYS Considerations

NET screens use DOS services. CONFIG.SYS specifies the parameters that affect DOS performance, so NET is also affected. Thus CONFIG.SYS parameters must be adjusted to compensate for NET's presence.

The CONFIG.SYS BUFFERS Parameter

BUFFERS specifies how many 528-byte areas, called DOS buffers, are allocated for transferring data to or from disk files to support DOS applications. There can be from 1 to 99 DOS buffers. The default for a workstation is 2 (3 for a PC AT).

Before DOS reads data from a device for an application, it inspects each buffer to see if it already contains the data. If one does, DOS immediately moves the data from it to the application's data buffer. Otherwise, DOS reads the data from the device into a DOS buffer and then moves the data to the applications data buffer, which takes much longer.

Alternately, before DOS writes any data to a device for an application, DOS checks these buffers to see if one of them contains old data. If so, DOS immediately moves the data from the applications data buffer into the DOS buffer. Otherwise, DOS obtains a new buffer and moves the data into it from the applications buffer. Note that the data are not always immediately written to the device. They remain in memory until the file is closed or until DOS needs the buffer for another disk request.

A large number of buffers can dramatically increase performance by satisfying data requests without disk retrievals. The increase is often most visible in data base processing, where applications request and update data randomly.

However, specifying too many DOS buffers can reduce performance. Too many buffers cause DOS to scan buffers unproductively for application data. After such a search, DOS must perform a relatively long disk read/write. In addition, each unnecessary DOS buffer consumes 528 bytes of memory, decreasing the memory available for DOS applications.

In conclusion, BUFFERS assists network processing only for machines operating as Servers. Machines operating in other configurations use the network buffers to satisfy network disk accesses. However, BUFFERS can still speed the accessing of local disk devices for such machines.

The CONFIG.SYS FCBs Parameter

FCBs controls the maximum number of files that can be simultaneously open using application file control blocks (FCBs). There can be from 1 to 255 FCBs available. The default is 4 (16 when the PC Local Area Network Installation Aid batch file is used). Each FCB table entry consumes approximately 53 bytes of storage.

This parameter is useful only for machines using file sharing. Otherwise, it has no effect.

The CONFIG.SYS FILES Parameter

FILES controls the maximum number of files that can be simultaneously open using file handles—from 8 to 255. The default is 8 (100 when the PC Local Area Network Program Installation Aid batch file is used to install NET on a fixed disk). Each file handle table entry consumes approximately 53 bytes of storage.

This parameter is useful only for machines operating as Servers and for machines that are using file handles, perhaps to process files on local devices. Note that Servers use file handles to open network files.

The CONFIG.SYS LASTDRIVE Parameter

LASTDRIVE specifies how many virtual and actual drives your machine can access simultaneously. The drives are specified as continuous letters ending with (and including) the letter specified on the LASTDRIVE parameter.

There can be up to 26 active drives; each entry in the drive table consumes approximately 77 bytes.

The CONFIG.SYS DEVICE Parameter

This parameter does not affect NET but is included for completeness. DEVICE specifies DOS device drivers that should be loaded and remain resident in memory until your machine is reset. The sizes of the device drivers vary.

Examples of some IBM device drivers are VDISK.SYS, ANSI.SYS, DXMA0MOD.SYS, DXMG2MOD.SYS, DXMT0MOD.SYS, and IBMCACHE.-SYS. Others are available from IBM and from other sources.

Chapter 14

PC Local Area Network Program
System Perspectives

This chapter discusses NET as a system. It is intended for readers who want to adjust NET's default parameters to improve its performance. Of necessity, the material is technical. Readers who are satisfied with their networks' performance need not read this chapter but should be aware of its contents for later reference. Remember the fundamental law of computer performance tuning:

First get the system to work correctly, then worry about improving its performance.

The specific topics we discuss in this chapter are:

- The relationship among calls, commands, and menus
- Memory considerations, including models of the workstation memory and NET memory
- NET application performance considerations
  - the effect of the /SES and /CMD parameters
  - NET file server processing
  - print server processing

THE RELATIONSHIP AMONG NET CALLS, COMMANDS, AND MENUS

NET menus provide a fill-in-the-blank approach to requesting NET services. NET commands are net requests that are presented via the DOS commands or via the NET menu fast-path command line. NET calls are NET requests that are presented by executing programs.

Figure 14-1 illustrates the three approaches to executing NET functions.

NET Calls

A complete discussion of these approaches is beyond the scope of this book. For further reading, consult the NET User's Guide, Appendix C, "Programming Interfaces," and the DOS Technical Reference Manual, Chapter 6, "DOS Interrupts and Function Calls."

The programming calls approach involves writing programs that present requests through the NET programming interface. Alternately, a program can build a NET command and invoke the DOS EXEC function to process it.

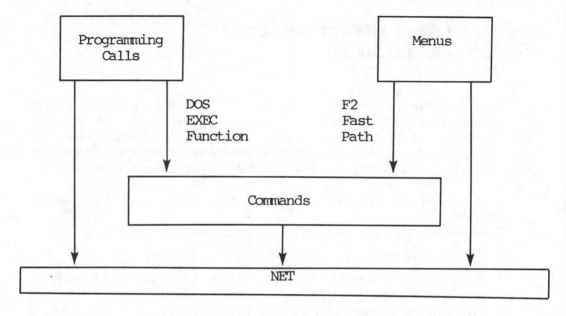

Figure 14-1 The relationship of NET calls, commands, and menus

NET Commands

A second way to invoke NET services uses the NET commands discussed in Chapter 13. As we noted, you can enter NET commands either from the DOS prompt or on the NET fast-path command line that appears when you press function key F2 within a NET menu.

The fast-path is extremely useful because you need not exit from your application. You simply obtain the NET menus via the network request keys, press function key F2, and enter the command. You can then resume your application by exiting the NET menus.

In general, you can do more with NET commands than with the NET menus. For example, NET START is the only way to specify 12 of the 18 NET START Server configuration parameters; the NET menus allow you to specify only 6 of them. In addition, network Server errors can be displayed only by NET ERROR, which is not a NET menu selection.

Finally, asterisks are allowed as passwords only in NET commands in a DOS Batch file. Otherwise, passwords must be contained in batch files that may not be secure.

NET Menus

The third and final way to invoke NET services is with the NET menus. They are useful because they present only options that are valid currently, keeping you from requesting services that cannot be provided.

Menus also provide capabilities that the commands do not. For example, you cannot change the print mode (number of lines per page and character size) on a network printer with a NET command. You must use the NET menus or the DOS MODE command. Menus also let you send messages as long as 1,600 characters, whereas NET SEND allows only 128 characters maximum. In addition, the only way a print Server can change the print queue—for instance, to delete an unwanted or problem listing—is through the NET menus.

Finally, you can save your machine's network configuration only by the NET menus (actually through a sequence of NET commands in your machine's AUTOEXEC.BAT DOS batch file.) Your machine can then automatically resume its current NET capabilities the next time it is reset.

MEMORY CONSIDERATIONS

Memory is a finite workstation resource, consumed by the hardware, DOS, device drivers, and applications. Typically, the more memory a workstation component has available, the faster it operates—but at the expense of other components. Thus, understanding memory use is essential to adjusting parameters to improve a system's performance.

Workstation Memory Model

Figure 14-2 illustrates how your workstation's memory is used after DOS has loaded itself, but before it has searched for your AUTOEXEC.BAT file. (Even with large memory devices available, many workstations such as the original PC family and the PS/2 models 25 and 30 will always be limited to 640K bytes.) Note two important things. First, there are many contenders for your workstation's memory, even before the first application is loaded. Second, the specifications in your system's CONFIG.SYS file may consume a lot of memory. These specifications also affect the performance and capabilities of your workstation.

NET Memory Model

After honoring all the CONFIG.SYS parameters, DOS searches for your machine's AUTOEXEC.BAT file. If you have saved your NET configuration, NET is then installed as a terminate-and-stay-resident application. (A terminate-and-stay-resident program is one that remains in memory even though it may seem to finish execution. It continues to "lurk" unobtrusively in the background and to execute requests as other programs execute. An example of a familiar terminate-and-stay-resident program is the DOS PRINT command, which continues to print data as other programs execute.) Before returning to DOS, the NET program is loaded, and space is reserved for all NET buffers.

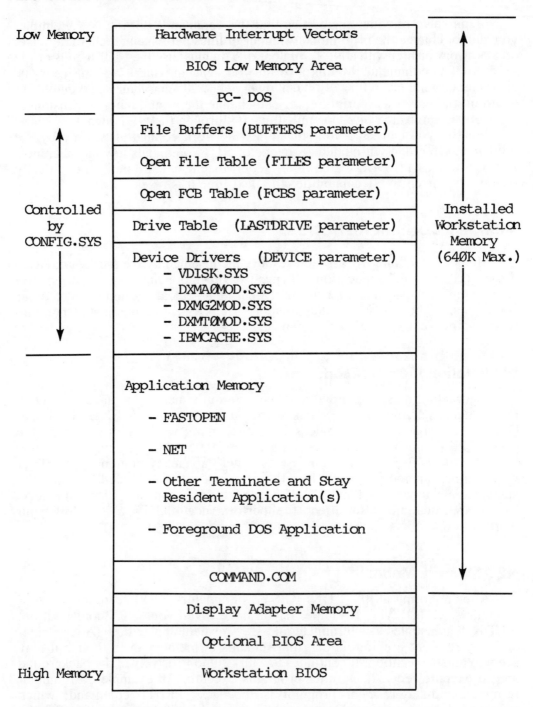

Figure 14-2 Conceptual model of workstation memory utilization

Up to a certain point, NET can improve its performance if more memory is available. However, NET's memory consumption reduces what is available for DOS foreground applications. So a balance must be drawn between NET's efficiency and the machine's applications processing. Optimizing NET's performance may well make the entire machine run slower by depriving applications of memory.

Here are the configuration memory requirements for NET 1.21, assuming the default parameters. The memory figures do not include memory requirements for PC-DOS and applications.

- Redirector—50K
- Receiver—68K
- Messenger—160K
- Server—350K

The following parameters do not affect other parameters or consume memory: /SES, /CMD, /TSI, /EXM, and /PRP.

Other parameters affect the values of other parameters or consume memory.

Parameters Applicable to All Configurations

- /SRV—Determines the size of the Server Table, consumes 70 bytes per entry, affects the /SES default
- /ASG—Determines the size of the Assign Table, consumes 90 bytes per entry, and affects the /PBx value(s)
- /NBC and /NBS—Determines the size of the USE Network Buffer, consumes the product of /NBC times /NBS bytes, and affects the /PBx value(s)
- /PBn—Determines the size of the user print-file transmission buffer(s). Its memory consumption is not well documented

Server and Messenger-Only Parameters

- /MBI—Determines the size of the Message Reception Buffer and consumes the specified amount of memory
- /USN—Determines the size of the Extra Name Table and consumes 600 bytes per entry

Server-Only Parameters

- /CAC—Determines the size of the disk data cache buffer, consumes 1,024 times the specified amount of memory

- /REQ and /RQB—Determines the size of the Request Buffer, consumes the product of /REQ times /RQB bytes, and affects the /PBx value(s) indirectly. If PBx is larger than /REQ, then /PBx minus /REQ bytes are not used

- /SHB—Determines the size of the file sharing and block lock buffer, consumes the specified amount of memory rounded up to the nearest 1K, and affects /SHL

- /SHL—Determines the size of the file sharing and block lock index table, consumes 90 bytes per entry, and affects /SHB

- /PRB—Determines the size of the single network buffer used by a Server's PSPRINT to process all print file requests for a shared printer, and consumes the specified amount of memory

- /SHR—Determines the size of the Device Share Table and consumes 350 bytes per entry

- /RDR—Determines the size of the Remote User Table and consumes no memory

Figure 14-3 provides an approximate way to calculate how much memory NET and DOS consume.

After NET is initialized and operating, DOS executes the AUTOUSER-.BAT file, which may load one or more DOS terminate-and-stay-resident programs. After the AUTOEXEC.BAT file completes execution, the remaining memory is available for foreground application use. You can determine how much remains by using the DOS CHKDSK command to analyze a nonshared disk device.

Summary of the Interrelationships Among NET START Parameters

The /SES default is affected by /RDR, /USN, and /SRV, as well as by the NET configuration.

The /CMD default is affected by /REQ and /USN, as well as by the configuration.

The PC Network LANA message transmission size is affected by /SES and /CMD.

The memory placement (standard or extended) of the server disk data cache buffer specified by the /CAC parameter is determined by the presence of the /EXM parameter.

The /PBx default is affected by /ASG, /SRV, /NBC, and /NBS, as well as

	NET Configuration Reguirement	=	_____
	Value of /SRV × 70	=	_____
All	Value of /ASG × 90	=	_____
Configurations	Value of /NBC × /NBS	=	_____
	Value of /PB1 + /PB2 + /PB3	=	_____
Messenger and	Value of /MBI × 70	=	_____
Server Only	Value of /USN × 600	=	_____
	Value of /CAC × 1024	=	_____
	Value of /REQ × /RQB	=	_____
Server	Value of /SHB	=	_____
Only	Value of /SHL × 90	=	_____
	Value of /PRB	=	_____
	Value of /SHR × 350	=	_____
	NET Memory requirements =		_____

Note: Not all parameters are valid for all configurations.

Figure 14-3 NET memory consumption guidelines

by other "conditions" not specified in the NET User's Guide. So you won't know what the default is.

The memory allocated for network buffers (for access of Server files by machines using a file Server) is bounded by the relationship:

/NBC times /NBS = 32K

The memory allocated for Server request buffers (to service machines using a Server's devices) is bounded by the relationship:

/RQB times /REQ = 48K

Finally, the memory allocated to service file and block locking activity is bounded by the relationship:

/SHB + (/SHL times 90) + size of DOS SHARE Command = 64K

NET PERFORMANCE CONSIDERATIONS

Predicting and modeling the performance of DOS applications that use NET Servers is an exercise involving advanced stochastic calculus of variations with respect to nonlinear multivariant manifold analysis. That's a technical subject for Ph.D. theses. The following discussion deals with the topic only conceptually. For more information, consult the NET User's Guide, Chapter 10, in the discussion titled "Controlling Server Performance."

The Effect of the /SES and /CMD Parameters

/SES and/CMD jointly affect the maximum packet size that a PC Network LANA adapter can transmit for printer and disk-sharing activities using its native NetBIOS ROM support.

NET File Server Processing

/NBC and/NBS are the most important performance parameters for a using machine. These services are provided by the REDIR.EXE DOS redirector extension, which is available to all configurations. A Server may simultaneously be a user of network devices, so these parameters also apply to Servers in that situation.

In the case of a shared printer, /NBC should be at least equal to the maximum number of open network files, while /NBS should be equal to the largest used Server's /RQB specification. Because /NBC and /NBS are not independently selectable, this may not be possible.

Figure 14-4 presents an overview of a machine using a file Server. It assumes that a user machine needs a file on a Server disk for subsequent processing.

Table 14-1 summarizes the various buffers and their relationships.

The process is:

1. The Server starts NET with NET START, specifying the size and number of Server Network Request Buffers in /RQB and /REQ.
2. The user starts NET with NET START, specifying the size and number of user Network Buffers in /NBC and/NBS.
3. The Server provides network access to the subdirectory with NET SHARE.
4. The user gains access to the Server's subdirectory with NET USE.
5. The user issues DOS file open and read requests to begin file processing.
6. The user's REDIR.EXE intercepts the calls and transmits the requests to the Server via the user's Network Buffers.
7. The user's network adapter transmits the requests to the Server's adapter using network packets.
8. The Server's adapter receives the requests and puts them in the Server's Network Request Buffers.
9. The Server's NET reads the file on the Server's disk, using standard DOS services and buffers. Performance may be enhanced by using FASTOPEN and a server disk data caching buffer specified by the NET /CAC parameter or the IBMCACHE.SYS device driver.
10. The file data are moved from the intermediate DOS buffers and placed in one of the Server's Network Request Buffers.

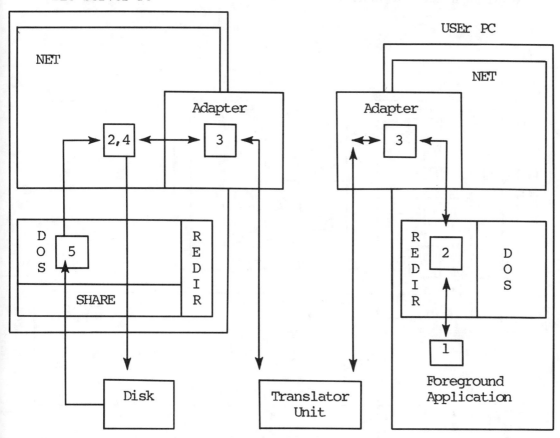

Figure 14-4 Conceptual view of a user machine processing a file on a server machine

Note: **On the File Server PC, buffers 2 and 4 are actually the same buffer used for two different purposes (receiving as well as sending).**

Buffers	Determined By
1 → Application	Application
2 → Network Buffers	/NBC and /NBS
3 → Adapter Transmission	/SES and /CMD
4 → Network Request	/RQB and /REQ
5 → DOS	CONFIG.SYS

Table 14-1 Relationship of the Buffers Illustrated in Fig. 14-6.

Note: **On the File Server PC, buffers 2 and 4 are actually the same buffer used for two different purposes (receiving as well as sending).**

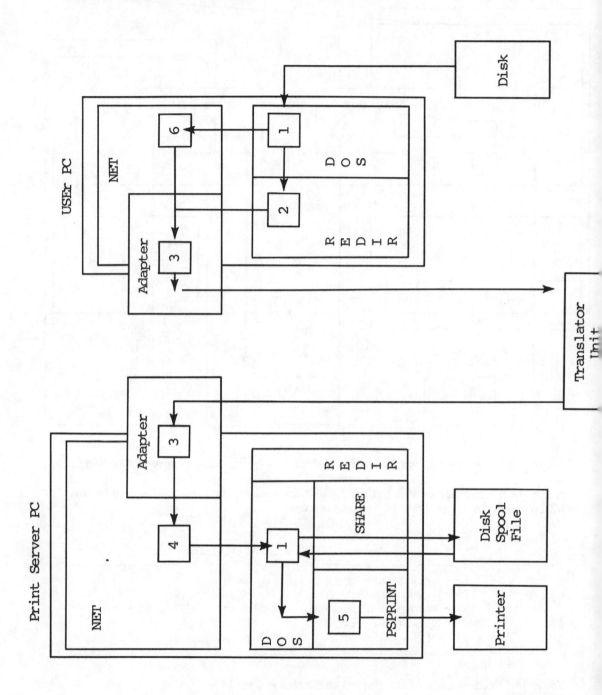

11. The Server's network adapter transmits the data to the user's adapter, using network packets.
12. The user's adapter places the data in one of the user's Network Buffers.
13. The user's NET moves the data in chunks to the application's buffer as the application requests them.
14. The DOS application receives and begins processing the data.

A similar process is used to transmit a file to the Server's disk from a user machine. Though each process is involved, owners of machines without fixed disks are likely able to process data as if they had suddenly acquired one.

Net Print Server Processing

Figure 14-5 presents an overview of a machine using a print Server. It assumes that a file on a local disk is transmitted to the print Server for processing, as follows:

1. The Server starts NET with NET START, specifying the size of the Network Request and PSPRINT Buffers with /RQB and /PRB.
2. The user starts NET with NET START, specifying the size of the Print-File Transmission Buffer with /PBx.
3. The Server provides network access to the printer with NET SHARE.
4. The user gains access to the Server's printer with NET USE.
5. The user issues a NET PRINT command to print the local file.
6. The file is read from the local disk using DOS services and buffers.
7. The data are moved from the intermediate DOS buffers to an internal buffer.
8. The data in the internal Buffer are fetched by the user's adapter and transmitted through the translator to the Server's adapter.
9. The Server's adapter places the data in the Server's Network Request Buffer.
10. Using DOS services such as SHARE, the Server's NET writes the data to the print queue located in a fixed disk, which involves an intermediate transfer through DOS buffers.

Figure 14-5 Conceptual view of a user machine transmitting a print file to a print-server machine

Note: **For performance reasons, NET PRINT bypasses REDIR since it recognizes that its output is going to a network printer. Thus, with NET PRINT, the /PBx specified buffer is not used. The /PBx buffer only is used for print data generated by applications.**

Buffers	Determined by
1 → DOS	CONFIG.SYS
2 → Print-File Transmission	/PBx
3 → Adapter Transmission	/NBC and /NBS
4 → Network Request	/RQB and /REQ
5 → PSPRINT	PRB
6 → NET PRINT Internal Buffer	NET PRINT

Table 14-2 Summary Relationship of the Buffers Illustrated in Figure 14-5.

Note: **For performance reasons, NET PRINT bypasses REDIR since it recognizes that its output is going to a network printer. Thus, with NET PRINT, the /PBx specified buffer is not used. The /PBx buffer is only used for print data generated by applications**

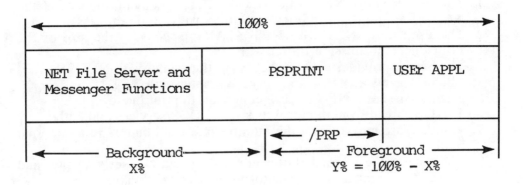

X and Y Determined by /TSI:fb	NOTE
$$X = \frac{v(b)}{v(b) + v(f)}$$	v(b) = number of ticks corresponding to a /TSI background specification of the integer b. v(f) = number of ticks corresponding to a /TSI foreground specification of the integer f.

Figure 14-6 Conceptual relationship between foreground and background processing time noting that PSPRINT's impact is generally unpredictable

11. Using DOS services, PSPRINT subsequently reads the data from the fixed disk print queue into the PSPRINT buffer. Again, this involves an intermediate transfer through DOS buffers.
12. PSPRINT eventually prints the data.

Table 14-2 summarizes the various buffers and their relationships.

BALANCING FOREGROUND AND BACKGROUND PROCESSING

As discussed earlier, all File Server and Messenger/Server message logging is achieved by background processing. However, NET conducts Print-Server activities in both background and foreground, along with DOS applications processing.

/TSI attempts to control the ratio of foreground to background processing. However, this is complicated by the fact that print services occur in both. Thus, once the foreground gains control, an application must contend with NET foreground PSPRINT activities, just as NET's other background functions must contend with PSPRINT activities. This situation is exacerbated when PSPRINT is printing on a high performance printer, such as IBM's 3812 Page Printer. In such cases, the/PCx:n parameter should be used to "throttle back" PSPRINT so other processing can proceed.

The ratio of printing to application processing is roughly determined by /PRP, which specifies the relative importance of PSPRINT activities and those of the Server's applications. Figure 14-6 summarizes the effects of/TSI and/PRP.

Finally, note that specifying /TSI = 00 disables time slicing and allows foreground activities to proceed only when there are no message logging or File Server activities to perform. Specifying/TSI = 00 is generally inadvisable for Print Servers.

Chapter 15

Other IBM LAN Software

This chapter rounds out the software discussion for IBM's LANs. It provides an overview of several LAN connectivity offerings, such as IBM's PC Network 3270 Program, IBM's remote NetBIOS access facility, and IBM's asynchronous communications server.

IBM's LOCAL AREA NETWORK SUPPORT PROGRAM

The IBM Local Area Network Support Program provides IBM's LAN adapters with PC-DOS device drivers that allow them to operate on their networks. It also provides applications with several levels of application programming interfaces. One of the most important of them is the NetBIOS programming interface.

What is NetBIOS?

A workstation's BIOS serves as an insulator between applications programs and hardware. It allows programs to execute on continually evolving hardware, without patches or updating. In the same way, NetBIOS shields network application programs from the actual IBM LAN adapter hardware.

NetBIOS provides a well-documented procedure by which a workstation program can make requests of an adapter. The procedure consists of filling in a request block and signaling the adapter to process the request. This approach presents a consistent architecture for requesting network services amidst diverse and evolving adapter hardware technologies.

Many LAN vendors besides IBM have adopted the NetBIOS interface. It has passed its first step in becoming an international, de facto standard for invoking LAN services, regardless of the network.

To reinforce this trend, IBM has stated that every IBM LAN will be able to run programs written using NetBIOS services. So, applications you develop should be portable to the IBM Token-Ring and to General Motors' MAP manufacturing token bus.

NetBIOS Services

A program can request four types of adapter services of a NetBIOS supported adapter:

- General Support, which resets the adapter, requests adapter status, and cancels previous requests
- Name Support, which adds and deletes names from a table of names, referred to as the NetBIOS Name Table
- Message Transmission and Receipt services, which include
  - Session Control, which establishes and terminates sessions, oversees data exchange, and provides session status
  - Datagram Support, which transmits and receives datagrams

These services are accessible from high-level languages such as C and PASCAL. Their existence means that programmers can write their applications without having to continually reinvent network system operation code. Moreover, the services are independent of the operating system. Thus, for example, they can be accessed from OS/2 Extended Addition applications, as well as from PC-DOS.

Name Support

In a LAN, each adapter receives all messages, regardless of the intended recipient. Obviously, an adapter must have a way to identify messages that are meant for it and to discard the remainder. This function is achieved by allowing each adapter to be named on the network. Each message can then include the identities of transmitting and receiving nodes.

An adapter allows its node to be known by as many as 17 different names. Sixteen of these can be specified by programs executing in the workstation; the adapter remembers them in a table called the Name Table. This table can be altered or even completely cleared under workstation program control. The table is also cleared every time the node is rebooted.

The 16 individual names can be either unique names specific to the node or group names shared by several nodes. Regardless of the type, names can be no more than 16 characters long. Lowercase letters and uppercase letters are distinct, and names can also include special characters and spaces, for instance Greg__Schwaderer__
Melissa__Ann_____

Since hexadecimal values are also allowed as letters within names, the total number of possible names is about 3.37 times 10 to the 38th power. Since it would take quite a while to randomly guess a confidential unique name (don't try), this approach provides a fair degree of natural security.

Unique Names

When a workstation program requests that a unique name be added to the Name Table, the adapter first broadcasts it on the network to see if any other node is currently using it. If another adapter is using the name, it complains across the network, and the first adapter notifies its workstation program that the name cannot be used.

In the absence of complaints, the first adapter adds the name to the Name Table as a unique name and so notifies the workstation program. The adapter must then remain vigilant, so that it automatically complains if some other adapter subsequently attempts to use the name.

The selection and use of unique names can present problems that may require central coordination across a network. For instance, two Charlies may want to use
Charlie‗‗‗‗‗
as a network name. One Charlie can learn who the other one is by using an adapter status inquiry. This inquiry returns, among other things, the permanent node name of the node using the name Charlie.

Group Names

A group name lets several nodes share a name, such as DepartmentL43Cal. This allows messages to be routed to entire groups, such as an entire department, rather than to individuals, reducing network traffic.

When a workstation program requests the addition of a group name to the Name Table, the adapter first broadcasts it on the network to see if any other node is currently using it as a unique name. If another adapter is doing so, it complains across the network, as with unique names. The first adapter then notifies its workstation program that the name cannot be used.

In the absence of complaints, the first adapter adds the name to the Name Table as a group name and so notifies the workstation program. The adapter must then remain vigilant, so that it can complain if some other adapter subsequently attempts to use it as a unique name. However, if another adapter attempts to use the name as a group name, no complaint is issued.

The Permanent Node Name

The seventeenth name, called the Permanent Node Name, is guaranteed to be different from every other adapter name in the world. It is permanently etched in the adapter's memory, just as an adapter's unique serial number is permanently affixed to its exterior.

The Permanent Node Name is essential in high-security applications, as it guarantees that a message came from a specific adapter or will be received by one or both. Using unique names cannot guarantee this type of natural security, because a workstation that should be using a unique name may be turned off. Another workstation would then be able to impersonate the authentic one by adding and using the same unique name. Preventing such a situation is one of the duties of the network administrator.

Adapter Status

An adapter provides its status to workstation programs on request or in response to a status request from another adapter addressing it by one of its names. In the second case, the requesting adapter could be located in a network control center that provides a single point of network management. The following status information is provided:

- The Permanent Node Name of the target adapter
- Message and error statistics, as well as the time interval during which they were gathered
- Manufacturing version of the adapter card
- Current contents of the Name Table (this is where you learn if a unique name is being used by more than one person)
- Jumper settings (if any)
- On-line test results

An operational network allows an adapter to verify that its transmitter is not permanently on. Adapters whose transmitters are permanently on disrupt the network; we call them "screaming" or "babbling" adapters or adapters with "constant carriers" or "hot carriers." Such an adapter disrupts the network because its constant transmission keeps other adapters from transmitting (as discussed under CSMA/CD in Chapter 3).

PC Network adapters continually monitor their own operation and the behavior of the network. When the network adapters detect a constant carrier signal for more than 30 seconds, indicating a hot carrier, all adapters immediately test to see if their own transmitter circuitry is at fault. (Thirty seconds is enough time for typical network maintenance tests.)

The hot-carrier test requires each adapter to transmit a short message to itself without turning on its transmitter. When the message is transmitted, the offending adapter and all other adapters are aware of the identity of the failing adapter, and each workstation is appropriately notified.

A final PC Network on-line test is called the *missing-carrier detection test*. If an adapter is trying to transmit but cannot detect its own transmission, its transmitter is assumed to be dead.

- Session Status

More specific transmission information can be obtained from an adapter with a session status request. However, another adapter cannot issue such a request across the network because it may present a security exposure in some environments in which communications patterns are confidential. Such a request can come only from the adapter's own workstation and be sent only to another workstation.

Message Transmission and Receipt

Once an adapter has added its name(s), it can use it (them) or the Permanent Node Name to exchange data with other nodes. The actual transmission rate is 2 million bits per second (250,000 characters per second).

Coaxial cable's transmission characteristics, the network's frequency modulation technique, and the adapter's error recovery capabilities make the probability of a transmission error less than one chance in a trillion. This is one error every 500,000 seconds (about 1,800 hours), at most.

An adapter transmits in a low-frequency range (channel) centered at 50.75 MHz and receives in a high-frequency range centered at 219 MHz. Because of the characteristics of the CSMA/CD access method, an adapter must operate as a full-duplex device—that is, a device capable of sending and receiving simultaneously.

Message traffic is handled in two ways: as session traffic and as datagram traffic.

Session Support

When two network nodes need to exchange data on a continuing basis, it is usually advantageous for them to establish a session. Doing so allows each node to exchange data more capably under extensive adapter vigilance in the spirit of the ISO seven-layer reference model discussed earlier. Sessions are like telephone calls, except that an adapter can also talk to itself for testing or diagnostic purposes.

Once in session, a node can send data to the other node by referring to a unique assigned session number (conceptually a unique telephone circuit) in its transmission request. The session number is assigned to a session by the adapter and provided to the workstation program during notification that the session has been established.

A given adapter can conduct a maximum of 32 simultaneous sessions, using any or all of its maximum of 16 names. It can have several simultaneous sessions with the same adapter or with different adapters. Again, each individual session would have a unique assigned session number to keep the various sessions from becoming confused.

As you might expect, considerable session-level support is required by layered architecture. Session support allows your workstation to engage in productive parallel processing, such as spreadsheet processing, while the network adapter concurrently handles much of the communications processing.

Datagram Support

If a network node needs to send a single or infrequent short message (up to a maximum of 512 characters) to another node, it is often advantageous to avoid the overhead of establishing a session. Instead, you can take a shortcut by sending a datagram. Unrestricted by the maximum session limit of 32, a datagram potentially allows a node to communicate with every node on the network.

You should think of a datagram as a "send and pray" message. There is no guarantee that the node will ever receive it, though it will have all the transmission error checking of a session message. Datagrams are simply transmitted on a best-effort basis. If they do not find a home, well, that's life in the big network. Even if it does arrive safely, the recipient adapter does not automatically acknowledge receipt. The receiving workstation must initiate such acknowledgment.

Finally, the sender can address a datagram to a specific node or to all network nodes. In the second instance, we call it a *broadcast datagram*.

NOVELL ADVANCED NETWARE/PCN

In November 1985, IBM announced it would market Advanced NetWare/ PCN, a high-performance alternative to the PC Local Area Network Program. Nodes using Advanced NetWare/PCN exclusively cannot communicate with nodes that use the PC Local Area Network Program exclusively, though the two programs can operate simultaneously on the same network.

Advanced NetWare/PCN has features not found in the PC Local Area Network Program, as well as faster performance in some environments. This product is also of interest because it operates on other communication products, such as the IBM Cluster.

Advanced NetWare/PCN uses a centralized management approach to control network names. In addition, it provides a system that allows messages to be delivered to a user's mailbox without the user being active on the network.

The cost of a single Advanced NetWare/PCN license substantially exceeds that of a single PC Local Area Network Program license. However, an Advanced NetWare/PCN license applies to up to 50 machines on a network. Thus, an Advanced NetWare/PCN license may prove more economical for networks having more than 20 nodes. Licensing is enforced by a hardware "key card" that must be installed in file Servers; a Server can support multiple user machines with various network services.

For more information on Novell's Advanced NetWare/PCN, contact:

Novell, Incorporated
1170 North Industrial Park Drive
Orem, Utah 84057
U.S.A.

Telephone: (800) 453-1267
              (801) 226-8202

IBM'S PC NETWORK ANALYSIS PROGRAM

The IBM PC Network Analysis Program provides a workstation using a PC Network LANA card with the functions necessary to watch PC LANA network traffic rates and decide which workstation–server pairings provide maximum performance. Specifically it permits:

- Monitoring broadband PC Network message activity—It can monitor the origin, destination, and size of messages, which is useful in determining Server loads and identifying network bottlenecks. The collection of this information is user-specified, and up to 32 adapters can be monitored simultaneously.

- Monitoring broadband PC Network operational errors for user-designated adapters—The program obtains the status of remote adapters using a technique similar to the NetBIOS Remote Adapter Status Command. This process obtains detailed information regarding errors that an adapter has experienced.

- Selectively logging message traffic statistics for subsequent analysis—The information can be reviewed on-line, or printed using a simple BASIC program provided as an example. Information includes: the Current Network Status (that is, the percentage of network utilization, the approximate number of network-caused delays experienced by users, the packet traffic statistics for monitored adapters, and the percentage of adapters experiencing errors exceeding a user-specified threshold); the log of notices issued within the specified period; the traffic pattern report that, as a security precaution, says nothing about the data contained in the messages; and the directory of powered-on adapters with location and owner information.

- Maintaining adapter location and owner information

- Monitoring adapter errors and issuing a notice when a threshold is exceeded

In summary, the PC Network Analysis Program can assist a network installation in problem determination, problem prevention, and planning. These capabilities are critical in large, complex networks.

The program results in less than 5 percent increased traffic on a network. It requires at least DOS 3.1 and IBM's EZ-VU Runtime Facility. It can operate only on an original PC Network LANA, not on the IBM Token-Ring or other IBM LANs. For more information, contact your local IBM representative or obtain the following IBM publications: IBM PC Network Analysis Program User's Guide (SC23-0782); IBM PC Network Analysis Program Quick Reference Card (SC23-0785); and PC Network Analysis Program Technical Guide (GG24-1727). You can also obtain information about courses on the IBM PC Network Program Analysis Program directly from IBM.

IBM'S PC NETWORK 3270 PROGRAM

The PC Network 3270 program allows a workstation to communicate via a dedicated or switched SDLC link with an IBM SNA/370 mainframe host. (If you do not understand the previous statement, you probably do not need to read the following discussion.)

Through emulation, the workstation communicates with the host as if it were an IBM SNA 3274-51C controller with an attached IBM 3278 display and IBM 3287 printer. Alternately, the workstation can be a node on a PC Network and also act as a network gateway Server for other nodes. In any event, NET should be started before the PC Network 3270 program is started on a gateway or any of the workstation using it as a gateway.

There can be more than one PC Network 3270 gateway on a PC Network. Each gateway can control up to 32 sessions with the host; a given gateway user node can be attached only to a single gateway at a given time. Provisions exist for the workstations and the host to exchange data files, as well as messages. Because the PC Network 3270 Program uses the NetBIOS interface, it can operate on the IBM Token-Ring as well.

For more information, contact your local IBM representative or obtain the following IBM publications: IBM PC Network 3270 Program Reference (S544-2286) and PC Network 3270 Emulation (GG24-1695).

IBM's LOCAL AREA NETWORK ASYNCHRONOUS CONNECTION SERVER PROGRAM

The IBM Local Area Network Asynchronous Connection Server Program allows asynchronous communication devices such as the IBM 3101 terminal to connect to a LAN workstation operating the IBM Local Area Network Asynchronous Connection Server Program. The attaching device can then request LAN services. In this mode, the server is configured to be an inbound server.

Alternately, the server workstation can be configured to be an outbound server. In this configuration, LAN workstations can connect to the server and request asynchronous communication connections with devices or services outside the LAN, such as an IBM RT/PC.

The IBM Local Area Network Asynchronous Connection Server Program requires a dedicated machine and can coexist on a LAN with other workstations operating the IBM Local Area Network Asynchronous Connection Server Program or the IBM Asynchronous Communications Server Program.

IBM's ASYNCHRONOUS COMMUNICATIONS SERVER PROGRAM

The IBM Asynchronous Communications Server allows a network work-station to become a network modem server. Using a special publicly documented communications protocol, called the IBM Asynchronous Communications Server Program Protocol, applications in other network workstations communicate with the modem server using NetBIOS command requests.

A network can have more than one modem server. A server can control up to two modems simultaneously. And each modem can conduct an independent asynchronous communications session over traditional telephone lines or CBX connections. A modem server does not have to be a dedicated server.

IBM's REMOTE NETBIOS ACCESS FACILITY PROGRAM

The IBM Remote NetBIOS Access Facility Program allows a stand-alone PC or PS/2 workstation to connect to a participating LAN server workstation; the connection uses an asynchronous communication link and allows the connecting workstation to participate in LAN activities as if it were actually part of the LAN.

Using the Remote NetBIOS Access Facility Program in each workstation, the attaching workstation is configured as a Remote NetBIOS Access Facility Program Remote Facility and the LAN server workstation is configured as a Remote NetBIOS Access Facility Program LAN-Gateway Facility. In both cases, the Remote NetBIOS Access Facility Program operates as a background application and each machine requires its own Remote NetBIOS Access Facility Program license.

The appearance of LAN connectivity is achieved by the Remote Facility configuration forwarding NetBIOS requests to the LAN-Gateway facility where they are executed. The results of the NetBIOS requests are returned to the Remote Facility when they are available.

The LAN-Gateway can recognize up to 255 connecting machines and can support only two simultaneous connections with Remote Facilities. A Remote Facility can be configured to connect with up to ten LAN-Gateway Facilities but can connect to only one of them at a time.

IBM TOKEN-RING NETWORK/PC NETWORK INTERCONNECT PROGRAM

The IBM Token-Ring Network/PC Network Interconnect Program interconnects two NetBIOS LANs and allows up to 16 workstation applications on one LAN to establish communication sessions with up to 16 workstation applications on the other LAN. The IBM Token-Ring Network/PC Network Interconnect Program provides this service by acting as an intermediary between each of the communication applications.

Hence, if applications A, B, and C on one LAN need to communicate with applications X, Y, and Z on the other LAN, the IBM Token-Ring Network/PC Network Interconnect Program poses as application X, Y, and Z to A, B, and C on the first LAN while it poses as application A, B, and C to application X, Y, and Z on the other LAN.

To configure the program, an operator specifies the following information:

- The unique network names that can use the facility
- The largest message size that can be passed
- Transmission time-out values
- The maximum number of concurrent sessions that can be supported

The IBM Token-Ring Network/PC Network Interconnect Program does not officially support baseband IBM PC Networks. However, unless an application program specifically looks for the type of PC Network adapters it is using (baseband versus broadband), it is difficult for them to detect any difference between baseband IBM PC Network adapters and their broadband counterparts. Hence, it is a good bet the Token-Ring Network/PC Network Interconnect Program will interconnect baseband PC Networks to Token-Rings, though any subsequent problems will be the responsibility of the users.

ADVANCED PROGRAM-TO-PROGRAM COMMUNICATION FOR THE IBM PERSONAL COMPUTER (*APPC/PC*)

APPC/PC provides workstations IBM System Network Architecture (SNA) Logical Unit 6.2 (LU 6.2) over IBM LANs or Synchronous Data Link Control (SDLC) connections. APPC/PC allows workstations using it to communicate with other workstations that are also running it. In addition, workstations can also communicate with other systems that are providing APPC support. These include:

- IBM System/36 systems
- IBM Series/1 systems
- IBM System 370 CICS systems

After installing and running APPC/PC, applications make requests to APPC/PC through APPC/PC verbs using a process similar to the way applications make NetBIOS requests. APPC/PC uses an adapter programming interface (DLC) that is different from NetBIOS, so APPC/PC operates independently of NetBIOS.

IBM LAN MANAGER PROGRAM

The IBM LAN Manager Program is a local area network management and problem-determination program for IBM LANs that operate with the IBM LAN Support Program. The LAN manager allows users to maintain network records, analyze LAN problems, and monitor network conditions. The workstation operating the LAN Manager Program can:

- prepare the LAN Manager for operation by defining its operating environment, passwords, etc.
- generate network event and activity log reports that contain adapter and media problem information such as probable cause and recommended actions to take to resolve the problem
- display/set system options and definitions
- query the current status of any or all network workstations
- monitor, and remove adapters from the network
- test network paths
- display the order of adapters on a Token-Ring
- display/set soft error logging and conditions
- manipulate Token-Ring bridges
- reinitialize the LAN Manager Program and reopen its workstation adapter

The IBM LAN Manager can operate stand-alone or as an application under IBM's network management program NetView/PC. Operating as a NetView/PC application allows the IBM LAN Manager to forward network information to an IBM mainframe host operating NetView and provides a remote console function for the LAN Manager workstation.

The IBM LAN Manager also coordinates its activities with the IBM Token-Ring Network Bridge Program.

IBM ENHANCED COMMUNICATION FACILITY

The IBM Enhanced Communication Facility (ECF) provides LAN workstations a cooperative processing facility with IBM mainframe hosts. The host can provide data storage and print support for LAN workstations. Workstation applications access these services as though they were provided by local devices. The IBM Enhanced Communication Facility requires software in both the host and workstation.

ECF's cooperative processing approach allows host applications to access certain types of workstation data as mainframe data. This allows text files to be readable on both host and workstation displays—even though the machines use different data codes (EBCDIC and ASCII respectively). The translation is selective and can be disabled as appropriate.

IBM TOKEN-RING NETWORK BRIDGE PROGRAM

The IBM Token-Ring Network Bridge Program interconnects two independent Token-Rings and selectively passes messages between the rings. It provides LAN workstations network and supervisory functions such as:

- ring number identification information, which replaces the adapter's default
- network statistics for both attached rings, which can be analyzed by the IBM LAN Manager Program
- network configuration information, which can be analyzed by the IBM LAN Manager Program
- problem-determination information, which can be analyzed by the IBM LAN Manager Program
- performance information, which can be analyzed by the IBM LAN Manager Program
- Message path traversal information for selected messages

Some programs, such as NetBIOS, transmit special network supervisory messages called limited-broadcast messages. Generally, more than one instance of an individual limited broadcast message should not appear on any individual network. If two networks share more than one bridge, it is possible each bridge could place a limited-broadcast message from one network on the adjoining ring. To prevent this, you can specify whether a bridge operating under the IBM Token-Ring Network Bridge Program can pass limited-broadcast messages.

IBM TOKEN-RING NETWORK TRACE AND PERFORMANCE PROGRAM

The IBM Token-Ring Network Trace and Performance Program provides visibility to IBM Token-Ring Networks traffic and performs user data-throughput measurements. A traffic trace function allows analysis of application programs that use different protocols on the ring and a performance function provides insight into the ring's utilization by all stations or a user-selected subset. When tracing begins and ends, a special message is sent to the IBM LAN Manager for logging as a measure of network security.

The IBM Token-Ring Network Trace and Performance Program requires an IBM Token-Ring Network Trace and Performance PC Adapter II or an IBM Token-Ring Network Trace and Performance Adapter/A.

IBM PC NETWORK PROTOCOL DRIVER

The IBM PC Network Protocol Driver allows PC Network II and PC Network II/A broadband adapters to communicate using PC Network LANA protocols. The IBM PC Network Protocol Driver Program is used in lieu of the IBM Local Area Network Support Program. Appendix C discusses PC Network LANA protocols in greater detail.

Section 7

Custom Broadband Networks for Establishment Communication

Chapter 16

Advantages of Broadband Networks

Large custom broadband networks may cover more area and have more nodes and services than networks that use the IBM PC Network Translator Unit or the IBM PC Network Cabling System exclusively. Such networks can be used in establishments that must meet a wide range of communications needs, including training, security, and image handling, as well as voice and data communications.

CABLE TELEVISION INDUSTRY EXPERIENCE

The forerunner of large custom broadband networks is the cable TV industry. When it began operation in 1949, it had to meet unprecedented communications requirements on an unprecedented scale. Because these requirements continue in today's industry and parallel the needs of establishment communications systems, it is useful to review them and examine the solutions.

Accommodating the Unknown

Cable TV companies must accommodate unpredictable growth in metropolitan areas. To be prepared for the unknown requires extreme network flexibility. Furthermore, a network must also accommodate unanticipated levels of electromagnetic interference and radio frequency interference (EMI/RFI). And, finally, signal-reflection problems must be minimized to allow enormous geographical scope.

Solution: Select branching-tree topology using coaxial cable and directional couplers to achieve maximum flexibility while minimizing signal reflection.

Hostile Environments

Cable TV networks are big, so there is economic pressure to minimize component costs. However, these inexpensive parts must be rugged at the same time. This combination is difficult to achieve.

Moreover, signal strength decreases (attenuates) as cable temperature increases (1 percent per 10 degrees Fahrenheit increase as a rule of thumb), so the requirement to withstand temperature variations across the network is not an idle, academic consideration.

Solution: Develop cables and connectors suited to virtually every environment, including stringently specified military and government secure environments.

Building Code Compliance

Building codes vary wildly across the United States. Cable TV companies must be able to comply with a spectrum of them.

Solution: Develop over 150 types or grades of cable, including Teflon-coated, so cables comply with virtually any building code.

Component Reliability

In some instances, network cables must be buried several feet below the ground. Since cable TV networks generally cover wide areas, complete cable and component redundancy is prohibitively expensive.

It is also expensive to dig up several yards of cable to find a failing 6-inch section or connector. Clearly, network components must function reliably, even though they are deeply buried for decades, perhaps under lawn sprinkler systems, roads, and sidewalks.

Solution: Design passive components (tilt attenuators, attenuators, taps, and splitters) that have a standard mean time between failure of 30 to 40 years, varying types of cables for varying longevity requirements, and signal amplifiers with a mean time between failure of nearly 20 years.

Traditionally, the biggest problems with broadband networks have been faulty connector installation and careless operators of backhoes and trenchers that sever outside trunk lines. Fortunately, such equipment seldom enters offices!

Media Signal Sharing

A cable TV company cannot economically dedicate a cable to each TV station. Thus, each cable must have substantial bandwidth that many signals can share.

Solution: Divide the enormous bandwidth of coaxial cable into frequency ranges. Use frequency modulation to transmit individual signals within single channels in accordance with the industry standard channel/frequency assignment table.

Remote Power

Since cable TV signals lose signal strength as they radiate, amplification is necessary. In addition, amplifiers should also compensate for the impact of temperature fluctuations. However, amplifiers require electrical power, which may be difficult to provide if the cable is buried or otherwise inaccessible.

Solution: Devise coaxial cable that can unobtrusively transmit AC electricity as well as normal signals to neighboring amplifiers. Design amplifiers that have adaptive capability (equalization and gain [amplification]) to compensate for temperature variations.

Isolation

Cable TV systems should not fail totally because of a problem in one small geographic area. The network must be relatively insensitive to problems such as shorts, and it should be able to operate while it is being expanded or maintained. As an analogy, one would not want to shut down an entire city's water supply to repair or add a water main in a distant suburb.

Solution: Use a branching-tree topology that naturally provides enormous isolation between sections of the network, and develop techniques for real-time maintenance.

Low-Cost Components

While cable TV components must be of extremely high quality, the enormous geographic coverage of cable TV networks mandates that they be inexpensive.

Solution: Establish stringent component standards that are widely accepted, resulting in an extremely cost-competitive industry that produces components at commodity prices.

Typical 1987 component prices for a broadband LAN are:

- $0.25 per foot for a 1/2-inch cable
- $26.00 for an outside tap
- $800.00 to $1,500.00 for an amplifier
- $24.00 for an eight-way inside drop
- $10.00 to $70.00 for a drop cable

The wide variety of cable types also makes it easy to select the best cable for price-sensitive network applications.

Low Skill Level

Because cable TV networks are so large, it is essential to minimize the skill level to install and maintain them.

Solution: Develop network technology using standardized modular components that are easy to understand, install, and repair. This also minimizes training and maintenance costs.

BROADBAND NETWORKS

No single type of LAN is perfect for every application or environment. Each has its unique advantages. But the capabilities of a broadband network significantly overlap those of virtually all other network types, as you will learn in this chapter. For instance, its strengths overlap those of twisted pair and fiber-optic networks. This makes a broadband network a strong contender for any local area network application.

For example, a broadband PC Network consumes no more than 5 percent of the transmission capacity of many broadband systems, which means it is only one of many services that a broadband network can carry within your establishment. The over 95 percent of transmission capacity remaining is available for independent and unrelated services, and should be administered as a corporate resource.

The advantages of broadband networks include:

- Extensive and comprehensive geographic coverage
- Ease of expansion
- Enormous transmission bandwidth
- Natural migration path for new devices
- Mixed service support
- Low cost
- High reliability
- Benefits of a mature technology
- Interchangeable parts

EXTENSIVE AND COMPREHENSIVE GEOGRAPHIC COVERAGE

The flexibility of the wiring arrangement (branching-tree topology, discussed in Chapter 3) used by broadband networks exceeds that of any other wiring scheme. In addition, because broadband networks are balanced networks, the distance between node connections is irrelevant, unlike the case with other types.

With a branching-tree topology, a network can blanket enormous geographic areas—about 30 square miles for a broadband PC Network. Splitting allows a tributary branch to be extended to a node, in contrast to other networking approaches, which require the entire network trunk to be diverted for even a single node. Diverting the entire network trunk becomes a critical issue in large networks because of length restrictions.

Here are a few hypothetical examples of the services that a broadband network could carry:

- A chemical corporation could connect hundreds of buildings spanning a major metropolis. The network would provide in-house education on TV, computer data and electronic mail, environmental monitoring, corporate sales records, production information, and computer network services.

- A military base spread out over a huge area could use its network for depot shipping and receiving data, gate security, fence sensing devices, communications systems, military computer linkage, records, inventory, emergency planning, two-way communications with vehicles, and in-house video.

- A manufacturing facility, covering millions of square feet, could be wired so that the maximum distance from any point to a network connection is 100 feet or less. It could provide production schedules, time and attendance records, inventory, TV scanners for security, environmental and pollution monitoring, and loading dock security.

- An insurance company could be integrated on several floors in each of multiple buildings with thousands of outlets, so that the maximum distance from any device to an outlet is 20 feet. Its network services could include document preparation, electronic mail, financial and stock market information, database access and other on-line services, video conferencing, and news wire services.

- A hospital could use its network for billing information, monitoring of intensive care equipment, a paging system, linkage with paramedics, accessing Medline and other on-line services, databases for a poison control center, an organ bank, patient records, FM radio, TV, up-to-date information on the diet status of patients, control of the building's heating and air conditioning, monitoring of air purification and particulate count, and data stored on video disks.

All of these examples are possible today, and some describe existing networks.

EASE OF EXPANSION

There are two approaches to expanding a broadband network. First, provisions for network expansion can be designed into the original plan, by doubling or tripling the projected number of network outlets. The cost of additional installation is often negligible, since the labor to simultaneously install two or more drop cables is nearly the same as for one.

In addition, several large branches can be split off the main trunks near potential expansion areas (such as undeveloped building sites) and immediately terminated. This "overdesign" allows large expansions at a future date without having to know how many taps or signal amplifiers will ultimately be needed. The cost in this case is also usually negligible.

Second, if future requirements are completely volatile, broadband networks can be expanded as required and rebalanced, usually without disruption of operation. Typically, only a new section must be balanced, not the existing system. In fact, because of its flexibility, a broadband network is perhaps the strongest solution to your needs under these circumstances.

ENORMOUS TRANSMISSION BANDWIDTH

Broadband networks have transmission capability second only to that of fiber-optic cable (which has severe tapping, installation, and repair restrictions). Even single-cable split-band (e.g., mid-split) broadband networks usually have capabilities that exceed those of baseband systems by a factor of twenty (2,000 percent). If that were not enough, the transmission capability of broadband network components is still growing.

High-quality coaxial cable has virtually unlimited bandwidth; broadband network frequency restrictions are often due to the limitations of amplifiers and filters. Some manufacturers started shipping bandwidth amplifiers exceeding 550 MHz in 1986.

NATURAL MIGRATION PATH FOR NEW DEVICES

Broadband networks can easily accommodate a variety of adapters that may have differing speeds, signaling techniques, or other characteristics. So they provide a natural migration path for new network devices, which lets you add new services and devices in the future, without disrupting existing services. (In contrast, baseband approaches mandate that all adapters exhibit identical behavior.)

MIXED SERVICE SUPPORT

Frequency division multiplexing modulation permits a broadband network to provide a wide variety of services—the larger the bandwidth, the greater the variety.

As you may recall, the network bandwidth is divided into channels that are usable independent of each other. That is, one channel may be used for television, another for FM radio, a third for a broadband PC Network, a fourth for telephone service, a fifth for another local area network using token-bus access, and a sixth for a public intercom system. This independence lets a

Broadband PC Network coexist on the same cable with a manufacturing shop floor network, such as General Motors' MAP.

In addition, broadband networks use standard cable TV connectors. So any connection point on the network can provide any of the services, without requiring centralized coordination. This means that a given port could be used at one time to provide an in-house educational TV connection and at another time for a PC Network connection.

Alternatively, a device can easily be disconnected and moved to a new location. After reconnection, work can resume immediately, again without centralized intervention or coordination. Certainly this degree of device mobility enhances an establishment's flexibility in staffing, relocation, and rapid reorganization.

Data

Broadband media have varying resistance to electrical noise. You are allowed to choose different types of cable for different types of environments and applications, such as remote or inaccessible safety equipment, fire alarms, environmental sensors, heating and cooling controls, time and attendance collectors, and energy management systems.

Broadband media are especially attractive in electrically noisy or sensitive manufacturing shop floors and process control areas. With additional protection for the cable, broadband networks have even been used in nuclear energy plants and corrosive areas.

Voice

The geographical independence of broadband network devices means a broadband network telephone can retain its number when moved from one location to another, without a PBX switchboard or wiring-closet change. Broadband networks can additionally support other audio applications, such as public address systems, AM/FM radio, and background music. However, this capability comes at a price that is put in perspective later in this chapter. For the present, voice transmission is generally more practical over a twisted-pair network.

Images

Broadband networks support concurrent distribution of commercial television, in-house VCR, and live broadcasts for education or security. The ability to move television receivers or use them in any of these roles enhances your establishment's visual communications.

LOW COST

Despite their overwhelming advantages, broadband networks are extremely price-competitive with other networks because they use the same cables, connectors, and other components that are mass-produced for commercial cable TV networks. Such components are readily available from a variety of local suppliers at commodity prices, usually resulting in connection costs averaging $150 to $200 per port. The actual attachment of the nodes to the network also requires an adapter card with a broadband modem that, in the case of the IBM PC Network, can be purchased or built economically.

In addition, a variety of companies within the industry (see Appendix F) can design broadband networks that address both current and future needs. Finally, the proliferation of cable TV has created a pool of experienced, semiskilled people who can install and maintain broadband networks.

HIGH RELIABILITY

Broadband networks naturally inherit the demanding degree of reliability that cable TV networks require. This degree of reliability includes a mean time between failure of 18 years for network amplifiers and 30 to 40 years for passive components (connectors, directional couplers, splitters, and attenuators). The natural isolation inherent in a broadband network insures that most failures affect only a small portion of the network. Also, the isolation properties of a network's directional couplers provide natural protection against sabotage.

In addition, broadband networks can have efficient systems, called *status monitoring systems,* for determining problems in which large numbers of devices are involved, beginning with large areas, such as buildings, then moving to specific floors and even offices where the problem device is located. As a direct consequence, the average mean time to repair for a large network can be about 15 minutes.

Since broadband networks are so reliable and quick to repair, a second or redundant system is not required. For establishments that require redundancy— police and fire departments, hospitals, and nuclear power plants, for instance— the total costs more than double. In addition, such backup networks must be checked regularly themselves to insure they are operational.

Finally, the natural immunity of coaxial cable to electrical noise and the inherent reliability of the PC Network's frequency modulation combine to provide superior reliability for data transmission in virtually any broadband LAN environment.

BENEFITS OF A MATURE TECHNOLOGY

Broadband and cable TV components have been in active design, improvement, and use for over 30 years, meeting the demands of cable TV. This record has resulted in a variety of forgiving, rugged, reliable, and off-the-shelf components suitable for use in a variety of environments, featuring insensitivity to electrical noise and extremes of humidity and temperature. These benefits allow the design of a single broadband network that can operate in a variety of application environments, such as door security, environmental sensors, badge readers, and access control alarms.

As you have seen, the mean time between failures of passive components is measured in decades. Amplifiers, though shorter-lived (18 years), are moderately priced and designed in a modular manner to facilitate immediate repair, replacement, and subsequent repair by an authorized vendor.

All broadband network components are widely available in a variety of forms to meet any fire or building regulations. Finally, security tools and connection approaches have been developed to satisfy requirements of the military and governmental security.

INTERCHANGEABLE PARTS

The wide availability of broadband network components insures vendor independence. All passive components are built to cable TV industry standards and are universally interchangeable. In addition, amplifiers and devices offer similar operating characteristics among vendors.

VOICE AND TV IN PERSPECTIVE

While broadband networks can support sound and visual transmissions, it is important to place them in perspective. Television consumes substantial bandwidth, which is why it is not widely available on most other LAN approaches. As for audio applications, it is not unusual to expect two broadband channels—one in the return direction and one in the forward direction—to support 300 simultaneous telephone conversations. (Typically, most phones are idle, so this capacity supports thousands of telephone handsets.) Since a midsplit system has only 18 return channels, this means that 5,400 conversations completely consume the return bandwidth of a midsplit system.

The same situation applies for two-way TV. Because television requires a 6-MHz bandwidth channel, there can be a maximum of 18 channels on a broadband network, unless frequency reuse techniques (described later in Section 5) are used to increase the signal count.

As a direct consequence, many establishments have found it advantageous to run wires from remote cameras to the broadband network headend and place the TV signal on the network there. Where feasible, this strategy frees a return channel for other purposes. Such a method is especially valuable for a security system in which several cameras are used and monitored from a single location—which is precisely the opposite configuration from that in a traditional broadband network.

A final application that consumes substantial bandwidth for a few users is video conferencing, essentially a point-to-point application. The bandwidth required to conduct multisite conferencing can be reduced by freeze-frame, delta action, or sophisticated compression techniques at some cost and at the expense of some animation.

Many users appreciate video conferencing's numerous advantages. But they report seeing what the camera is pointed at—not necessarily what they want to see. In other words, be sure that your establishment wants, needs, and will use video conferencing at a level that justifies the requisite consumption of reserved bandwidth.

In the final analysis, broadband is good for receiving remotely generated audio and video signals. But it is substantially stronger for broadcasting them on the network because of the inequality between the number of return and forward channels.

A FINAL NOTE

In the unlikely event that a broadband network's capacity proves too limited, techniques discussed in Section 5 will allow reuse of frequencies in various situations. These techniques provide ways to achieve greater effective bandwidth for the network.

Chapter 17

A Broadband Primer

This chapter discusses custom broadband network installation, and the relationship between broadband LANs and traditional cable TV networks. What follows is a primer on the wiring concepts that are important to broadband networks having custom cabling or commercial translators. If you have ever had the pleasure of installing a lawn sprinkler system, you are already at the head of the class.

LAWN SPRINKLER HIGH TECHNOLOGY

Consider the problem of installing an underground lawn sprinkler system in a yard. First, you want to obtain materials (pipe, connectors, joints, sprinkler heads, etc.) as inexpensively as possible. Of course, you want them to be durable as well. No one wants to dig up the yard every year. Second, the parts should be available anywhere at commodity prices. This obviously requires mass production and a large number of customers. Third, the parts should be adaptable to a wide variety of environments and shapes of lawns. Fourth, because it is aggravating to dig up and fix subterranean leaks, the components must last a long time. Beginning to sound familiar?

To install the system you must first survey your lawn. Then you must decide on the shape of your sprinkler system, its topology. You could install a star-shaped system, but that would require the most pipe. Alternately, you could choose a single-bus system, but that could also consume a lot of pipe. More important, a failure in the main pipe would make the entire sprinkler system fail. Thus, this approach does not offer much fault tolerance.

Eventually, you will probably decide on a branching-tree topology. This approach has good fault tolerance and (potentially) minimum pipe costs. This does not necessarily mean that the system uses a minimum amount of pipe, just that its total cost is minimum. In contrast to the single-bus approach, you can use smaller, cheaper pipe at the ends.

Having selected the general topology, you must now choose materials. Usually, the choice is between metal or plastic pipe. Most people choose plastic, because it is cheaper. In addition, plastic pipe is easy install and repair, requiring fewer tools and less skill.

For example, if a plastic pipe breaks, it is easy to remove a short section and repair it or bypass it altogether. This does not require the skills of a brain surgeon, but it helps to be handy.

You should now place the sprinkler heads to give the yard a uniform spray. However, there are problems to ponder first. If a sprinkler head gets too much water pressure, it pops out of the ground in a fleeting effort to go into orbit. A geyser of water then erupts from the empty socket, seriously reducing the water pressure to all nearby sprinkler heads. Even though distant sprinkler heads still function, the pressure must be be carefully regulated across the entire system to avoid fiascoes like this.

Alternately, a sprinkler head that does not get enough pressure dribbles water over a fraction of its assigned coverage area. Clearly, we need a way to balance water pressure across the entire system. We can do this with pipes of different diameters.

Pipe Fluid Friction Loss

A wide sprinkler pipe has less *fluid friction,* or *distance loss,* than a narrower one. This means there is less power loss when the water travels through a wide pipe than when it travels the same distance through narrower pipe.

In a well-designed system, long pipes that transport water to the branch (or drop) pipes should be wide, whereas the drop pipes should be narrower (and less expensive). This approach greatly decreases the effect of distance loss and insures that all sprinkler heads draw the same amount of water under normal conditions.

In contrast, the single-bus approach mandates wide sprinkler pipe everywhere. Because wide pipe is more expensive per foot, the branching-tree approach is usually cheaper. Moreover, smaller pipe is more flexible, and therefore easier to handle and install.

Insertion Loss

Another type of loss, called an *insertion loss,* occurs where components are inserted in the system. For example, insertion loss occurs at the sprinkler heads, because each of them siphons off part of the water pressure.

In addition, insertion loss occurs at right-angle joints because of increased fluid turbulence. Fluid turbulence also appears at T junctions (two-way splitters) and four-way intersections (three-way splitters).

System Installation

Now it is time to install the pipes. First you dig the trenches. You then put the pipes in the trenches and connect them carefully, remembering that faulty connector attachment is a common problem. Finally, you install the on-off valves to provide a reliable supply of water from the municipal water main.

Note that you do not cover up the pipes in the trenches yet. You do this only after testing the system by hooking it up to the water system for a wet run.

Directional Couplers

Many water utilities prohibit direct connection of a lawn sprinkler system to a public water supply. This is because systems may allow muddy water to flow into the main water supply after they are turned off. Thus, the tap that connects the system to the water main must be a directional tap. That is, it must prevent water from returning to the main system.

At last, you attach your directional tap to the water main, go to the convenient location (the headend) where you have installed the valve(s), and turn on the water. Any problems should be easy to see, since the pipes are still uncovered and accessible. Assuming everything works, you cover up the pipes and begin to use your sprinklers.

Subsequent Expansion

Before expanding a system, you must realize that you cannot indiscriminately add or remove sprinkler heads. To do this would modify the system's characteristics and alter its balance.

It would have been better to plan for expansion when you designed the system. How? By using wider pipes than you needed and adding some pipe stubs.

SPRINKLER SYSTEMS AND NETWORKS

Now let's see what sprinkler systems and networks have in common.

Network Attenuation: Passive Loss and Cable Loss

A broadband network has two types of signal strength loss (attenuation). The first, called *flat, insertion,* or *passive loss,* occurs when a signal passes through an attenuator, connector, splitter, directional tap, outlet, or other network components.

Flat loss comes from the decrease in strength for signals of all frequencies (Fig. 17-1), resulting in the flat curve on the graph. This type loss is called passive because it is caused by passive (nonelectrically powered) network components. And insertion loss means the components are inserted in the path of the signals, just as some components were inserted in the water sprinkler system.

The second type of attenuation is called *cable loss,* because it occurs as signals travel along cables. Unlike flat loss, cable loss is frequency-dependent and varies with temperature and cable characteristics. Coaxial cable loss always increases with frequency, as indicated in Figure 17-2.

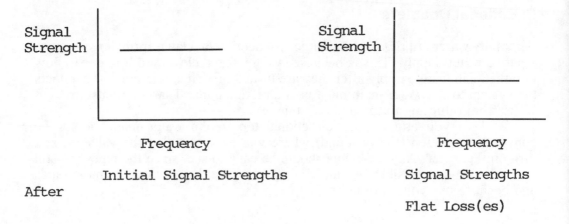

Figure 17-1 Flat loss

Cable loss is due to a phenomenon called *skin effect,* which results from the behavior of electrical signals as they travel in a wire. A very low frequency signal tends to travel through the entire cross section. However, higher-frequency signals flow nearer the outer part of the wire, avoiding its center.

This tendency decreases the wire's effective cross-section. Since thinner wires attenuate signals faster than thicker wires, higher-frequency signals attenuate more rapidly. Research has shown that attenuation loss varies approximately with the square root of a signal's frequency.

A coaxial cable's loss characteristics are expressed in terms of the attenuation of one or more high-frequency (typically 400 MHz) signals at a specific temperature per 100 feet at 68 degrees Fahrenheit.

Though signal strength curves differ for different types of cable, they always tilt down with increasing frequency. Thus, we refer to a cable type's unique

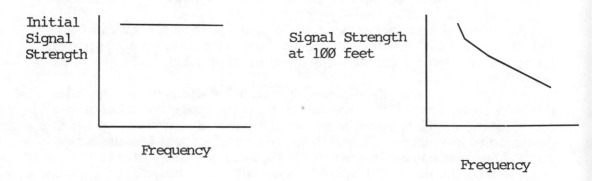

Figure 17-2 Typical cable loss

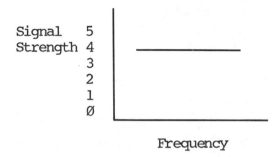

Figure 17-3 Graph of initial signal strengths

signal strength loss characteristic as its *cable tilt,* because it tilts to the right. Finally, for a given type of cable, signal strength loss increases with increasing temperature, typically 1 percent per 10 degrees Fahrenheit.

Network Balancing (Alignment)

Since broadband networks operate as balanced networks, designers must compensate for both flat loss and cable loss. This compensation permits nodes to receive signals within a range of strengths set system-wide, a process sometimes called *aligning*.

Amplifiers can compensate for flat loss, but compensating for cable loss is trickier. In Figure 17-3, assume a range of frequencies is transmitted at the same strength onto the network. When the signals eventually reach an amplifier, a graph of their strengths resembles Figure 17-4.

Amplifier components called *equalizers* adjust the arriving signals to make them again uniform in strength (Fig. 17-5). These equalizers are similar to the

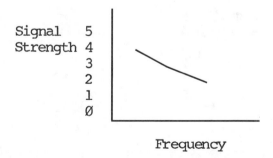

Figure 17-4 Signal strength due to cable loss

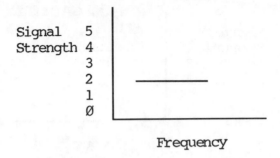

Figure 17-5 Signal strength after equalization

ones found in many home stereos; they modify the volumes of selected frequency ranges to bring the total sound into "balance." In technical language, they create a flat response across the range of frequencies.

In broadband networks, equalizers have attenuation characteristics that are the opposite of the cable's. That is, they attenuate lower frequencies more than higher frequencies, resulting in a uniform signal strength as illustrated in Figure 17-6.

As a final step, the amplifier's boosting circuits strengthen all the signals (Fig. 17-6). Since amplifiers strengthen all frequencies by the same amount, equalization must occur first. Otherwise, lower-frequency signals might be too strong. The results would be overloading of the amplifier circuits and signal distortion.

Finally, note that equalization is accomplished by tilt attenuators like those included in the IBM PC Network Cabling System Distance Kits. Technically speaking, these equalizers are not part of the network amplifiers, though they often are packaged in the same housings.

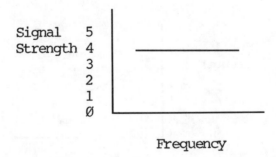

Figure 17-6 Signal strength after amplification

BROADBAND VERSUS SUBSCRIPTION CABLE TV

Because broadband local area networks have so much in common with subscription cable TV networks, it is important to contrast the two. First, subscription cable TV has traditionally been a unidirectional broadcast-only network. Some networks allow limited two-way communication, usually to accommodate future applications.

In cable TV systems, all signals flow from a headend to network taps. Only limited provisions exist to send data to the headend from a network node, primarily as an aid in locating problems. Furthermore, cable TV networks often face special government regulation as public utilities, which may further restrict their capabilities.

In contrast, broadband local area networks are privately owned, bidirectional networks that are generally unregulated. They may observe the cable TV industry channel and frequency assignment table out of economic convenience. This observance allows them to use off-the-shelf components for television transmission. Despite the fact that broadband networks use the same components as cable TV systems, their bidirectional nature mandates different designs.

Cable TV networks typically use a true three-level hierarchical branching-tree topology consisting of trunks, branches, and feeder cables. Because a cable TV network is essentially unidirectional, its design optimizes transmission of signals traveling in the forward path.

Cable TV network amplifiers gently amplify signals as they travel down the trunk cables. This minimizes distortion but makes the signals more vulnerable to external noise. When the signals reach the feeder cables, they are amplified strongly. Thus, in a cable TV network, 98 percent of the signal noise is injected on the trunk lines and distortion from amplification occurs on the feeder lines. This approach is unsuitable for a bidirectional network.

In contrast, large establishment broadband networks typically use a two-level modified branching-tree topology. The top level of the hierarchy is called the *backbone* and the lower-level elements are called the *distribution systems*. The headends are called the *main metropolitan LAN* (MLAN) headend and the *sub/small LAN* (SLAN) headend, respectively. The backbone and the distribution systems are individual branching-tree networks. However, the nodes on the backbone cable are the distribution systems.

A distribution system connects to the backbone trunk at a single point using special components (bridges or channel processors, discussed later). They purify node signals originating in the distribution system. The purification process presents a uniform strength signal to the backbone network, even though signals arrive at the connection point with varying strengths. The uniform signal strength enhances the backbone's capability to deliver the signal to the headend with minimum distortion and noise. The final result is that, in contrast to cable

TV systems, broadband network backbones and distribution systems introduce equal noise and distortion.

History shows that many establishments were surprised by the quiet but pervasive penetration of informally acquired PCs in their facilities. If history is any guide, many such establishments will again be surprised by the number of PC Networks that are operational without formal management knowledge. Most likely, these networks will be installed on an ad hoc basis and exhibit all the characteristics of unplanned topsy-turvy growth.

Since many departmental networks will use the IBM PC Network Cabling System, we must discuss how to salvage the installation investment, if a more full-featured network becomes necessary. The solution is surprisingly easy.

THE ESTABLISHMENT BACKBONE NETWORK

As previously discussed, establishment-wide custom cable networks that integrate existing networks are called backbone networks. When an establishment provides its backbone network, it should have directional couplers installed adjacent to existing IBM PC Network Translator Units. These directional couplers should be calibrated to accept the signal levels that are present at the translator units. The existing translator units can then be removed and the connection hardware attached to the backbone network.

Note that a backbone network also allows distribution of TV signals. While these signals are not available on the previously autonomous networks' wiring, they are obtainable directly off the backbone network. Thus, the presence of autonomous PC Networks that use the IBM PC Network Cable System presents no permanent obstacle to incorporation of other types of transmission.

However, the integration of multiple autonomous networks into a single network implies a substantial level of traffic. Under these conditions, it becomes increasingly important to conserve transmission capacity by eliminating unnecessary traffic. The idea of traffic conservation introduces the three interrelated concepts of frequency reuse, subnetworks, and bridges.

Frequency Reuse

Frequency reuse allows a transmission channel to be simultaneously used differently in different parts of the network. For example, as you may recall, a midsplit broadband network has fewer return channels than forward channels. The limited number of return channels could cause a potential problem if several departments needed to simultaneously broadcast television programs to the headend for subsequent rebroadcast.

For example, suppose an establishment has six departments that provide television broadcasts. Ordinarily this would require six return channels. Now suppose that the establishment backbone network contains six main trunk cables.

In this situation, the six different departments could transmit their broadcasts using the same channel frequency but each on a different trunk cable. Provided the signals were intercepted and moved to separate frequencies via channel converters before being rebroadcast, the system would function perfectly. Only one return channel would be required.

Subnetworks

Subnetworks are networks that can receive signals from the headend but not transmit signals to it. Subnetworks are useful because they do not consume any of the backbone network's capacity but can benefit from its presence. An example is a custom cable PC Network for a large establishment that could receive TV signals from a backbone network but whose message traffic was prevented from reaching the backbone.

While a subnetwork like this would not allow establishment communication of PC Network messages, it does allow multiple PC Networks to operate at capacity simultaneously, without interfering with one another.

Bridges

A bridge is a special device used to connect two similar networks indirectly. In the current discussion, a bridge would connect a backbone network to an existing departmental distribution network, as an alternative to connecting the departmental network directly to the backbone. The bridge could then forward traffic from the department onto the backbone network. It would not forward strictly local traffic.

Because a bridge intercepts messages on the departmental network and places them on the backbone network, the backbone translator sees only one adapter instead of all the departmental adapters. Thus, many departmental networks could participate on the backbone, each having many nodes.

Channel Processors

A less expensive alternative to a bridge is a channel processor. Channel processors do not shield the backbone from the departmental network amplifier and node noise. However, they insure that the backbone receives a uniform-strength, rebuilt signal. This tends to minimize the impact of noise.

Level Stabilizers

A final signal purification component is called a *level stabilizer*. Like the channel processor, it presents a uniform-strength signal to the backbone network. However, a level stabilizer does not rebuild the signal as does a channel processor and costs significantly less as a result.

Chapter 18

Equipment for Custom Broadband Networks

With this chapter, the reader becomes familiar with the remaining components for custom networks. The components that form a large custom cable broadband network can be divided into two categories: headend components and distribution network components.

HEADEND COMPONENTS

Headend components are the central point of origin for all signals transmitted on the forward path and the final destination for all signals traveling on the reverse path. The headend determines the offerings of the network because it determines what services are available and whether they are one-way or two-way. Because the headend components are a critical point in a network, they should always receive clean, reliable power.

Headends usually have backup frequency translators and switch units that rapidly make the backup translators operational on the network. One function that is typically near the headend is the network control center.

Network Control Centers

A network control center is a central maintenance and monitoring location. It contains the equipment needed to diagnose network problems and test for components that are near failure. It usually has some or all of the following diagnostic equipment:

- Frequency counter, which measures and displays the frequency of a network signal at its port
- Time domain reflectometer, which locates shorts and breaks in cables
- Sweep signal generator, which generates constant signals of a desired frequency for transmission on the network and analysis on a spectrum analyzer
- Spectrum analyzer, which graphically displays network signals
- Field strength meter, which displays the amplitude of a signal at a given frequency
- Signal egress detector, which detects network emissions

One of a control center's most significant activities is to operate a status monitoring system.

Status Monitoring Systems

A status monitoring system is a LAN that operates on a broadband network. Its function is to gather operating statistics on network components. To do this, nodes called *transponders* are placed within amplifier housings and other key network points. The information gathered is transmitted to a central node in a network control center.

A status monitoring system can help determine rapidly the cause and location of a network failure, resulting in substantially decreasing mean time to repair. It can also help identify network components that are approaching failure levels.

Some transponders control circuits that allow the temporary disconnection of a branch from the network on command from the control center. This capability can help locate a screaming modem or other disturbance. In such a situation, the affected trunk can remain disconnected until the problem is fixed, allowing the remainder of the network to resume operation.

Status monitoring systems are generally available from network amplifier manufacturers. They are designed to work with their specific products. Needless to say, procedures to determine network problems should be well documented and tested before a network becomes operational.

DISTRIBUTION NETWORK COMPONENTS

The headend signals are delivered to the nodes by the remaining components, which are collectively called the distribution network components. They can be further divided into three categories:

- Cable components—all trunk, distribution (feeder), and drop cables
- Active components—those components that require power, such as network amplifiers and status monitoring systems. Networks that have active components are called active networks. Note that the terms sub-split, mid-split, and high-split have meaning only in active networks.
- Passive components—those components that do not require power, such as attenuators. Networks composed only of passive components, such as the IBM Cabling Components, are called passive networks.

Cable Components

As cable components do not require power, they are not active. However, they do not exhibit flat loss attenuation, so they are not included in the passive category.

Modern cable designs are the result of decades of design effort using high-technology materials. Figure 3-6 shows a cable's components.

A cable's transmission characteristics depend on the center conductor being a uniform distance from the outer conductor. Thus, cable must be protected from crimping, kinking, and extreme stretching during installation to insure this distance is preserved over the entire length of the cable.

Active Components

All amplifiers are active components and usually are in the primary source of noise in networks. Because an amplifier can work only on a signal traveling in one direction, broadband network amplifiers actually consist of two amplifiers in a single housing, one for the forward path and one for the reverse path.

The input signals are fed to the amplifiers after passing through a *diplexer,* a component that separates the two signal bands. Note that amplifiers in the reverse direction need not be as powerful as those in the forward direction. The cable loss is lower because of the lower frequency, reducing the need for signal amplification. Thus, amplifiers must be correctly oriented to work properly.

Amplifiers are measured by four primary operating characteristics:

- Gain, which is the difference between the strength of the original (input) and the amplified signals (output). The gain may be set manually or automatically as temperature variations dictate. It is stated in dB.
- Output level, which is the maximum strength signal that the amplifier can emit, stated in dBMv
- Noise introduction, which is the amount of extraneous noise added to the signals during amplification, stated in dB
- Distortion introduction, which is the amount of signal distortion produced during amplification, stated in dB

Amplifiers are usually powered remotely by electricity transmitted over the network. They fall into one of four functional classifications:

- Trunk amplifiers, which are on the main trunks of the distribution network. They are of the highest quality.
- Bridging amplifiers, which drive branch cables. For problem determination, they may have circuits that allow branches to be temporarily disconnected from the network by command from a central point.
- Line extender amplifiers, which boost the signals between bridging amplifiers and tap outlets
- Internal distribution amplifiers, which are like line extender amplifiers but can be plugged into a standard 110-volt wall outlet

Note that the noise added to a signal in each amplifier accumulates until it reaches its final destination. The headend is subjected to the accumulated noise of every return path amplifier, whereas a network node is subjected only to the noise that accumulates from the forward amplifiers between it and the headend. Return path amplifiers must be of at least the same quality as the forward path amplifiers.

Passive Components

There are many types of passive components, including attenuators, connectors, directional couplers, taps, splitters, filters, outlets, and terminators.

Attenuators

Attenuators were discussed in Chapter 9. They reduce the strength of all signals by a constant amount.

Connectors

Connectors link components. Traditionally, they are the weak link in a broadband system and cause 75 percent of all system outages as a result of either failure or incorrect installation.

Dozens of types of connectors can be used in a network. However, most conform to industry standards. Connectors should be carefully selected and attached to cables to insure reliable network operation. Beware of subtle variations in cables that require the use of specific connectors.

Directional Couplers

Directional couplers divert part of the signal traveling on the forward path on one cable onto a secondary cable. In addition, they route signals traveling on the reverse path of the secondary cable to the headend (via the first cable) after attenuating them. This is a selective method of splitting the cable path. As discussed in Chapter 9, directional couplers must be installed in a specific orientation to function correctly.

Four parameters describe the operating characteristics of a directional coupler:

- Insertion loss, which is the difference in signal strength between the trunk-in cable and the trunk-out cable due to the presence of the directional coupler
- Tap value, which is the difference in signal strength between the trunk-in cable and the tap cable

- Isolation, which is the level of signal separation the coupler provides between the return path signals on the trunk out cable and those on the tap cable

- Directivity, which is the difference between the isolation loss and the tap loss

Taps

Taps divert part of a signal from a distribution cable and deliver it to a drop cable after decreasing its strength. One form of tap, called a *multitap,* combines a directional coupler with a splitter. In this scenario, multiple drop cables are supplied with signals, while the individual ports are isolated and independent from each other. A multitap can pass power, but the power along the distribution cable is isolated from the drop cables.

Splitters

Splitters were discussed in Chapter 9. Their function is to divide an input signal's power from the forward direction into two or more output signals of the same strength. Alternately, a splitter receives two or more input signals from the reverse direction, combines them, and passes the result onto the headend.

Taps versus Splitters

Both taps and splitters are directional components and provide isolation. However, their functions are different. Taps remove a small percentage of power from a branch, leaving most of it intact. This amounts to a small sampling process and is seldom achieved with extreme electrical precision. In contrast, splitters are responsible for dividing input power among the all outputs and accomplish this with great precision.

Filters

Filters are used to prevent and allow signals from reaching components. There are four different types of filters:

- Bandpass, which allow signals between two frequencies to pass while attenuating all others

- Bandstop, which attenuate signals between two frequencies while allowing all others to pass

- High pass, which allow signals above a given frequency to pass while attenuating all others
- Low pass, which allow signals below a given frequency to pass while attenuating all others

A high-pass and a low-pass filter are combined to make diplexers, components used to separate signals traveling on the forward and reverse paths for amplifiers. Other filters can attenuate specific channels or frequencies.

Outlets

Outlets are the actual network connection points between a node and a drop cable. It is important to terminate unused network taps to minimize signal ingress to return path. Doing so also keeps signals from radiating from (egressing) open ports.

Terminators

Terminators are components used to discard unwanted network signals, by converting their energy to gentle heat. Terminators are important because they facilitate network balancing, eliminate network signal reflections, and minimize undesirable signal ingress and egress.

Chapter 19

Custom Cable Installation Considerations

This chapter discusses the planning and installation of custom cable networks. Of the several topics, the first, the Fundamental Theorem of Broadband Network Design, is by far the most important and is difficult to overemphasize: Do not try to design or install a large complex custom cable network without qualified assistance.

PROFESSIONAL DESIGN

Just as "only a fool is his own lawyer," you might well leave the design of a complex broadband network to qualified professionals. Effective network design requires a level of experience beyond being "intuitively obvious to casual observers with a moment's reflection."

Specifically, because a broadband network operates as a balanced network, transmission signal levels must be uniform for all frequencies. As sections likely use different lengths and types of cable, each of which has different loss characteristics, the effort quickly becomes involved.

Toss in the directionality of amplifiers, splitters, and directional taps along with the need for later expandability, and neophyte network designers can and usually do become overwhelmed. Just as it is difficult to become proficient in a sport by watching videotaped instruction, you will likely find it difficult, and unprofitable, to design a network based on academic knowledge.

Qualified consultants are readily available who have proven skills, automated design tools, and experienced engineering staffs. The result will almost certainly be quick, error-free design that allows subsequent network expansion with minimal disruption. Using such a consulting service could easily result in your network becoming operational far sooner than otherwise.

In addition, after calculating all the expenses of designing your own network, you may discover that it costs less to have a consultant do the job. Finally, because of their wide base of experience, consultants will likely install, for example, amplifiers so that they can be quickly serviced or even removed. Such serviceability cannot be retrofitted without great difficulty.

Finally, with a properly designed and tested network, you should be provided with documentation on cable routes, network calibration values, servicing procedures, bill of materials, and schematics, as well as spare components placed at appropriate network points. Be sure your contract network design or installation includes this.

OUTSIDE REVIEW

If you elect to design your own network, have a qualified independent design consultant review your work. We know of a network design team for one major firm that did this reluctantly only to learn that nearly half the network had been inoperative as designed.

Remember, a large broadband network is a major asset. Thus, upper management is likely to review how well it works. An improperly designed network can result in large extra costs, wasted time, and unhappy users.

PRELIMINARY PLANNING

Required Network Services

The first step in planning a network is to develop an understanding of its requirements. Thus, you need to identify the services (current and future) users need. Effective planning includes developing an understanding of how information is exchanged in your establishment and how the network changes this. It can be much easier to provide voice, video, and other services later, if the initial design makes provisions for them.

Detailed Maps and Layouts

Next, you should acquire or develop a complete set of detailed building maps and floor plans on which to design the network.

Plan for Growth

Any network design should provide for substantial excess network capacity beyond current and future perceived requirements. The provisions should be easy to activate with minimal disruption.

Remember, network utilization can quickly exceed the wildest expectations. You should always try to design for twice your current needs and reserve at least 30 percent of the frequency spectrum to accommodate later growth and node movement.

Luckily, because of the low cost of broadband network components, you can include substantial reserve capacity inexpensively in the original design. Excess capacity provisions include placing directional couplers in convenient locations with branches that are immediately terminated and extra taps.

If you cannot include excess capacity in your initial network, you can retrofit it, though with somewhat more expense and difficulty. In the case of large complex networks, the effort usually involves a two- or three-day rebalancing effort every few years. Rebalancing can often be accomplished while the network is operational.

NETWORK DESIGN CONSIDERATIONS

Armed with your requirements and a detailed facility layout, you should now begin your design. Serviceability, fault isolation, and redundancy should be primary considerations. The design must observe regulatory requirements. In the United States, for instance, you must follow the regulations discussed in Section 15 of the Federal Communications Commission's (FCC's) Master Antenna TV regulations, as well as regulations of the Federal Aviation Administration (FAA). These regulations cover such matters as reserved frequency use and acceptable levels of network signal leakage.

As in the water sprinkler analogy, your design usually has a branching-tree topology with multiple trunk lines radiating from the headend. This approach allows you to run all trunk lines outside of buildings rather than having to loop them completely through the building to each network tap.

Thus, unlike with baseband systems, you can provide each building with signals delivered by a distribution cable that is attached to a trunk cable. The distribution cable approach insures a natural degree of network failure isolation. For convenience in balancing, each distribution leg should consist of equal cable lengths, though this is not required.

For expandability, all passive components should be able to pass a 550-MHz signal at the very minimum. Individual components, such as the PC Network, that must operate at specific frequencies are allocated their frequencies first. Then other network signals that can be tuned to operate at various frequencies are assigned to the remaining frequencies.

To prevent organizational misunderstanding, you should establish a formal process to allocate frequencies on an establishment-wide basis. Doing so minimizes the chance of network channels being allocated in an unorganized way.

Finally, after checking local building codes, you should select the various network components by vendor, item, and model number.

NETWORK INSTALLATION DOCUMENTS

The previous design step should result in the following documents:

- A complete bill of materials that assigns a unique identifier to each component. Where possible, this identifier should be permanently visible on the component.

- A table of network signal levels present at all component connections, specified by unique component identifiers and directional orientation. This table facilitates design verification during installation.

- Accurate maps indicating all cable routes and component installation locations with unique component identifiers.
- Detailed drawings of every splitter, with all taps clearly identified and associated with a specific cable that is uniquely labeled on each end. These drawings facilitate later maintenance efforts.

PROFESSIONAL INSTALLATION

Just as it is a good idea to involve a professional consultant in the design of your network, you should give considerable thought to having a professional firm install it. Having your network professionally installed helps avoid installation errors such as misoriented amplifiers and directional taps, and increases the chances that components are accessible for convenient, rapid servicing. Again, network serviceability is difficult to retrofit. Rack mounting of components where possible or quick-release mounting of amplifiers eventually repays your establishment in reduced mean-time-to-repair efforts.

In addition, professional installation decreases the likelihood of cable damage that results in mechanical or structural return loss. Such loss is exhibited by the presence of unwanted signal reflections and standing waves in a network. It is usually the result of one of three cable installation errors:

- Clamping a cable too tightly with a support bracket, thereby exceeding its rated pressure limit
- Pulling a cable too hard during installation or abruptly stopping a cable spindle from spinning while it is dispensing its cable, thereby exceeding its rated tensile strength limit. Tensile strength is also exceeded when a cable sags unsupported across a long distance.
- Exceeding the minimum bending radius of cable, resulting in kinks. A cable's minimum bending radius is generally twelve times the cable's diameter.

In both the pulling and sagging scenarios, the cable can "hourglass" or stretch, so that sections are permanently narrower than the manufactured width.

Remember, while coaxial cable is durable, it is not indestructible. The transmission capability of coaxial cable depends on the center conductor being a specified distance from the outer conductor.

NETWORK CERTIFICATION

Once installed, a network should be tested by an independent group or consultant to insure the appropriate frequency response is present across the network and, finally, detailed procedures should be developed and certified before the network becomes generally available for use.

Chapter 20

Extending IBM PC Network Cabling Systems

The IBM PC Network Cable System is adequate for many small networks. However, occasionally it may be necessary to have a node more than 1,000 feet from the Base Expander. Furthermore, your establishment may need to interconnect departmental PC Networks, each of which uses the IBM PC Network Cabling System. This chapter discusses general techniques to meet these objectives.

DISCLAIMER

The following material presents techniques that work, but IBM does not support them. If you use them, IBM's maintenance procedures and service literature may no longer apply to your network.

One technique describes how to extend the radius of a cable kit up to 2,000 feet. Note that if you use this method to extend your network outside a building, you must obtain all necessary licenses and observe applicable electrical (such as lightning protection or grounding), fire, and safety regulations. If you are unfamiliar with these regulations, consult an expert or cable TV consultant.

ATTENUATION REVIEW

As you may recall, a broadband network has two types of attenuation: flat loss and cable loss. Flat loss is caused by passive components and attenuates signals of all frequencies by a constant amount. Attenuators intentionally "throttle down" a signal, so that it will not overpower an amplifier.

Cable loss is the attenuation that occurs as a signal travels down a cable. The amount varies with signal frequency; the attenuation is greater at higher frequencies. Different types of cable have different loss characteristics. A wider cable generally has less cable loss per unit length than a narrower one.

DISTANCE KITS

Distance kits and cables are available with the IBM PC Network Cabling system to provide an easy way to install a PC Network. With them users do not need to worry about balancing, because distance kits designed to work with only RG 11 cables cable at one of three specific distances.

Distance kits have both attenuators and equalization components, called tilt attenuators, with specific strengths calculated to work with specific lengths of

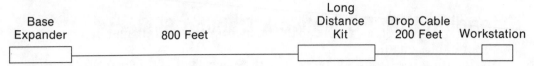

Figure 20-1 Suggested use of a long distance kit (Assuming a 200 foot drop cable.)

cable that connect them to a Base Expander. Figure 20-1 shows a Long Distance Kit used to connect a node located 1,000 feet from a Base Expander. In this figure, signals from the PC to the Base Expander travel along 1,000 feet of cable, encountering two Long Distance Kit tilt attenuators along the way.

SLIPKNOT EFFECT

You should note that signals would also travel 1,000 feet along the cable and encounter the two tilt attenuators if the components were connected in the manner shown in Figure 20-2. These examples are only a few of a multitude of connection scenarios.

In each option illustrated in Figure 20-2, if the kit were located the suggested 800 feet from the translator, a longer drop cable would not be permitted. Since a

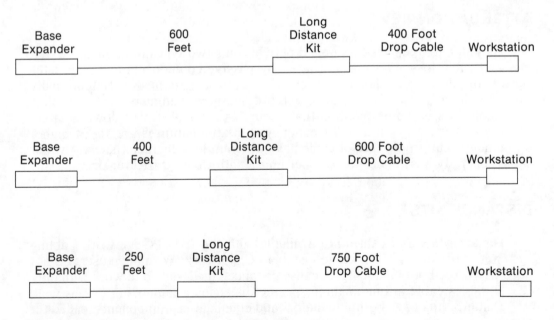

Figure 20-2 Alternate uses of the long distance kit

Long Distance Kit may attach as many as eight drop cables, locating it closer to the Base Expander forces you to use longer drop cables to maintain a constant 1,000-foot cable length.

By locating the Long Distance Kit the suggested 800 feet from the Base Expander, you can use shorter drop cables, potentially resulting in large cable savings. However, the nodes must then be within 400 feet of each other. Thus, while using an alternate cabling arrangement makes longer drop cables necessary, using long drop cables allows nodes to be located correspondingly further apart. And since the Long Distance Kit could actually be placed anywhere along the 1000 foot cable, its position could vary, much like the position of a slipknot on a rope.

In summary, each alternate design allows nodes that are further apart to share a Long Distance Kit, but with the trade-off of correspondingly longer drop cables.

EXTENDING THE RADIUS OF A CABLE SYSTEM NETWORK

The previous discussion showed that the position of the Long Distance Kit can vary, provided that the overall cable length remains constant. In addition, the design of all distance kits assumes the use of RG-11 cable.

Cables other than the specified lengths of RG-11 have different loss characteristics for which the distance kits are not specifically designed to compensate. However, the specified lengths of RG-11 cable produce a predictable attenuation loss figure for which the distance kits can compensate.

To understand the implications of this, assume that you have located a Long Distance Kit 990 feet from a Base Expander, which allows you to attach drop cable with a maximum length of 10 feet. As we have seen, this scenario works because the Long Distance Kit is designed to compensate for the cable loss that occurs on 1,000 feet of RG-11 cable.

Suppose now that you can find a cable with one half the loss rate of RG-11 cable. You would then be able to replace the 990-foot section of RG-11 cable with 1,980 feet of this low-loss cable, because it would produce the same amount of total loss. Thus, a node could be located 1,990 feet (1,980 + 10) from the translator. More generally, this rule can be stated as:

$$\text{800 Feet} < \left(\frac{\text{New Type Cable Length}}{2} \right) + \text{RG-11 Cable Length} < \text{1000 Feet}$$

This approach can be applied to cables with other amounts of loss as well. Finally, note that you must also obtain and attach appropriate connectors to the new low-loss cable.

CONCLUSION

This chapter has presented a simple way to extend the radius of networks using the IBM PC Network Cabling System. Though such an extension implies rebalancing, the effort is minimal because of the availability of cable distance kits and the general topological simplicity of such networks.

Appendices

Appendix A Subdirectory Concepts

The PC Network Program relies heavily on PC-DOS's subdirectory capabilities when sharing a fixed disk across a PC Network. It is therefore important to understand PC-DOS subdirectory concepts in file server environments. The following explanatory material is excerpted from Computer Insights' SCOUT file search program documentation with the permission and courtesy of Computer Insights, P.O. Box 110097, Pittsburgh, Pennsylvania 15232.

When the IBM PC was first announced, it and its operating system (PC-DOS 1.0) could use only single-sided diskette drives. That is, while each diskette clearly had two sides, you could use only one side of any diskette for reading or writing your files.

If you were lucky enough to have more than one diskette drive, you had to tell PC-DOS what drive was the *default drive*. This drive (a: or b:), also called the *current drive,* was the diskette drive PC-DOS would use to find your program and data files unless directed to use another diskette drive.

Set aside on each diskette was a small area, called the *directory,* that had the name, location, and size of each file on the diskette. Each such diskette directory could keep track of up to 64 files that, together, used about 160KB (163,840) characters of information.

Things were pretty simple then. Each diskette had one small directory for a cozy community of up to 64 resident files. If you wanted to list your files, you could invoke the PC-DOS 1.0 DIR command and the file names would appear, each on a separate line.

Thus, if you had the maximum of 64 files on a diskette, you would have had about two and one-half screens worth of names to look at as they raced up the screen. The PC also had to do a little work reading the directory to find your files, especially if they were at the end of the directory. But, all in all, it was very fast and, as mentioned, pretty simple. Programs therefore began to be written with the following simple rules in mind:

- File names consisted of up to eight characters
- File names could be followed by a three-character extension
- The current drive could be overridden by prefixing the file name and extension with another diskette drive designator

When IBM later announced double-sided diskette drives for the PC, it also announced a new version of its operating system, PC-DOS 1.1, that could use new double-sided drives. This allowed the PC to read and write data files on both sides of a diskette. Because the usable space doubled to 320KB, it was natural for the directory to be expanded also, since most files tend to be small and 64 of them often might not fill up a 320KB diskette. So, the directory was expanded to allow 112 files on a double-sided diskette and other information—the time and date of each file's creation—was also included in the directory.

This good news also came with some side effects on the DIR command. Suddenly, instead of up to two and one-half screens of file names in a directory, the DIR command had to display up to four and one-half screens of file names, along with their associated creation dates. Anticipating this could get a bit tough on your eyes, the PC-DOS 1.1 DIR command arrived with two new options.

First, you could use a /P option that directed PC-DOS to display one screen's worth of file names with their creation dates and wait for you to press a key, signaling PC-DOS to display the next screen and pause as before, until the entire directory had been displayed. Alternately, you could use the /W option to direct PC-DOS to display all the files names without creation dates on a single screen by listing 5 file names on each line.

No doubt about it, diskette capabilities had gotten better in many ways with PC-DOS 1.1. And, as you might suspect, the amount of work it took PC-DOS to find a file's entry in the larger directory also increased. But things were still very fast, because the speed of diskette reading and writing improved with PC-DOS 1.1. Indeed, things were getting bountiful as the PC tracked the pace of technology. As the PC's popularity exploded, increasing numbers of programs were written for it using (you guessed it) the same simple file-naming rules.

In early 1983, IBM announced the IBM PC XT and a new version of PC-DOS, PC-DOS 2.0. PC-DOS 2.0 continued the trend of expanding the capabilities of the diskette drives by allowing a single-sided diskette to hold 180KB of data and a double-sided diskette to hold 360KB worth of data. However, the number of directory entries, 64 and 112 respectively, stayed the same.

In addition, the XT had a fixed disk drive that could hold over 10MB (10,000,000) characters of information. This meant that the storage capacity of this disk drive was over 28 times the amount of data that a double-sided diskette could hold and a whopping 56 times the amount of data on a single-sided diskette. Clearly, things were going to have to be approached in a new way.

Consider the dilemma. If the fixed disk had one large directory, it might take PC-DOS 2.0 a very long time to find file entries. This would result in extended directory searches and an overall slowdown. On the other hand, if the fixed disk had a small directory, then a great deal of space on the disk could be wasted when the directory was completely filled with small files. The solution was going to require more than one directory, but how should these directories be arranged?

Let's look at the following analogy:

Suppose you had hundreds of manila folders stored away in a storage facility. If you wanted to have a messenger fetch a particular folder, you would perhaps say, "Get on the elevator, go to the third floor, find the blue room, locate filing cabinet six, open the third drawer, and get the XYZ folder." The messenger would get on the elevator, push the third floor button, get off on the third floor, find the blue room using a floor map, locate the correct filing cabinet using a filing cabinet guide, open the third drawer, and, if things went well, find the XYZ folder using the drawer index. After a while you could shorten this type request to

\FLOOR3\BLUEROOM\CABINET6\DRAWER3\XYZ

Note that this type of arrangement would allow the messenger to find a different XYZ folder if you gave a different request, such as

\FLOOR3\BLUEROOM\CABINET4\DRAWER3\XYZ

or as

\FLOOR3\BLUEROOM\CABINET6\DRAWER2\XYZ

This type of approach is referred to as a hierarchical directory structure in computer literature because there is more than one level of directory involved. Here, there are four: the elevator floor buttons, the individual floor maps, the cabinet guides, and the drawer indexes.

This approach is precisely how PC-DOS 2.0 and all later releases of PC-DOS manage your files on the hard disk (and interestingly, on diskettes too, if you so desire).

PC-DOS 2.0 ushered in a new era in data management for the IBM PC by using hierarchical directories. Although things got a bit more complicated, there were some immediate benefits. For example, the hierarchy allowed smaller directories with faster directory searches as well as accelerated backup and recovery procedures using the new PC-DOS 2.0 BACKUP/RESTORE commands.

The BACKUP/RESTORE implications of hierarchical directories were important because you could group files that did not change often and back them up only when they did change. Multiple directories also allowed for more flexible usage of the fixed disk and a method of organizing related files. Naturally, they also introduced some new terminology.

The main directory, the elevator buttons in the previous analogy, is always referred to as the *root directory*. A root directory may have 112 entries in it for diskettes and over 500 for the fixed disk. Each entry may be for a file or for another directory called a *subdirectory*. While root directories have a fixed number of entries, subdirectories can have a variable number of entries, limited only by the size of the disk or diskette. Subdirectories can also have subdirectories that can have subdirectories, and so on. What all this means is that a disk or diskette can now have more than one directory, causing some interesting complications.

Remember the concept of the current drive? Well, in PC-DOS 2.0 you now had an additional concept called the *current directory*. PC-DOS 2.0 would look in only one directory on the current drive, the current directory, for a program, and give up if it did not find it. To select your current directory you would use the new PC-DOS 2.0 command CD. Since you might be disappointed if PC-DOS repeatedly had trouble finding your programs, PC-DOS 2.0 also provided a new command called the PATH command.

Using this command allowed PC-DOS to look elsewhere for your programs and batch files, if it did not find them in the current drive's current directory. In effect it said "If you don't find the program here, try here, then here, then here. . . ." Each place PC-DOS would look would be specified by a fully qualified directory name. In the analogy above, such a directory would be

\FLOOR3\BLUEROOM\CABINET4\DRAWER3

which would contain the XYZ file you desired. That works fine for finding programs, but when it comes to data files, there are a few remaining observations and problems.

First, a subdirectory's PATH name does not include a drive specifier because the drive specifier is considered information to the drive name. This allows you to have subdirectories with the same name on different drives, perhaps allowing rapid file backup and archiving procedures. Thus, the subdirectories

c:\source\asm\test1.asm
d:\source\asm\test1.asm

are distinctly different though they have the same PATH name, because the drive specifier (c: and d: respectively) is not considered part of the PATH name.

Second, the PATH command only helps PC-DOS find program and batch files but gives no assistance at all when a program goes looking for a data file. Even though programs can request PC-DOS to find a data file by fully identifying the directory it is in, you might recall that quite a few programs were written before PC-DOS 2.0 and fixed disks came along. As a result, most programs still adhere to the simple naming conventions described earlier. Thus, file names such as

c:\source\asm\test1.asm

may simply have too many characters for many existing programs to swallow. This gives rise to many untidy solutions. For example, you can have copies of the same file in several directories, so that the file is accessible as you change current directories. Or you can copy a file into the current directory each time you use it and delete it when you are done. Or finally, you can forget subdirectories altogether and put everything in the root directory.

While this list of alternatives is not complete, it is uniformly unappealing. Clearly what is needed is a PATH-like function for data files, and this is why file search programs and the PC-DOS APPEND command were subsequently created.

Appendix B

The IBM PC Network Broadband Maximums

The broadband PC Network is available for a variety of environments with varying restrictions. While provisions exist within the LocalNet/PC architecture to address these and other limitations, the reason for the restrictions can be confusing.

This appendix discusses the restrictions you may associate with the PC Network. For more information on the LocalNet/PC architecture, refer to Appendix C, "PC Network Adapter and Protocol Details."

SEVENTY-TWO PCs ON AN IBM CABLING SYSTEM NETWORK

A network that uses the IBM PC Network broadband cabling components exclusively can support a network of 72 nodes:

- Eight nodes can be attached to the connection hardware included with each PC Network Translator Unit
- Eight nodes can be attached to each of the eight cable kits that can be attached to the Base Expander

ONE THOUSAND PCs PER FREQUENCY CHANNEL; THREE THOUSAND ON A NETWORK

The IBM PC Network Broadband uses a 1-persistent CSMA protocol, permitting an adapter to transmit as soon as it has something to transmit, provided the channel is idle. To minimize the probability of packet collisions, adapters must generate a carrier signal of a specified strength as quickly as possible; the carrier then reserves the channel for the adapter. The longer the delay (*latency time*) to generate a proper strength carrier signal, the greater the "collision window" or probability of a collision.

Clearly, the proper strength carrier signal must be quickly generated. That is, its "rise time" must be short. However, just as a car's tires screech when the car is accelerated too quickly from a stop, if a carrier is produced too quickly, a modem also generates unwanted frequency by-products in the process. Thus, an adapter is given a "rolling start" by never turning off the transmitter completely, even when the adapter is idle. The rolling start allows the adapter to achieve a short rise time without the undesired frequency by-products, or tire screeches in the analogy.

Thus, adapters are always transmitting at a weak signal, referred to as the *clamp down level,* even when idle, and produce what is known as a *carrier leakage.* While the leakage is minimal for a single adapter, the leakage that accumulates at a channel's headend from all adapters on a channel may not be. As a result, a channel cannot support an unlimited number of adapters; the PC network supports 1,000 adapters on a channel.

However, if a midsplit network has the appropriate custom translator and bridging capability, the network can support all three PC Network broadband channel pairs—each supporting 1,000 nodes. This allows a suitably configured network to support up to 3,000 total nodes.

FIVE KILOMETERS MAXIMUM NETWORK RADIUS

The 100-Microsecond Golden Nugget

The actual radius of a broadband PC Network is limited only by the maximum allowable round-trip delay to the translator and back on a network channel. The PC Technical Reference Manual indicates that this maximum allowable delay is 100 microseconds (millionths of a second). Assuming that a signal travels across the network at two thirds the speed of light, this certainly allows a network radius greater than 5 kilometers. The exact radius is left to the reader as an interesting exercise with the following thoughts.

The Length of a Bit

A popular poster has a caricature of Albert Einstein in a policeman's uniform with the caption "186,000 miles per second is not only a good idea, it's the law." When signals travel down a cable, they actually travel about 67 percent of the speed of light, due to what is referred to as the network propagation delay, or about 124,000 miles per second across a broadband network. Hence, when adapters transmit at 2,000,000 bits per second on a network, one second's worth of data (2,000,000 bits) spans 124,000 miles. This means that one bit's signal on the network stretches about 327 feet from the beginning to end.

The Minimum Packet Length

Networks are limited in radius to a finite distance for a number of reasons, such as component capability. Another reason for restricting a network's radius is for network efficiency in detecting collisions.

Consider two nodes that are physically close to each other but located 10,000 miles from the headend on a hypothetical bozo network. If the first node starts transmitting a short message to the second node, the second node does not immediately hear the transmission because the signal must travel 20,000 miles to the headend and back. This transit takes a great deal of time. However, since nodes are unaware of how how far they are from the headend, there is no allowance for such long transit delays.

Suppose the first node finishes transmitting and, by sheer coincidence, the second node begins to transmit to another network node before the first message arrives at either node. Both nodes eventually receive the first message about the same time. The first node checks to see if there was a collision and, assuming there was none, detects none. It subsequently assumes the message arrived safely at its destination, the second node.

However, when the second node receives the first message, it is listening for its own transmission and is unaware that the message that it is receiving originated from another node. Because the transmissions are different, the second node assumes the message is the result of a collision of its transmission with another message, stops transmitting, and discards the message that would have arrived safely. This is somewhat less than efficient communication.

For collision detection to work, it is imperative that all messages completely "fill the network" before their transmission finishes. That is, a transmitter must begin to receive its own transmission before the transmission is complete, regardless of where it is on the network. This is achieved by restricting the size of the network or by requiring all packets to be greater than a minimum size.

MINIMUM PACKET LENGTH VERSUS NETWORK SIZE VERSUS TRANSMISSION SPEED

Since messages must fill the network, clearly the minimum packet size, network radius, and transmission rate are all inseparably related. If a given size of network has a slow transmission rate, the bits are "longer," allowing smaller minimum packet sizes to fill the network. Conversely, larger packets allow a larger network radius, assuming a constant transmission speed. Faster transmission speeds require smaller networks or larger packet sizes.

To increase the efficiency of collision detection, a network architecture can specify that collisions must occur within the first few transmitted characters of any message; otherwise the message is assumed to be collision-free. This has the effect of decreasing the minimum packet size and perhaps the network radius.

Appendix C

PC Network Adapter and Protocol Details

This appendix presents technical details regarding the broadband PC Network adapter and the original PC Network layered architecture. Some of the information can be found in the PC Network Technical Reference Manual. However, the material discussing the PC Network's layered architecture was extracted from "Executive Overview of Sytek Inc.'s 'LocalNet/PC,'" available from the Marketing Department, Sytek, Inc., 1225 Charleston Road, Mountain View, California 94043.

The architectural material is most illuminating and is largely absent from the PC Network Technical Reference Manual. It continues to be important because it describes the protocols that the IBM PC Network Protocol Driver provides. Note that the discussion presents an architectural capability that is substantially in excess of the announced PC Network's current capabilities.

As an example, generally available Sytek documentation indicates the architecture supports a network radius of over 7 miles, allowing a network to span over 150 square miles. Investigation into why the PC Network was announced as only spanning 3 miles reveals that the announced radius was restricted by available CATV components. This subject is further discussed in Appendix B, "The IBM PC Network Maximums."

OVERVIEW

The original IBM PC Network is a derivative implementation of a more general communications architecture known as the Sytek LocalNet/PC architecture. This architecture is tailored to meet the requirements of distributed applications on broadband networks within a wide variety of personal computer LAN environments. These environments range from modest, small business networks to campus-size networks serving thousands of users. The architecture provides mechanisms that allow interconnection of separate subnetworks into a unified system via a mixed services trunk.

LocalNet/PC adapter card implementations such as the IBM PC Network use Sytek technology and packaging that allow data transfer up to several times the true "effective rate" of other approaches. This data transfer is achieved by performing higher-layer data communication activities on the LAN network adapter card rather than relegating them to the PC; the adapter card is often more powerful and better suited to these tasks than the PC it serves.

A LocalNet/PC adapter card requires a single long slot and contains a radio frequency (RF) 2-Megabyte-per-second frequency shift keyed (FSK) modem with supporting digital logic. It employs a 6-Megahertz Intel 80188 microprocessor that handles the upper levels of a five-layer protocol. A separate Intel 82586 chip processes lower protocol levels that provide services such as HDLC message framing. A custom Sytek chip performs the CSMA/CD access to the physical media.

Each card can support up to 32 separate sessions to other network nodes. Name service is included on the card, and each card can be known by up to 16 aliases. Applications can interface directly to the session layer of the card, allowing a measure of operating system independence.

THE 16K RAM

The 16K RAM memory is used to contain data buffers as well as the Name Table. It also provides the 80188 with a hardware stack area and program pointer storage area. This 16K of memory resides within the 80188's memory address space and does not consume any of the PC's memory.

THE 32K ROM

The 32K ROM contains Sytek proprietary code that implements the network protocol. The program logic uses the 16K RAM for temporary storage. This 32K of code resides within the 80188's memory address space and does not consume any of the PC's memory. The protocols are also provided by the IBM PC Network Protocol Driver Program.

THE 8K NETBIOS

The 8K NetBIOS is an IBM copyrighted code that controls the adapter interface from the PC side. This 8K of code resides within the PC memory address space and uses segment arithmetic which precludes it from operating in 80286 protected mode. Part of this code is listed in the PC Network Technical Reference Manual.

PC NETWORK ADAPTER JUMPERS

The jumper settings determine the adapter number (zero or one), IRQ level (2 or 3) of the adapter. In addition, they activate and deactivate the NetBIOS on the card (if two adapters are in a PC, only one can have an active BIOS) as well as the Remote Program Load feature. These options are discussed further in Appendix D, "PC Network Adapter Hardware Considerations and Jumper Settings."

THE 32 X 8 ROM

The 32 x 8 ROM contains the Permanent Node Name that is unique for every adapter. Each IBM PC Network adapter has a unique external serial printed on the card. In addition, each adapter has another unique identification number called the Permanent Node Name that is different from every other PC Network's Permanent Node Name—an electronic fingerprint of sorts.

Unlike the external serial number, an adapter's Permanent Node Name is invisibly etched in an adapter's memory. It consists of ten bytes of binary zeros followed by six unique bytes of hexadecimal values.

Since the Permanent Node Name is guaranteed to be unique, it provides a useful mechanism to guarantee the identity of a calling PC. You can fetch an adapter's Permanent Node Name by sending a special inquiry command to the adapter. This is what the PC Network Remote Control programs do to display your adapter's Permanent Node Name and to help insure that your PC is protected from unauthorized access.

LOCAL NET/PC ARCHITECTURE LAYER DETAILS

Each layer within the LocalNet/PC architecture uses the services provided by lower-level layers and provides a service usable by higher layers. Thus, the discussion starts with the lowest layer and proceeds toward the higher layers.

Physical Layer

As presented in the subsequent Network Layer discussion, provisions exist within the LocalNet/PC architecture to accommodate a variety of transmission media. However, broadband coaxial cable is the primary transmission medium used by current implementations of LocalNet/PC. On this medium, signals on any given channel must propagate in a single direction. A "two-way" broadband system organizes its channels by splitting the set of available frequencies into "upstream" and "downstream" channels.

On such a cable system, bidirectional channels are created by pairing an upstream channel with a downstream channel. The difference between the two frequencies is referred to as the *offset*. A broadband headend easily pairs two channels by converting all signals received on a given upstream channel to the corresponding frequencies within the band of the downstream channel.

In its broadband implementation, LocalNet/PC uses a bidirectional channel as a single shareable logical channel. Each node on the LocalNet/PC network includes a radio frequency (RF) modem that transmits at 47.75 to 53.75 MHz and receives at 216.00 to 222.00 MHz. Many such modems can be configured on the network that transmit and receive on this pair of frequencies. Custom headends convert signals on the transmit channel to corresponding signals on the receive channel. Consequently, all nodes (including the transmitting node) are able to receive any transmitting node's signal.

The primary LocalNet/PC modulation technique is frequency shift keying (FSK), which signals binary one and zero bits by shifting a transmitted signal's frequency between two closely spaced frequencies. This modulation technique is relatively simple to implement and is tolerant of electromagnetic noise and interference prevalent in many broadband cable environments.

The LocalNet/PC architecture can support any number of alternative transmission schemes. However, for cost and reliability, it is likely that 2 MB per second FSK broadband channels will remain effective for some time to come.

Link Layer

The primary link level protocol within LocalNet/PC is the Link Access Protocol (LAP), which is responsible for CSMA/CD handling, message framing, error detection, and address recognition.

CSMA/CD Handling

LAP is responsible for insuring that the potential multiple transmitters on a channel do not interfere with each other by simultaneously transmitting data. LAP accomplishes this by using the popular Carrier Sense Multiple Access with Collision Detection (CSMA/CD) technique, discussed in Section 1 of this book.

Message Framing

LAP is responsible for the basic framing of transmitted information. This means that, before transmission, messages are enclosed within a larger message, called a *frame* or *packet,* in a way that allows the identification of the frame's beginning and end. This is achieved via the same message framing technique used in a popular transmission protocol known as HDLC.

In HDLC, the start and end of a frame are signaled with a "flag byte" that consists of a 01111110 bit pattern. During a frame's transmission, LAP inserts a zero after any data bit sequence of five successive ones; upon reception of a frame, LAP strips away any zero that follows five ones.

This *zero insertion* technique, sometimes referred to as *bit stuffing,* allows bytes that have the same bit pattern as a flag byte to be sent as data within the frame. Thus, the receiving LAP interpreter can be sure that any received flag must be a true-beginning or end-of-frame indicator.

Error Detection

Error detection is accomplished using a 32-bit cyclic redundancy check (CRC) polynomial and generation process that complies with the IEEE 802 standards for local network error detection. This polynomial is the same polynomial used by ETHERNET and provides a four-character check value that accompanies each transmitted frame and is checked upon receipt. (Discussion of how the CRC is generated is beyond the scope of this book, though a complete discussion can be found in C Programmers Guide to NetBIOS, Howard W. Sams Co., Inc., 1988, by W. David Schwaderer.

If a received frame contains an invalid CRC, the frame is discarded; it is the responsibility of higher level protocols within the LocalNet/PC architecture (such as RSP) to recover from lost-frame errors.

Address Recognition

In LocalNet/PC, each node may receive all broadcasts on the network. To properly discard unwanted messages, each node is assigned a unique 48-bit address and is responsible for recognizing certain addresses within received frames.

A LAP component, referred to as a *LAP interpreter,* places the address of a message's intended recipient (destination) node in the first 48 bits of a transmitted frame following the start flag. Upon reception of all frames, LAP checks the destination address and ignores packets intended for other nodes.

In addition, LAP allows higher protocols to request that one or more "group addresses" be enabled. A group address is a 48-bit address with the least significant bit 1. Multiple nodes may simultaneously have the same group address enabled. When a frame is sent to a group address, all LAP interpreters authorized to use that address accept the frame. An address of all ones represents a "broadcast," which can be received by any node on the network.

LAP's Other Media Considerations

The LocalNet/PC architecture allows for link level protocols besides LAP, which may be desirable if other transmission media are used. Specifically, the following discussion of the LocalNet/PC network layer describes various mechanisms that allow the interconnection of distinct cable systems via microwave or other point-to-point links.

Across a point-to-point link, it is appropriate to use a specialized link level protocol. The LocalNet/PC architecture requires only that such a link level protocol provide a service similar to that of LAP. Thus, any link level protocol used within LocalNet/PC should provide the same error detection capabilities as LAP, and need not provide for any error recovery.

Network Layer

While a network may contain multiple links of varying transmission media types, the individual link protocols that apply to each link only provide for the transfer of packets from one node on the link to another node on the same link. If a packet is transmitted from a node on one link to a node on another link, it is necessary to transcend single link protocol procedures and invoke the packet routing procedures of LocalNet/PC's network layer—the Packet Transfer Protocol (PTP).

As an example, note that a single broadband cable system usually can support multiple 2-Mb-per-second channels. This is true in large networks requiring more capacity than a single 2-Mb-per-second channel can provide. Thus, a LocalNet/PC installation on a single broadband cable system may actually consist of multiple, distinct channels, and the integration of multiple such channels into a single network requires the ability to route packets from one channel to another.

Alternately, it is possible to integrate multiple cable systems into a single LocalNet/PC network. Conceptually, the fact that the cable systems are distinct is irrelevant, since a multicable network can be viewed as a collection of distinct channels on the same cable. Even though channels may reside on physically separate cable systems, there is nothing logically different about this from the seemingly simpler case of the multichannel single cable system.

Although the exact routing mechanisms used by PTP to handle interchannel and intercable transfers has not been presented, it is not hard to imagine the equipment required to handle the routing in these cases. Clearly, the interchannel routing can be achieved by providing a packet switch with interfaces to multiple channels on the cable system. The packet switch would receive packets on one channel and transmit them on a second. If the packet switch also incorporates an interface to a point-to-point line to a second switch on another cable system, the goal of intercable routing is achieved.

Within the LocalNet/PC architecture such a packet switch is called a *bridge*. PTP can therefore be viewed as the protocol that is responsible for the routing of packets through bridges.

A multicable LocalNet/PC may have another type of link in addition to broadband channels: a point-to-point link between pairs of communicating bridges. Such links have their own link level protocol rather than LAP. Conceptually, this alternate protocol is handled by a bridge's PTP similar to the way broadband channels LAPs are handled.

Bridges (or more precisely, the PTP implementations within the bridges) perform the packet routing functions between broadband channels and between those channels and the point-to-point link to tie the pieces into a single integrated network.

Having described the network environment in which PTP routes packets, we can examine some of the detailed mechanisms designed into this network level protocol.

Send and Pray

One of the basic goals of a layered architecture is to avoid placing too much function into any single layer, thereby allowing each layer to effectively address a smaller task. Given this design principle, the LocalNet/PC architecture does not incorporate any error recovery mechanisms within PTP, since PTP's real responsibility is packet routing. Error recovery (using acknowledgments and retransmissions) is placed within the higher-level transport layer, since this mechanism can best be handled in conjunction with other transport layer responsibilities such as flow control.

Consequently, the data delivery service provided by PTP to the LocalNet/ PC transport layer is essentially a "best-effort" service. This means the transport layer protocols cannot assume any packet delivered to PTP for routing automatically reaches its destination. This level of service provided by PTP is sometimes referred to as "send and pray."

Since PTP is not required to provide error recovery operations, the operations of the PTP interpreters within bridges are straightforward. First, a packet arrives at a bridge via one channel. Next, the PTP interpreter examines the packet to determine its ultimate destination, and then the packet is forwarded onto the "best" channel for the next leg of its journey.

To make the decision regarding the next channel to use for forwarding a particular packet, bridges use a *routing table*. If a packet is one of a stream of packets between the same source and destination, PTP incorporates the concept of a "network connection" to improve the switching efficiency of the bridges.

Network Connections

When a network connection is established, the communicating bridges exchange pointers to their appropriate routing table entries. These pointers accompany subsequent messages and allow bridges to locate correct routing information without requiring routing table searches, thereby dramatically improving routing performance.

Datagrams

PTP also supports a datagram mode, which handles packets individually without requiring a network connection. LocalNet/PC bridges can simultaneously support both operational modes.

Broadcast Discovery

For broadband cable media, PTP includes an additional consideration for "frequency agile modems." This type of modem can tune to any one of a set of possible channels under software control.

Given the existence of such modems on a network, the channel on which a specific unit is currently operating is generally unpredictable. Consequently, PTP supports an operational mode for both datagrams and network connection establishment known as *broadcast discovery*.

In broadcast discovery, bridges broadcast a packet onto all network channels while searching for the destination node. If a network connection is required, a set of "trial routes" for the connection are set up within the bridges, one of which is chosen when the first packet in the return direction is exchanged. PTP mechanisms ensure that these broadcast packets are not transmitted on a given channel more than once. In this and other ways, PTP clearly provides LocalNet/PC with the ability to support large numbers of nodes; the use of bridges allows many channels and cable systems to be integrated into a single network.

The amount of PC code required for full PTP support is minor. Consequently, the cost of including PTP in all network nodes is negligible, compared with the significant migration and expansion benefits inherent in the LocalNet/PC architecture. Network growth, accomplished by the simple addition of bridges to an already existing installation, is easily achieved, since PTP bridging provisions are automatically present in each user device.

Transport Layer

There are two protocols within the LocalNet/PC transport layer: the Datagram Transport Protocol (DTP) and the Reliable Stream Protocol (RSP).

DTP provides a best-effort datagram service built upon PTP's datagram services. The simpler of the two, DTP enhances PTP's basic service by incorporating a higher-level addressing structure, allowing datagrams to be directed to specific entities within a node (i.e., specific session layer protocols). In contrast, PTP only addresses datagrams to nodes. DTP's services allow more than one session layer protocol the ability to use datagrams.

The other protocol within LocalNet/PC's transport layer, RSP, provides the ability to establish a transport-level virtual connection with any other RSP user. Such virtual connections are managed by RSP in a way that guarantees reliable delivery of PC application data, requiring flow-control procedures that ensure senders do not flood receivers with more data than they can handle. RSP also supports a transaction operation that allows users to send requests and receive responses in a reliable fashion.

RSP's connections are established at the request of an initiating user through the exchange of RSP control packets with the remote node. During this initial packet exchange, various relevant connection information is exchanged, such as an 8-bit "connection ID" used to identify the particular connection. Since prior knowledge of the destination node's specific channel may not exist, the connection initiation packet is sent by invoking PTP's broadcast discovery service. Future packets on the connection subsequently use the established PTP network connection.

Once a connection is established, RSP procedures guarantee reliable data delivery by attaching a sequence number to each transmitted packet. When a set of packets has been correctly received, the receiving RSP interpreter indicates an acknowledgment within a special field available within packets going in the reverse direction. Each acknowledgment can acknowledge multiple packets and can be piggybacked along with any user data transferred to the other side of the connection.

A transmitting RSP interpreter maintains a copy of each packet sent until it is acknowledged and repeats a transmission if a timely acknowledgment is not received. The transmitting RSP interpreter may also "poll" the receiver, requesting an explicit acknowledgment of all current packets correctly received.

Flow control is handled using a *sliding window technique*. Two communicating RSP interpreters continually exchange a *current window value* contained in special RSP control fields within packets. A current window value indicates how many more packets can be received by the other node. A transmitting RSP interpreter does not send more packets than a receiver indicates can be handled, thus insuring that packets do not unnecessarily flood the receiver.

RSP's connection establishment packets can include user data. This allows session level protocols to use this service for sending a single request packet when anticipating a particular response. This is called a *request/response transaction*. By using request/response transactions, the benefits of request/response automatic retransmissions, as well as the ability to broadcast a request to a number of potential nodes, is obtained without establishing a network connection.

The request/response transaction service is implemented within RSP as part of the normal connection establishment sequence. A session level protocol may ask RSP to attempt to open a new connection, while giving RSP some additional data to pass along in the connection request. When an RSP interpreter receives an incoming connection request that contains user data, the data are passed to the session level for examination. Using this information, the session level protocol interpreter can decide whether to accept the connection request, reject the connection request, or ignore the connection request.

If the session protocol directs RSP to accept the connection, the connection is established through the completion of normal RSP procedures. If RSP is told to reject the connection, an explicit "connection rejected" packet is sent to the initiating RSP interpreter. Both these cases allow for the inclusion of additional session level data to be passed back to the initiating session protocol interpreter. Finally, if RSP is told to ignore the connection request, it takes no further action.

Since normal RSP connection establishment procedures include automatic retransmission of connection establishment requests if a response is not forth-coming, session level protocols do not initiate transaction retransmissions. By using the "reject" operational mode at the responder's node, simple request/response exchanges are achieved. If necessary, connections can be established for further exchanges of data by using the "accept" mode. By using the "ignore" mode, multiple potential responders can receive the same request, even if only some of them choose to respond; the rest can ignore it.

Session Layer

The session level is the topmost layer in the LocalNet/PC architecture. It contains four protocols that provide distinct communications services to PC applications. They are:

- The Session Management Protocol (SMP)
- The Name Management Protocol (NMP)
- The User Datagram Protocol (UDP)
- The Diagnostic and Monitoring Protocol (DMP)

In LocalNet/PC, PC applications are viewed as software that executes on the PC processor, either as a part of BIOS or as an actual application code. This PC-based software can access the services of LocalNet/PC via procedure calls or interrupts to the session level protocols.

Session Management Protocol (SMP)

The Session Management Protocol (SMP) provides its users with basic stream-oriented services for reliable data transfers. SMP uses an RSP virtual connection to support a user's session. Consequently, session data transfer is handled reliably and in a flow-controlled manner. Applications can send and receive session data using buffer sizes appropriate for their particular environments, without worrying about how to break the data into packets for transmission; SMP performs the actual packetization and depacketization.

Associated with this SMP packetization service is a logical message marking service, which allows the user to identify logical data boundaries within the session's stream. SMP also permits referring to destinations by meaningful symbolic names rather than 48-bit network addresses, provided that those names have already been registered through the Name Management Protocol.

Name Management Protocol (NMP)

The Name Management Protocol (NMP) provides fundamental name registration and name query functions. These functions support the use of symbolic names by other session level protocols.

One of the major requirements for a distributed LAN architecture is an optional independence from any centralized service that would disable the entire network if it failed. Consequently, name management within LocalNet/PC does not depend on a single "name server" but is a distributed service. However, it is also necessary to insure that no two nodes both register the same name for different services. A service to prevent name conflicts is easy to provide with a centralized name server but is somewhat more difficult in a distributed name management system.

In addition, it is also necessary to support both an exclusive and a nonexclusive registration for names. For example, certain servers on a LAN may provide identical services, such as a capability to access remote public data bases. You may wish such servers to be identified via the same symbolic name (such as "modem").

Alternately, some servers may provide a unique service (such as a particular disk server) and must be identified by unique symbolic names. Therefore, the name conflict prevention mechanism for a personal computer LAN must deal with both naming requirements.

NMP prevents name conflicts by using the addressing capabilities of lower-level protocols. Whenever a user requests a particular name be registered at his node, NMP algorithmically derives a group address from the name's character string. The algorithm is described in The PC Network Technical Reference Manual, Appendix C, in the discussion titled "Packet Processing."

This group address is enabled at the local node, and an NMP name claim packet is transmitted to the group address. Since any node that previously registered the name has enabled the group address, the packet is received by all such nodes, and an appropriate name claim response packet is returned. If such a response indicates that another particular node has registered the name for its own exclusive use, the name is not registered at the new node.

NMP uses the transaction services of RSP to support the name claim and response procedure. This insures that a name claim is repeated numerous times if no response is forthcoming, protecting against name conflicts arising because of name claim packet bit errors. In the name claim response procedure, the responding NMP interpreter directs its local RSP interpreter to ignore the incoming connection request if the name is not registered, or to reject the request if the name is already exclusively registered. A name claim transaction never leads to the establishment of an RSP connection.

The name query operation also uses the underlying RSP transaction service. However, in this case an RSP connection may be established to support a session with the desired named destination. This is accomplished similarly to the name claim procedure, except that the responding side may direct RSP to accept the incoming connection request. Note that if multiple nodes have the same name registered (nonexclusively), a session would be established with only one of them.

In the unlikely event that the name conflict prevention mechanisms fail (due perhaps to an improbable circumstance of all name claim packets being lost due to bit errors), it is still desirable to detect such a conflict on an exclusive name. This name conflict detection service is provided by NMP during the name query operation.

If a node has a name exclusively registered, and it accepts the connection associated with an incoming name query, then a name conflict condition is signaled if the connection acceptance fails to complete properly. Such a situation is most likely to occur if another node has also registered the name exclusively. Consequently, NMP responds by deregistering the given name, indicating to its local user that a potential name conflict was detected.

Although the primary application of the LocalNet/PC architecture requires a distributed approach to name management, in other environments a centralized naming authority is desired (perhaps for specialized access control purposes). NMP has been designed to allow the incorporation of a centralized naming authority if required. Nodes then may be added to the network but must go through the centralized authority before gaining access to particular services. Other nodes could continue to operate according to the distributed name procedures as usual.

The remaining two LocalNet/PC session layer protocols provide relatively straightforward services, and they are both built on top of the underlying datagram services of DTP.

The User Datagram Protocol (UDP)

The User Datagram Protocol (UDP) provides basic datagram services to application programs. User applications that have no need for a reliable session can use this service for data exchange. However, as with all datagram services,

UDP transfers are provided only on a best-effort ("send-and-pray") basis, and all responsibility for acknowledgments, timeouts, retransmissions, and flow control must be assumed by these applications. UDP enhances the underlying DTP service by allowing destinations to be identified by symbolic names, rather than by network addresses.

The Diagnostic and Monitoring Protocol (DMP)

The Diagnostic and Monitoring Protocol (DMP) provides for the exchange of node status and network statistics information. User applications may request information regarding the local adapter or regarding a remote node's adapter.

Remote nodes may be identified by name or address, and specific DMP packets are exchanged between the DMP interpreters to deliver the desired information across the network to the user. This information includes the names currently registered and current performance statistics.

Appendix D

PC Network Adapter Hardware Considerations and Jumper Settings

HARDWARE SUMMARY

This discussion is intended for individuals who would like to understand the function of the various PC Network adapter components. With that in mind, we assume the reader's familiarity with basic PC hardware concepts.

80188 Processor

A PC Network adapter contains an on-board Intel 80188 microprocessor. Operating at a 6-MHz clock speed, the 80188 has a self-contained timer, interrupt controller, and DMA capability. It is used to control the PC Interface Controller, Sytek Serial Interface Controller, 82586, bus interface logic, and some communications functions.

82586 Coprocessor

The 82586 is a high-performance data-serializing and deserializing circuit. This is the same circuit that is used to perform the identical function for many ETHERNET networks. Operating at 6 MHz, its functions include memory fetch and packetizing of data, link level packet recognition, error recovery and retry, and HDLC responsibility.

HDLC duties involve error detection (CRC) and bit stuffing responsibilities. The use of HDLC permits the adapter to detect an end of frame independently of the modulation signal.

Sytek Serial Interface Controller (SIC)

Operating at 14 MHz, the Sytek Serial Interface Controller handles NRZI encode/decode responsibilities and CSMA/CD control, as well as hot-carrier and no-carrier detection.

F-type Connector

The F-type connector is a standard cable TV connector that attaches the adapter to the 3-meter RG-59 attachment cable.

FM FSK Modem

The PC Network adapter modem is a full-duplex frequency shift keyed (FSK) modem that transmits modulated NRZI serialized data from the SIC in a 6-MHz channel with a center frequency of 50.75 MHz. The modem receives modulated signals in a 6-MHz channel with a center frequency of 219 MHz and provides a serialized bit stream to the SIC. The modem is compatible with video signals on other frequencies.

PC Host Interface Controller (HIC)

The PC Host Interface Controller is a VLSI gate array that is used to operate the interface between the adapter and the PC from the adapter side of the interface.

HARDWARE CONCEPTS

PC Network adapters use various PC resources during their operation: memory addresses, I/O space addresses, interrupt levels, and DMA channels. However, other adapters may also attempt to use these same resources and cause interference with the PC Network adapter.

Since PC Network adapter cards have jumpers you can set to resolve many of these conflicts, you should understand what these resources are, their purpose, and how to determine which, if any, other adapters may be also using them.

Memory Addresses

A PC's INTEL 8088 microprocessor can address over 1 million memory addresses, each containing an information character of program or data. Some of these addresses are used for the PC's BIOS, screen adapters, and other logic that accompanies adapter cards. The PC Network adapter requires addresses 0xCC000 through 0xCDFFF for its extended BIOS logic.

!/O Space Addresses

A PC has 1,024 ports, or special input/out addresses that can be used to pass data to and from adapters. These addresses are different than the PC's memory addresses.

The PC Network adapter requires port addresses 0x360 through 0x36F for proper operation. Port addresses 0x360 through 0x368 (low I/O range) are reserved for adapter zero, and port addresses 0x368 through 0x36F (high I/O range) are reserved for adapter one.

Interrupt Levels

A PC is frequently interrupted by events such as adapter data arrival or keyboard keystrokes. These events are internally prioritized into eight levels of priority, or interrupt requests (IRQ), 0 through 7, and presented to the PC as a processing interrupt at the corresponding level of priority (16 levels, 0 through 15 for a PC AT—IRQ2 actually appears as IRQ9 in an AT but is changed to an IRQ2 by the BIOS). You can think of this process as similar to living in a house that has eight separate doors, each dedicated to a special delivery service and each with its own doorbell.

An individual PC Network adapter requires exclusive use of its selected interrupt level, separate from any other adapter, including a second PC Network adapter. It can use either IRQ3 or IRQ2.

Direct Memory Access (DMA) Channels

Direct memory access provides a high-performance way of moving data to and from adapters. A PC has four DMA resources, called *channels* (and the PC AT has seven), each of which can be programmed to transfer data from one adapter to and from memory independently.

The PC Network adapter uses DMA channel 3 but does not require its exclusive use.

EXTENDED BIOS MEMORY ADDRESS RANGE CONFLICTS

The PC Network adapter 32K NetBIOS ROM consumes PC memory addresses between x'CC00 0' (CC00:0000 in segment: offset notation) through 0xCDFFF (CC00:1FFF in segment:offset notation). These addresses have been reserved by IBM for the PC Network adapter and are unchangeable. Other non-IBM cards may have ROMs (or EPROMs) residing within this same address range that would interfere with the PC Network Adapter.

If you wish to check for possible extended BIOS address range conflicts, use DEBUG's 'D' (Dump) command to display memory addresses starting at 0xCC00:0000 before your PC Network Adapter has been installed. If repeating hexadecimal patterns are displayed, these addresses are available for use by the PC Network NetBIOS. Otherwise, a conflict exists.

I/O ADDRESS RANGE CONFLICTS

Currently, no IBM cards use the PC Network Adapter Card I/O addresses (x'360'to 0x36F). However, non-IBM cards may, and before installing one, you should determine whether its I/O addresses conflict with PC Network adapter cards.

If your documentation does not provide this information, you may try to empirically determine in-use addresses via the DOS DEBUG 'I' (input) instruction to see if any card responds on any of the addresses 0x360 to x'36F'. If these I/O addresses are not in use, you will likely get the same value from any address of the I/O address range in question.

These DOS DEBUG commands are documented in the DOS User's Manual. This attempt should be performed before installing a network adapter.

INTERRUPT LEVEL CONFLICTS

PC Network adapters can use interrupt levels IRQ2 and IRQ3 in PCs. The recommended IRQ level (and factory default) is IRQ2. The PC Network Adapter cannot share its IRQ level with any other adapter, including another PC Network adapter.

IRQ2 Conflicts

Representative of other IBM adapter cards that use IRQ2 are the 3278/9 Emulation Adapter (Part Number 1602507) and the Enhanced Graphic Adapter (Part Number 1501200).

IRQ3 Conflicts

Representative of other IBM adapter cards that use IRQ3 are the COM2: Asynchronous Communication Adapter (Part Number 1502074), the Binary Synchronous Adapter (Part Number 1502075), the SDLC Adapters (Part Numbers 1502090 and 1501205), the PC Cluster Adapter (Part Number 1501206), and the GPIB Adapter (IEEE-488 Adapter) (Part Number 6451503).

In addition, BASIC, BASICA, and compiled BASIC programs annihilate critical IRQ3 information before returning to DOS, disabling an adapter that is also using IRQ3. Thus, it is advisable to use IRQ2 whenever possible. However, if you use two PC Network adapters in a PC, one must use IRQ2 and the other must use IRQ3.

DMA CHANNEL SHARING

The Network Card shares DMA channel 3 with system unit expansion units and the fixed disk adapter of a PC XT. The PC AT uses the 80286 INS and OUTS instructions instead of DMA channels.

Some other IBM cards that use DMA channel 3 are the GPIB Adapter (IEEE-488 Adapter), the PC/XT-370 3277 Adapter (ANR Card), and the 5251 or 5253 Emulation Display Adapter.

If DMA channel 3 is busy, the PC Network Adapter NetBIOS uses program-controlled data transfer, reverting to DMA-controlled data transfer when DMA channel 3 becomes available.

PC NETWORK ADAPTER JUMPER SETTINGS

Figure D-1 illustrates the position of the eight PC Network Adapter jumpers W1 through W8 and indicates their factory settings. An "E" indicates the jumper is enabled (installed) and a "D" indicates the jumper is disabled (not installed).

Further information on the adapter jumpers is located in the Installation Instructions for the IBM PC Network Adapter (IBM PC, PC XT, and Personal Computer AT) booklet that accompanies each adapter. Also see the PC Network Technical Reference Manual, Chapter Three, in the discussion titled "Configurable Options."

The various jumpers and their meanings are:

1. Jumper W1—Remote Program Load
The PC Network adapter allows an adapter to Remote Program Load a PC if a diskette or fixed disk is not available to do so. To use an adapter's Remote Program Load feature, the W1 jumper must be removed. If this feature is used, PCs use the following search order: diskette, fixed disk, IBMNET-BOOT Network Remote Program Load Server, and ROM BASIC. Note that the remote program load feature is not supported by the PC Network Program.
2. Jumper W2—Reserved
3. Jumper W3—Interrupt Level 2 (IRQ2) Selector
A jumper on this setting (the factory default) enables the adapter to use IRQ2.

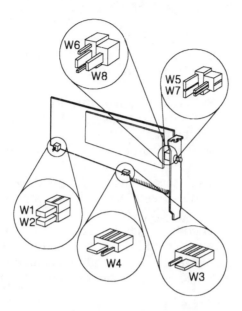

Figure D-1 PC network LANA adapter jumpers (Drawing courtesy of IBM Corp.)

4. Jumper W4—Interrupt Level 3 (IRQ3) Selector
Placing a jumper (the factory default) on this setting enables the adapter to use IRQ3.

5. Jumper W5—I/O Address Range Selector #1
This jumper selects the High I/O Address Range (0x368 to 0x36F) if it is jumpered with W7, and allows the adapter to respond to requests directed to adapter one. W5 should be jumpered if and only if W7 is jumpered.

6. Jumper W6—I/O Address Range Selector # 2
This jumper selects the low I/O address range 0x360 to 0x367 (factory default) and allows the adapter to respond to requests directed to adapter zero. W6 should be jumpered if and only if W5 and W7 are not jumpered.

7. Jumper W7—I/O Address Range Selector # 3
This jumper selects the high I/O address range (0x368 to 0x36F) if it is jumpered with W5, and allows the adapter to respond to requests directed to adapter one. W7 should be jumpered if and only if W5 is jumpered.

8. Jumper W8—BIOS ROM Enable
This enables BIOS ROM (factory default). If two adapters are installed, only one should have W8 jumpered, because the two adapters interfere with each other, and either ROM services the other. Note that PC Network Program uses only one adapter in a PC, even if two adapters are present.

Adapter Installation Verification

After you have installed the PC Network adapter in your PC, you should validate its proper operation. To do so, be sure that your adapter is connected to the network and that the network translator is functioning. Now, turn on your system unit.

The PC Power-On Self-Test (POST) process fails if your adapter cannot detect the presence of an operational translator. If it fails, you see a 3XXX error message appear on your screen (with a "Resume = F1" prompt). Assuming that your adapter passes the POST process, it is now appropriate to execute diagnostic tests on the adapter.

Place the Diagnostics diskette that is shipped with every PC Network Adapter in your A:. diskette drive. There is one version for the PC and one version for the PC AT. Alternately, you may use the PC Advanced Diagnostics (Version 2.06 or higher) accompanying the Hardware Maintenance and Service Manual. Now, restart your PC and follow the diagnostic menus.

If your PC Network Adapter(s) is operating correctly, a System Board 3000 message appears on your screen and disappears after running the Network Adapter test.

NETWORK SECURITY

The PC Network offers several levels of security. At the adapter level, packets are filtered by microcode logic. This means that though messages are broadcast on the network, only the intended recipient PC(s) actually sees them. In addition, the adapter's design makes snooping by adapters for unintended messages (or "promiscuous spy adapters") extremely difficult.

The use of unique network names and the Permanent Node Name also provides a measure of security. Finally, NET's use of passwords and access rights assists in providing network security. In the final analysis, if these measures are not sufficient, you may find encryption useful.

PC NETWORK HARDWARE FEATURES UNSUPPORTED BY NET

The PC Local Area Network Program does not support five PC Network hardware features:

- Remote Program Load—Your machine cannot use NET to load DOS.
- Specific User Datagram—You can send datagram messages only to a specific user.
- ROM Serial Number—NET does not use the Permanent Node Name.
- Group Support—NET uses only unique machine names.

  Multiple Adapter Support—NET can use only one adapter, even if more than one is present.

Appendix E

PC Network Program Summary

THE NET START COMMAND

NET START Command Parameter	RDR RCV	MSG	SRV	RANGE	DEFAULT	NOTES
/SRV - # of computers via USE	Y	Y	Y	1–31	2/3	2
/ASG - # of network devices	Y	Y	Y	1–32	5	
/SES - # of NetBIOS sessions	Y	Y	Y	2–254	varies	3
/CMD - # of NetBIOS commands	Y	Y	Y	2–254	varies	3
/NBC - # of network buffers	Y	Y	Y	1–64	4/2	4
/NBS - network buffer size	Y	Y	Y	512–32K	4K	1, 4
/PBx - print buffer size	Y	Y	Y	80B–16K	1K/512B	5

Table E-1 Summary of the NET START parameters

NET START Command Parameter	RDR RCV	MSG	SRV	RANGE	DEFAULT	NOTES
/MBI - message buffer size		Y	Y	512B–60K	1750B	6
/TSI - time slice int. fgd/bgd		Y	Y	00–99	54	
/USN - # of extra names		Y	Y	0–12	1	
/REQ - # Server msg receives			Y	1–3	2	7
/RQB - buffer sizes for /REQ's			Y	512B–32K	8K	7
/CAC - Server Disk Cache Size			Y	varies	112K	8
/EXM - Disk Cache Location			Y	N/A		
/SHB - buffer size locks/ blocks			Y	512B–60K	2K	
/SHL - # of locked file ranges			Y	20–1000	20	
/PRB - print buffer size			Y	512B–16K	2K	

Table E-1 Summary of the NET START parameters (*Continued*)

NET START Command Parameter	RDR RCV	MSG	SRV	RANGE	DEFAULT	NOTES
/PRP - bkg. print priority			Y	1–3	3	
/SHR - # of shareable devices			Y	1–999	5	
/RDR - # RDRs accessing Server			Y	1–251	10	

Table E-1 Summary of the NET START parameters (*Continued*)

Table E-1 notes:

1. **B corresponds to bytes, K to 1,024 bytes.**
2. **/SRV defaults to 3 for Servers and to 2 for other configurations.**
3. **The values of /SES and /CMD can be determined by the configuration and other parameter values.**
4. **The maximum settings of /NBC and /NBS are constrained by the relationship:**

$$(/NBC * /NBS) = 32K$$

5. **/PB1 defaults to 512 bytes for computers with less than 128K memory. For all others, it defaults to 1K bytes. /PB2 and /PB3 always default to 128 bytes.**
6. **/MBI has 2 default values: 1,600 if the PC Local Area Network Program is started from the menus, and 1,750 if the PC Local Area Network Program is started with a NET START command.**
7. **The maximum settings of the /REQ and the /RQB parameters are constrained by the relationship:**

$$(/REQ * /RQB) = 32K.$$

8. **/CAC varies from 128 to 15,232 if /EXM is present, and from 16 to 360 otherwise. (The value denotes K bytes.)**

Appendix F

Custom Broadband Network Vendors

The following listing of custom broadband network vendor organizations does not imply an endorsement or statement of their ability to provide services or equipment suitable to your establishment's satisfaction. The list is provided for readers who may wish to obtain additional information on custom broadband network design, installation, and available components from representative industry vendors. Thus, the list is not meant to be exhaustive or totally comprehensive in any sense, merely representative.

It is your responsibility to determine the fitness of any organization that provides any service or equipment to your establishment, including broadband network services and equipment. Other locally based organizations or distributors may provide services and equipment more suited to your requirements.

BROADBAND NETWORK DESIGN AND INSTALLATION VENDORS

Allied Data Communications Group, Inc.
5375 Oakbrook Parkway
Norcross, GA 30093
(404) 923-4866

Sytek, Inc.
1225 Charleston Road
Mountain View, CA 94043
(415) 966-7300

Clover Electronics
19353 Beech Daly Road
Detroit, MI 48240
(313) 535-2322

Allcom
1165 Massachusetts Avenue
Arlington, MA 02174
(617) 641-2770

Tele-Engineering
2 Central Street
Framingham, MA 01701
(617) 877-6494

RFI Electronics
360 Turtle Creek
San Jose, CA 95125
(408) 298-5400

C-COR Electronics, Inc.
60 Decible Road
State College, PA 16081
(814) 238-2461

Interactive Networks, Inc.
1757 Veterans Memorial Hwy.
Central Islip, NY 11722
(516) 582-8282

Marketechs
Wellesley, MA 02181
(617) 237-4343

Kel-Met
P. O. Box 17117
Pittsburgh, PA 15235
(800) 453-8081

BROADBAND NETWORK EQUIPMENT VENDORS

Brand Rex
Telecommunications Division
1600 West Main Street
Willimantic, CT 06226-1128
(203) 456-1706

C-COR Electronics, Inc.
60 Decible Road
State College, PA 16081
(814) 238-2461

General Instrument Corp.
RF Systems Division
4229 S. Fremont Avenue
Tucson, AZ 85714
(602) 294-1600

Magnavox
CATV Systems, Inc.
133 W. Seneca Street
Manlius, NY 13104
(315) 682-9105

RCA Cablevision System
8500 Balboa Blvd.
Van Nuys, CA 91409
(800) 423-5617

Theta-Com
122 Cutter Mill Road
Great Neck, NY 11021
(800) 528-4066

Cable Services Company, Inc.
2113 Marydale Avenue
Williamsport, PA 17701
(800) 233-8452
(800) 332-8545 in PA

Scientific Atlanta
Box 105027
Atlanta, GA 30348
(404) 441-4111

General Instrument Corp.
Jerrold Division
Hatboro, PA 19040
(215) 679-4800

Sylvania
CATV Division
1790 Lee Trevino
Suite 600
El Paso, TX 79936
(915) 591-3555

Sytek, Inc.
1225 Charleston Road
Mountain View, CA 94043
(415) 966-7300

Appendix G

PC Network Baseband and Token-Ring Component Vendors

The following listing of vendor organizations does not imply an endorsement or statement of their ability to provide services or equipment suitable to your establishment's satisfaction. The list is provided for readers who may wish to obtain additional information from representative industry vendors. It is your responsibility to determine the fitness of any organization that provides any service or equipment to your establishment. Thus, the list is not meant to be exhaustive or totally comprehensive in any sense, merely representative.

For PC Network Baseband and Token-Ring Wiring, Jack, and Connector Components:

Brand Rex
Telecommunications Division
100 S. Clay Street
Marion, NC 28752
(704) 652-5800

Virginia Plastics Company
3423 Aerial Way Drive
S.W. Roanoke VA 24018
(703) 985-3811

For PC Network Baseband Wiring Closet Components:

The Siemon Company
76 Westbury Park Rd.
Watertown, CT 06795-2523
(203) 274-2523

Appendix H

Sample Net Separator Page

The following example illustrates a NET separator page specification file. The example file illustrates how to print block characters at 17.1, 12, and 10 characters per inch. For page-length reasons, only one of these example portions should be used; NET acts unpredictably when the separator page definition size exceeds 512 bytes. The example works for an IBM Proprinter and the results may vary for other printers.

Please note that all comments must be deleted (between and including the /* and */ pair on the right of each line) for this file to work. Also, the underscore character (_) is the file escape character, and upper and lowercase letters are allowed after the file escape character.

Use caution when modifying this file. NET gives no error if it detects separator page specification error. It simply terminates interpreting the specifications and immediately begins printing the file in whatever print mode it is in, wherever it is on the separator page.

```
_          /* WARNING ===> Underscore (_) is the escape character <===      */
                          WARNING

                 /* ------------------------------------------------------------ */
                 /*                   WDSSEP4.SEP                              */
                 /*                                                           */
                 /* (C) Copyright 1985, 1988 W. David Schwaderer              */
                 /*     All rights Reserved                                   */
                 /*                                                           */
                 /* ------------------------------------------------------------ */

                 /* ----------------- Initialize the Proprinter ----------------- */
_h1B_h41_h0B     /* Esc + "A" + 12 ==> Store 6 Lines/Inch Default             */
_h1B_h32         /* Esc + "2 "      ==> Start Using Spacing Default            */
_h1B_h37         /* Esc + "7 "      ==> Select character set 1                 */
_h1B_h46         /* Esc + "F "      ==> Cancel Emphasized Print               */
```

```
_h1B_h48              /*  Esc + "H"      ==> Cancel Double Strike Print    */
_h1B_h54              /*  Esc + "T "     ==> Cancel Sub/Superscript Print  */
_h1B_h2D_h00          /*  Esc + "_ " + 0 ==> Cancel Continuous            */
                                                  Underscore
_h1B_h55_h00          /*  Esc + "U" + 0  ==> Select Bidirectional Printing */
_h1B_h57_h00          /*  Esc + "W" + 0  ==> Cancel Double Width Print     */
_0                    /*  Print Carriage Return and Line Feed              */

                      /*  -------- Print Block Character Lines at 17.1 CPI -------- */
_hOF                  /*  OFh ==> Select Condensed Print Mode(17.1 CPI)    */
_b                    /*  Select Block Character Mode                      */
_m                    /*  Select Double Width Block Characters             */
_LExample_0           /*  Print "Example" (7 Char Max if Double)           */
_1                    /*  Skip 1 Line                                      */
_s                    /*  Select Single Width Block Characters             */
_L1234567890123456_0  /*  Print "1234567890123456" (16 Char Max if Single) */
_u                    /*  Cancel Block Character Mode                      */
_0                    /*  Print Carriage Return and Line Feed              */
_2                    /*  Skip 2 Lines                                     */

                      /*  ---------- Print Block Character Lines at 12 CPI ---------- */
_h1B_h3A              /*  Select 12 Characters per Inch Printing(12 CPI)   */
_b                    /*  Select Block Character Mode                      */
_m                    /*  Select Double Width Block Characters             */
_LExampl_0            /*  Print "Exampl" (6 Char Max if Double)            */
_2                    /*  Skip 2 Lines                                     */
_s                    /*  Select Single Width Block Characters             */
_L123456789012_0      /*  Print "123456789012" (12 Char Max if Single)     */
_u                    /*  Cancel Block Character Mode                      */
_0                    /*  Print Carriage Return and Line Feed              */
_2                    /*  Skip 2 Lines                                     */

                      /*  ---------- Print Block Character Lines at 10 CPI ---------- */
_h12                  /*  Select Normal width characters (10CPI)           */
_b                    /*  Select Block Character Mode                      */
_m                    /*  Select Double Width Block Characters             */
_LExamp_0             /*  Print "Examp" (5 Char Max if Double)             */
_2                    /*  Skip 2 Lines                                     */
_s                    /*  Select Single Width Block Characters             */
_L1234567890_0        /*  Print "1234567890" (12 Char Max if Single)       */
_u                    /*  Cancel Block Character Mode                      */
_0                    /*  Print Carriage Return and Line Feed              */
_2                    /*  Skip 2 Lines                                     */

                      /* ----------------------- Print Your Name ----------------------- */
_h1B_h3A              /*  Select 12 Characters per Inch Printing(12 CPI    */
_h1B_h47              /*  Esc + "G" 56=> Select Near Letter Quality (NLQ)  */
LGreg and Melissa_0   /*  Print String                                    */
```

```
_1                              /*  Skip 1 Line                                        */
_h1B_h48                        /*  Esc + "H" ==> Cancel Near Letter Quality (NLQ)     */
_h12                            /*  Normal width characters (10 CPI)                   */
_L*---------- Printed at _t_L on _d_L ----------*_0 /* Date and Time When Printed       */
_0                              /*  Print Carriage Return and Line Feed                */
_2                              /*  Skip 2 Lines                                       */
                                /* ---- Print the Machine Name of the File Originator ---- */

_h0F                            /*  0Fh ==> Select Condensed Print Mode(17.1 CPI)      */
_b                              /*  Select Block Character Mode                        */
_s                              /*  Select Single Width Block Characters               */
_n                              /*  Print Origin Machine, must have <= 14Chars         */
_u                              /*  Cancel Block Character Mode                        */
_0                              /*  Print Carriage Return and Line Feed                */
_2                              /*  Skip 2 Lines                                       */

                                /* -------------- Print the File Queue ID Number -------------- */
_h0F                            /*  0Fh ==> Select Condensed Print Mode(17.1 CPI)      */
_b                              /*  Select Block Character Mode                        */
_m                              /*  Select Double Width Block Characters               */
_i                              /*  Print Queue ID Number                              */
_u                              /*  Cancel Block Character Mode                        */
_0                              /*  Print Carriage Return and Line Feed                */
_2                              /*  Skip 2 Lines                                       */

                                /* ------------- Clean Up before Printing the File ------------- */
_h12                            /*  Select Normal Width characters (10CPI)             */
_h1B_h32                        /*  Esc + "2"  ==> Start Using Spacing Default         */
_0                              /*  Print Carriage Return and Line Feed                */
_e                              /*  Eject to New Page—Could have many of these         */
```

Appendix I

IBM PC LAN Component Summary

This appendix summarizes IBM PC LAN hardware products.

IBM Token-Ring Network PC Adapter	6339100
IBM Token-Ring Network PC Adapter II	67X0438
IBM Token-Ring Network PC Adapter/A	69X8138
IBM Token-Ring Network PC Trace and Performance Adapter II	96X5773
IBM Token-Ring Network PC Trace and Performance Adapter/A	96X5774
IBM Token-Ring Network PC Adapter Cable	6339098
IBM Token-Ring 30-Foot Cable Assemblies	8642552
IBM 8228 Token-Ring Multistation Access Unit	6091014
PC Network Baseband Extender	72X8100
PC Network Baseband Adapter	72X8101
PC Network Baseband Adapter/A	72X8102
PC Network Baseband Wrap and Terminator Plugs	72X8103
PC Network Baseband 25-Foot Cable	72X8104
PC Network Baseband 25-Foot IBM Cabling System	72X8107
PC Network Baseband 25-Foot General Purpose Cable	72X8108
PC Network Adapter	8286171
PC Network Adapter II	72X8105
PC Network Adapter II/A	72X8106
PC Network Translator Unit	8286173
PC Network Transformer (120 Volt)	8286176
PC Network Transformer (230 Volt)	8286177
PC Network Base Expander	8286178
PC Network Short Distance Kit	8286179
PC Network Medium Distance Kit	8286180
PC Network Long Distance Kit	8286181
PC Network 25-foot cable	8286182
PC Network 50-foot cable	8286183
PC Network 100-foot cable	8286184
PC Network 200-foot cable	8286285

Appendix J

IBM PC Network Adapter II and Baseband Adapter Jumpers

The IBM PC Network Adapter II and Baseband Adapter have five jumpers that require setting. The individual jumpers consist of three pins numbered 1, 2, and 3 that are arranged vertically or horizontally. A jumper setting is selected by placing the jumper on either pins 1 and 2 or 2 and 3. Figure J-1 illustrates the relative location of the jumpers on an adapter.

A summary of the significance of jumper settings follows:

- W1: Pins 1 and 2 set interrupt level 2, pins 2 and 3 set interrupt level 3.
- W4: Pins 1 and 2 set primary adapter I/O addresses (620h to 627h), pins 2 and 3 set alternate adapter I/O addresses (628h to 62Fh).
- W5: Pins 1 and 2 set primary adapter memory address (memory address CC000 to CDFFF), pins 2 and 3 set alternate adapter memory address (memory address DC000 to DDFFF).
- W6: Pins 1 and 2 disable Remote Program Load (RPL), pins 2 and 3 enable Remote Program Load
- W7: Pins 1 and 2 enable the adapter ROM, pins 2 and 3 disable the adapter ROM. The adapter ROM is always located at address D0000 to D7FFF.

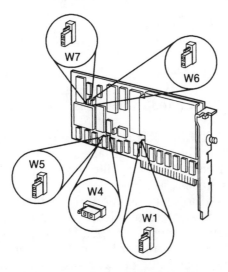

Figure J-1 PC network adapter II and PC network baseband adapter jumpers (Drawing courtesy of International Business Machines Corporation.)

Appendix K

DOS 3.1 File-Sharing Modes

DOS 3.1 allows a file to be opened in one of five file-sharing modes. If a file-sharing mode is not specified, the default-sharing mode depends on the file's attribute and on the way it was opened, as summarized in Table K-1.

The five sharing modes are:

Compatibility Mode—A file can be opened any number of times in compatibility mode, provided it is not already open in one of the other four sharing modes. If the file is already open in another sharing mode, an open error occurs.

Deny Read/Write (Exclusive) Mode—If a file is successfully opened in this mode, access to the file is exclusive. That is, the file must be closed before being opened in another mode.

Deny Write Mode—If a file is successfully opened in this mode, the file must be closed before a request for Write Access is granted. However, an attempt to open a file with Deny Write Mode when it is currently open in Write Access Mode fails.

Deny Read Mode—If a file is successfully opened in this mode, any other attempt to open this file requesting read access is unsuccessful until the file is closed. However, an attempt to open a file with Deny Read Access when it is currently open in Read Access Mode or compatibility mode fails.

Deny None Mode—If a file is successfully opened in this mode, any other attempt to open this file is successful. However, an attempt to open a file with Deny Read Access when it is currently open in compatibility mode fails.

Table K-2 illustrates the results of attempting to open a file that is already open in a given sharing mode. For more information on DOS sharing modes, read the discussion under the topic "3DH Open a file" in the DOS 3.1 Technical Reference Manual chapter "DOS Interrupts and Function Calls."

Read-Only Attribute

File Opened By	Access	Assigned Sharing Mode
FCB	Read/Write	Deny Write
Handle Read	Read-Only	Deny Write
Handle Write	Error	–
Handle Read/Write	Error	–

Not Read-Only Attribute

File Opened By	Access	Assigned Sharing Mode
FCB	Read/Write	Compatibility
Handle Read	Read/Write	Compatibility
Handle Write	Write	Compatibility
Handle Read/Write	Write	Compatibility

Table K-1 Assigned default sharing modes—Initial open

Subsequent Opens

		DRW			DW			DR			DN		
		I	IO	O	I	IO	O	I	IO	O	I	IO	O
D R W	I	–	–	–	–	–	–	–	–	–	–	–	–
	IO	–	–	–	–	–	–	–	–	–	–	–	–
	O	–	–	–	–	–	–	–	–	–	–	–	–

FIRST OPEN														
	DW	I	–	–	–	Y	–	–	–	–	–	Y	–	–
		IO	–	–	–	–	–	–	–	–	–	Y	–	–
		O	–	–	–	–	–	–	–	–	–	Y	–	–
	DR	I	–	–	–	–	–	–	–	–	–	–	–	Y
		IO	–	–	–	–	–	–	–	–	–	–	–	Y
		O	–	–	–	–	–	–	–	–	Y	–	–	Y
		I	–	–	–	Y	Y	Y	–	–	–	Y	Y	Y
		IO	–	–	–	–	–	–	–	–	–	Y	Y	Y
		O	–	–	–	–	–	–	Y	Y	Y	Y	Y	Y

Legend

Y - Subsequent opens are successful, else they are unsuccessful

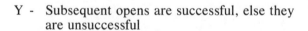

Sharing Mode -	DRW:	Deny Read/Write (Exclusive) Mode
	DW:	Deny Write Mode
	DR:	Deny Read Mode
	DN:	Deny None (Allow Read/Write)

Access Mode -	I:	Read-Only Access
	O:	Write-Only Access
	IO:	Read/Write Access

Table K-2 Consequences of opens subsequent to initial open

Appendix L

IBM Cabling System Wiring

The following is a summary of IBM Cabling System Data Cables used in IBM Token-Ring and PC Network Baseband LANS.

Type 1 (Data Only):

- Type 1 Data Cable—Two twisted pairs of No. 22 AWG (American Wire Gauge) solid copper conductors for data communication, each pair wrapped in metallic foil, enclosed in a braided metal cable shield covered with an appropriate nonplenum sheath.
- Type 1 Data Plenum Cable—Two twisted pairs of No. 22 AWG solid copper conductors for data communication, each pair wrapped in metallic foil, enclosed in a braided metal cable cable covered with an appropriate sheath.
- Type 1 Data Outdoor Cable—Two twisted pairs of No. 22 AWG solid copper conductors for data communication, each pair wrapped in metallic foil, enclosed in a corrugated metallic cable covered with an appropriate sheath. Suitable for aerial or underground installations.

Type 2 (Data and Telephone):

- Type 2 Data and Telephone Cable—Two twisted pairs of No. 22 AWG solid copper conductors for data communication, each pair wrapped in metallic foil, enclosed in a braided metal cable shield covered with an appropriate nonplenum sheath. Also included inside the cable are four pairs of No. 22 AWG solid copper conductors for telephone use.
- Type 2 Data and Telephone Plenum Cable—Two twisted pairs of No. 22 AWG solid copper conductors for data communication, each pair wrapped in metallic foil, enclosed in a braided metal cable shield cable covered with an appropriate sheath. Also included inside the cable are four pairs of No. 22 AWG solid copper conductors for telephone use.

Type 3 (Unshielded Telephone):

- Number 22 or 24 AWG solid copper twisted pairs
- Two twists per foot minimum

- A maximum of 28.6 ohms DC resistance per 1,000 feet (305 meters)
- Meets one of the following industry specifications:
  - ANSI/ICEA S-80-576-1983
  - REA PE-71
  - Bell Systems 48008
- Maximum attenuation per 1,000 feet (305 meters)
  - 4.00 dB at 256 KHz
  - 5.66 dB at 512 KHz
  - 6.73 dB at 772 KHz
  - 8.00 dB at 1000 KHz
- Impedance characteristics:
  - 90 to 120 ohms at 256 KHz
  - 87 to 117.5 ohms at 512 KHz
  - 85 to 114 ohms at 772 KHz
  - 84 to 113 ohms at 1,000 KHz

Type 5 (Fiber-Optic):

- Type 5 Fiber-Optics Cable—Two 100/140 micron optical cables suitable for indoor nonplenum use, outdoor aerial installation, or placement in dry waterproof conduits.

Type 6 (Patch Cable):

- Type 6 Data Cable—Two twisted pairs of No. 26 AWG stranded copper conductors for data communication covered together in metallic foil, enclosed in a braided metal cable shield, and covered with an appropriate nonplenum sheath. Used for patch cables only because of its flexibility.

Type 8 (Under Carpet):

- Type 8 Data Cable—Two parallel (not twisted) pairs of No. 26 AWG solid copper conductors for data communication. Each pair of conductors is individually shielded with copper shield. Requires an under-carpet Cable Connector Kit. Type 8 cable has two bending radius specifications. The on-the-flood minimum bending radius is 10 inches (250 mm); the minimum bending radius for going from the floor to a wall is 1.5 inches (38 mm).

Type 9 Data Cable (Lower-Cost):

- Type 9 Data Cable is a lower-cost alternative to Type 1 cable. It contains two shielded twisted pair data-grade solid or stranded copper conductors made from No. 26 AWG wire.

For more information on the IBM Cabling System, consult the IBM Cabling references in the Bibliography.

Bibliography

Edward Cooper, *Broadband Network Technology*. Mountain View, CA: Sytek Press, 1984.

A Building Planning Guide for Communication Wiring (G320-8059). Armonk, NY: IBM Corporation, March 1985.

John E. Cunningham, *Cable Television,* 2nd Edition. Indianapolis, IN: Howard W. Sams & Co. Inc., 1983.

DOS 3.3 Reference (80X0945). Armonk, NY: IBM Corporation, April 1987.

DOS 3.3 Technical Reference (80X0667). Armonk, NY: IBM Corporation, April 1987.

Executive Overview of Sytek, Inc.'s "LocalNet/PC." Mountain View, CA: Sytek Inc., 1985.

IBM Cabling System Catalog (G570-2040). Armonk, NY: IBM Corporation, October 1985.

IBM Cabling System Planning and Installation Guide (GA27-3361). Armonk, NY: IBM Corporation, October 1985.

IBM PC Local Area Network Program User's Guide (6139747). Armonk, NY: IBM Corporation, April 1987.

IBM PC Local Area Network Support Program User's Guide and Diskette Documentation (8575230). Armonk, NY: IBM Corporation, June 1987.

IBM PC Network Adapter Technical Reference (S68X-2265). Armonk, NY: IBM Corporation, April 1987.

IBM PC Network Adapter II Technical Reference (S68X-2223). Armonk, NY: IBM Corporation, April 1987.

IBM PC Network Adapter II/A Technical Reference (S68X-2263). Armonk, NY: IBM Corporation, April 1987.

IBM PC Network Analysis Program Technical Guide (GG24-1727). Armonk, NY: IBM Corporation, March 1985.

IBM PC Network Baseband Adapter Technical Reference (S68X-2267). Armonk, NY: IBM Corporation, April 1987.

IBM PC Network Baseband Adapter/A Technical Reference (S68X-2264). Armonk, NY: IBM Corporation, April 1987.

IBM PC Network Baseband Extender Technical Reference (S68X-2266). Armonk, NY: IBM Corporation, April 1987.

IBM PC Network Baseband Planning Guide (S68X-2269). Armonk, NY: IBM Corporation, April 1987.

IBM PC Network Broadband Planning Guide (S68X-2268). Armonk, NY: IBM Corporation, April 1987.

IBM PC Network Hardware Maintenance and Service (80X1000). Armonk, NY: IBM Corporation, April 1987.

IBM PC Network Technical Reference (6322505). Armonk, NY: IBM Corporation, 1984.

IBM PC Network Translator Unit and Cabling Options Technical Reference (S68X-2228). Armonk, NY: IBM Corporation, April 1987.

IBM Personal Computer Network Concepts and Support, IBM Course 77440 Textbook (SR28-0537). Armonk, NY: IBM Corporation, 1985.

IBM Personal Computer Seminar Proceedings, Vol. 2, No. 5. Armonk, NY: September 1984.

IBM Personal Computer Seminar Proceedings, Vol. 2, No. 8-1. Armonk, NY: May 1985.

IBM Token-Ring Network Administrator's Guide (GA27-3748). Armonk, NY: IBM Corporation, June 1986.

IBM Token-Ring Network Installation Guide (GA27-3678). Armonk, NY: IBM Corporation, June 1986.

IBM Token-Ring Network Installation Guide (GA27-3747). Armonk, NY: IBM Corporation, April 1986.

IBM Token-Ring Network Introduction and Planning Guide (GA27-3677). Armonk, NY: IBM Corporation, October 1985.

IBM Token-Ring Network PC Adapter Technical Reference (69X7830). Armonk, NY: IBM Corporation, 1986.

IBM Token-Ring Network Problem Determination Guide and Planning Documents (SX27-3710). Armonk, NY: IBM Corporation, June 1986.

IBM Token-Ring Network Technology (GA27-3732). Armonk, NY: IBM Corporation, January 1986.

IBM Token-Ring Network Telephone Twisted-Pair Media Guide (GA27-3678). Armonk, NY: IBM Corporation, May 1986.

Scout User Manual. Pittsburgh, PA: Computer Insights, 1985.

Ken Simons, *Technical Handbook for CATV Systems.* Hattsborough, PA: Jerrold Division, General Instrument Corporation, March 1968.

Norbert Straub, Werner Redle, and Oliver Sims, *PC Network and PC Network Program Introduction* (GG24-1691). Armonk, NY: IBM Corporation, March 1985.

Glossary

The following material is excerpted with the permission and courtesy of Sytek, Inc. from Sytek Press's *Broadband Network Technology* by Edward Cooper. In addition, some terms have been excerpted from the IBM PC Network Technical Reference Manual and the Token-Ring Network PC Adapter Technical Reference with the permission and courtesy of IBM.

Access channel control—The collection of logic and protocol machines managing data transfer between link stations and their medium-access control layers.

Access control byte—In the IBM Token-Ring, the byte following the frame's or token's start delimiter. The access control byte controls access to the ring.

Access priority—In the IBM Token-Ring, the maximum priority a received token can have for the adapter to use it for transmission.

Access method/procedure—The method/procedure/protocol used to gain access to the medium. The specified IEEE 802 standard medium access procedures are CSMA/CD (IEEE 802.3), Token-Passing Bus (IEEE 802.4), and Token-Ring (IEEE 802.5).

Active component—A component that requires electrical power to operate.

Active monitor—In the Token-Ring, a function in a single adapter that initiates token transmissions and provides token error recovery facilities. Any active network adapter can provide the active monitor function if the current active monitor fails.

Adapter—The circuitry, and its associated software, within a communicating device that enables the device to communicate on a network.

Adapter support interface—The software that provides a common application program interface and operates IBM LAN adapter cards in IBM personal computers.

Address—A number specifying a particular user device attachment point.

Alias—An alternate name your adapter can be known by on the network.

Allocation—In broadband networks, the assignment of specific frequencies for various communications uses. It divides the available frequency spectrum between competing services and minimizes interference among them. The manager of a broadband network must allocate the available bandwidth of the cable among different services for the same reason.

Amplifier—In broadband networks, a device that increases the power (amplitude) of an electrical signal. Amplifiers are placed where needed in a cable system to strengthen signals weakened by cable and component attenuation as they pass through the cable network. Midsplit systems use a forward and a reverse amplifier in the same enclosure to boost signals in both directions.

Appendage—In the IBM Token-Ring, an application program routine that assists in handling specific ring events.

Attach—In the IBM Token-Ring, connecting a device logically to a ring and participating in the ring's data passing protocol.

Attenuation—A decrease in signal strength between two transmission points.

Attenuator—A device that creates intentional attenuation.

Auto removal—In the IBM Token-Ring, the adapter removing a device from data-passing activities without human intervention.

Balancing—In broadband networks, adjusting the gains and losses in each path of a system to achieve nearly equal signal levels at all user outlets. Balancing also produces nearly equal inputs to the headend from transmitters connected anywhere in the network.

Bandwidth—The frequency range that a component, circuit, or system can pass. For example, a voice transmission by telephone requires a bandwidth of about 3,000 cycles per second (3 KHz). A television channel occupies a bandwidth of 6 million cycles per second (6 MHz).

Beacon—In the IBM Token-Ring, a frame indicating a serious network problem, such as a broken cable.

Beaconing—In the IBM Token-Ring, sending continuous beacon frames.

Baseband—A general term used to describe data-encoding techniques that preclude the sharing of a transmission medium with other signals. Baseband encoding techniques typically involve the use of media voltage levels to encode data.

BIOS—Basic Input/Output System.

Branch cable—In broadband networks, an intermediate cable distribution line in a broadband coaxial network that either feeds or is fed from a main trunk. Also referred to as a feeder.

Bridge—A specialized device connecting and routing messages between different instances of the same type network.

Broadband—A general term used to describe wide bandwidth equipment or systems that carry signals occupying a large proportion of the electromagnetic spectrum. A broadband communication system can accommodate television, voice, data, and many other services.

Buffer—A memory area used to perform communication input/output operations.

Bypass—Eliminating a component from a network by forcing the communication path to go past it.

Cable kit—In broadband networks, an IBM cabling component consisting of an eight-port splitter and attenuators used to connect personal computers to a network.

Cable loss—In broadband networks, the amount of RF signal attenuation by a given coaxial cable. The amount of cable attenuation is mainly a function of signal frequency and cable length, though temperature also has an effect. High frequencies have a greater loss than low frequencies, according to a logarithmic function. Cable losses are often calculated and specified for the highest frequency carried on the cable.

Cable powering—In broadband networks, supplying operating power to active CATV equipment (for example, amplifiers) with the coaxial cable. This AC or DC power does not interfere with the RF information signal.

Cable tilt—In broadband networks, the variation of cable attenuation with frequency. The attenuation of a length increases with frequency; therefore, the amplitude of an RF sweep signal measured at the end of a length of cable is greater at low frequencies than it is at high frequencies. When viewed on a spectrum analyzer, the waveform tilts downward to the right.

Cable TV—A communication system that simultaneously distributes several different channels of broadcast programs and other information to customers via coaxial cable. Previously called Community Antenna Television (CATV).

Carrier—A signal that is altered in a way that conveys information.

Carrier sense multiple access with collision detection (CSMA/CD)—A communication medium access technique that allows many different transceivers (transmitters and receiver combinations) to share a single channel without requiring a central transmission allocation authority. All transceivers monitor the channel (carrier sense) and do not transmit when receiving a signal. Whenever the channel is idle, any transmitter can transmit (multiple access). If two or more transmitters begin transmitting during the same period, their signals collide and their associated receivers detect that a collision has occurred (collision detect). They cease transmitting and wait for a short time before trying to retransmit the data.

Cascade—In broadband networks, the number of amplifiers connected in a series in a trunk system.

CATV—See Cable TV.

Central Retransmission Facility (CRF)—In broadband networks, the location of broadband equipment that processes RF signals for network retransmission in the forward direction.

Checksum—A value that when ORed with a sum calculated from accumulating all bits in a field yields a zero result.

Coaxial cable—A single cable with two conductors separated a uniform distance having a common longitudinal axis. The inner conductor (center conductor) carries information signals; the outer conductor (shield) is grounded for those signal frequencies to prevent interference. The shield and center conductor are separated by an insulating dialectic made of polyethylene.

Completion code—The final result value returned by an adapter following an request.

Composite video signal—The complete video signal. For monochrome systems, it comprises the picture, blanking, and synchronizing signals. For color systems, it includes additional color synchronizing signals and color picture information.

Constant-value loss—The network flat loss caused by passive devices. The attenuation is constant for all frequencies.

CRC—See Cyclic redundancy check.

CRF—See Central Retransmission Facility.

Cross modulation—A form of signal distortion in which modulation from one or more RF carrier(s) is imposed on another carrier.

Crosstalk—Energy undesirably transferred from one circuit to another. The circuit transferring the energy is called the disturbing circuit. The circuit absorbing the energy is referred to as the disturbed circuit.

CSMA/CD—See Carrier sense multiple access with collision detection.

Cyclic redundancy check—A numeric value derived from a message's bits used to check message transmission errors.

Data frame—See Frame.

Datagram—A particular type of message that relies on the best effort of the link layer and requires no explicit acknowledgment from the receiver. Datagrams may be sent to a particular network node, group of nodes, or broadcast indiscriminately for general reception. In the latter case, the datagram is referred to as a broadcast datagram.

Data link—A physical connection, such as a wire or a telephone circuit, that connects one or more communicating network devices.

Data link control—An IEEE protocol containing the IEEE Logical Link Control (LLC) sublayer.

Data link layer (or level)—In ISO/OSI, the layer providing the functions and procedures establishing, maintaining, and releasing network element data link connections between two communicating entities.

Data rate—The rate of information transfer, usually expressed in bits per second (bps) units.

dB—An abbreviation for decibel, used as a relative unit of measure between two signals on a logarithmic basis. dB is an expression of a ratio between an input level and an output level.

dBmV—An abbreviation for decibel millivolt. The level at any point in a system expressed in dB above or below a 1 millivolt/75 ohm standard is the level in decibel millivolts (dBmV). Zero dBmV is equal to 1 millivolt across 75 ohms.

Default—The default value of a setting is the one used in the absence of any specification.

Delimiter—A bit pattern defining the limits of a message or, in the instance of the IBM Token-Ring, a token or frame.

Directional coupler—In broadband networks, a passive device used in cable systems to divide and combine RF signals. It has at least three signals and lines: trunk-in, trunk-out, and tap. The trunk signal passes between the trunk-in and trunk-out lines with little loss. A portion of the signal applied to the trunk-in line passes to the tap line, in order to connect branches or outlets to the trunk. A signal applied to the tap line is attenuated and passes to the trunk-in line and is isolated from the trunk-out line. A signal applied to the trunk-out line passes to the trunk-in line and is isolated from the tap line. Some devices provide more than one tap output line (multitaps).

Direct memory access—A high-performance way of moving data to/from a PC adapter.

Distribution amplifier—In broadband networks, an amplifier used to increase RF signal levels to overcome cable and flat loss in signal distribution.

Distribution panel—In the IBM Token-Ring, a rack-mounted wiring board providing a patch panel function.

DLC—See Data link control.

DMA—See Direct memory access.

Downstream—In the IBM Token-Ring, the direction of data flow. The downstream node from a given node is the next node to receive a frame or token. Also, see Upstream.

Drop cable—See Drop line.

Drop line—In broadband networks, a flexible coaxial cable that connects a network tap to a user's outlet. Also referred to as a drop cable.

Drop line device—In broadband networks, any external device attached to the coaxial network through a drop line (for example, an RF modem, television set, or audio modulator).

Dual cable—In broadband networks, a type of broadband local area network that uses two branching-tree networks. Each network carries signals traveling in one direction, opposite to the direction of the other network. See also single cable.

Echo—See Reflection.

Egress—See Signal egress.

Ending delimiter—In the IBM Token-Ring, a specially formatted byte indicating the end of a token or frame.

Equalization—In broadband networks, a means of modifying the frequency response of an amplifier or network to compensate for distortions in the channel. The ideal result is a flat overall response. This slope compensation is often done by a module within an amplifier enclosure.

Equal-split—See High-split.

Faceplate—A plate for mounting network and telephone jack connectors. In the case of the IBM Token-Ring, faceplates come in two varieties, wall-mounted and surface-mounted.

F connector—In broadband networks, a standard, low-cost 75-ohm connector used by the CATV industry to connect a coaxial cable to equipment.

FDM—See Frequency division multiplexing.

Feeder cable—See Branch cable.

Filter—In broadband networks, a circuit that selects one or more components of a signal depending on their frequency. Used in trunk and branch (feeder) lines for special cable services such as two-way operation.

Flat loss—In broadband networks, equal signal strength loss across a system's entire bandwidth, such as that caused by attenuators.

Flooded cable—In broadband networks, a special coaxial CATV cable containing a corrosion-resistant gel between the outer aluminum sheath and the outer jacket. The gel flows into imperfections in the aluminum to prevent corrosion in high-moisture areas.

Forward direction—In broadband networks, the direction of signal flow in a cable system that is away from the CRF or headend.

Frame—In the IBM Token-Ring, the unit of transmission created when a node appends data to a token. It includes starting and ending delimiters, source and destination addresses, routing information, information, control information, and cyclic redundancy check characters.

Frame check sequence (FCS)—A multibyte cyclic redundancy check (CRC) field computed from several fields of a network message.

Frame status (FS)—In the IBM Token-Ring, a frame byte following the end delimiter byte indicating whether the destination adapter received the frame.

Frequency—The number of times a periodic signal repeats itself in a unit of time, usually 1 second. One Hertz (Hz) is one cycle per second; kilohertz (KHz) is one thousand cycles per second; megahertz (MHz) is one million cycles per second; gigahertz (GHz) is one billion cycles per second.

Frequency division multiplexing (FDM)—A method of dividing a communication channel's bandwidth among several subchannels with different carrier frequencies. Each subchannel can carry separate data signals.

Frequency response—The change of a signal parameter (usually amplitude) with frequency.

Frequency shift keying—A modulation technique that signals information by varying the frequency of a carrier signal. This form of modulation is resistant to the effects of external interference.

Frequency translator—In a two-way broadband system, an active device at the headend that receives RF signals traveling in the reverse direction from devices connected to the network, converts them to higher frequency signals above the system's guard band, and sends them in the forward direction.

FSK—See Frequency shift keying.

Full duplex—A communication connection that allows simultaneous transmissions in both directions.

Gateway—A device and its associated software that connects two different types of networks and performs protocol translation, so that data from one network can be transmitted on the other.

Hard error—A serious persistent network error requiring network reconfiguration or that the source of the error be removed before the network can resume reliable operation.

Harmonic distortion—In broadband networks, a form of interference caused by the generation of harmonic signals according to the relationship N(f), where N is an integer greater than 1 and f is the original signal's frequency.

Headend—In broadband networks, the facility that contains a cable system's electronic control center, generally the antenna site of a CATV system. It usually includes antennas, preamplifiers, frequency converters, demodulators,

modulators, and other related equipment that receive, amplify, filter, and convert incoming broadcast television signals to cable system channels. In two-way broadband systems, the headend houses at least the frequency translator. The term *headend* is sometimes used synonymously with the equipment located at this central site.

High frequencies—In two-way broadband network, frequencies allocated for the forward direction, 160 MHz to 400+ MHz in a midsplit system.

High-split—In broadband networks, a frequency division scheme used in some two-way cable systems. Reverse path signals come to the headend between 5 to 174 MHz; forward path signals go from the headend between 232 to 400+ MHz. No signals are present between 174 and 232 MHz (the guard band). The frequencies have not been standardized. Also referred to as equal-split.

Host concept—Many protocols, such as IBM's SNA for example, employ some large data processing facility host as part of the network.

Hot carrier—A condition that occurs when a transmitter is locked in transmit mode.

Hub—In broadband networks, the same as a headend for bidirectional networks, except that it is more centrally located within the network.

Idles—In the IBM Token-Ring, signals transmitted on a ring when frames and tokens are not being transmitted.

Inbound—The cable carrying signals to the headend in a dual cable system.

Ingress—See Signal ingress.

Insert—In the IBM Token-Ring, to make an adapter active (attach) on a network.

Insertion loss—In broadband networks, the loss of signal level in a cable path caused by insertion of a passive device such as a directional coupler; equal to the difference in signal level between input and output of such a device.

Isolation loss—In broadband networks, the amount of signal attenuation in a passive device from output port to tap outlet port.

LAN—See Local area network.

LANA—An original IBM PC Network adapter.

Link—The logical connection between nodes including end-to-end link control procedures.

Link connection—The physical components and protocol machines lying between communicating link stations on a link. These include any switched or leased physical data circuits, local area networks, or X.25 virtual circuits.

Link station—A node's protocol machine-managing procedure elements required for data exchange with another link station.

Lobe—In the IBM Token-Ring, a section of cable connecting a device to an access unit.

Lobe receptacle—In the IBM Token-Ring, a wiring concentrator outlet that connects a lobe.

Local area network—A privately owned and operated high-speed data communications network operating in a limited geographic area that does not extend across public rights-of-way.

Local busy—An adapter state occurring when an adapter cannot handle additional frame activity for one or more of its link stations.

Local Session Number—The number assigned to each NetBIOS session established by an adapter. Each session receives a unique number distinguishing it from any other active sessions.

Logical Link Control Protocol Data Unit (LPDU)—The unit of information exchanged between link stations in different nodes consisting of the destination service access point (DSAP) and source service access point (SSAP) address fields, the control field, and the optional information field.

Low frequencies—Frequencies allocated for the reverse direction in a two-way broadband system, 5 MHz to 116 MHz in a midsplit system.

LPDU—See Logical link control protocol data unit.

LSN—See Local session number.

MAC—See Medium access control

MAC frame—In the IBM Token-Ring, frames containing information about the status of the ring or one of the ring adapters.

Main trunk—See Trunk line.

Medium—A physical carrier of signals.

Medium access control (MAC)—The DLC subcomponent supporting medium-dependent functions using the physical layer services, including the medium access port, to provide services to the logical link control layer.

Memory mapped I/O (MMIO)—A method of accessing input and output ports as if they were memory locations.

Midband—In broadband networks, the part of the electromagnetic frequency spectrum that lies between television channels 6 and 7, reserved by the FCC for air, maritime and land mobile units, FM radio, and aeronautical and maritime navigation. Midband frequencies, 108 to 174 MHz, can also be used to provide additional channels on cable television systems.

Midsplit—In broadband networks, a frequency division scheme used in some two-way cable systems. Reverse path signals come to the headend between 5 to 116 MHz; forward path signals go from the headend between 168 to 400+ MHz. No signals are present between 116 and 168 MHz (the guard band).

Modem—A modulator-demodulator device. The modulator codes digital information onto a carrier signal by varying the amplitude, frequency, or phase of that carrier. The demodulator part extracts the digital information from a similarly modified carrier signal.

Monitor—In the IBM Token-Ring Network, the function required to initiate token transmissions and to provide soft-error recovery in the event of lost tokens, lost circulating frames, or other ring problems. All ring stations have this capability.

Multitap—In broadband networks, a passive distribution component composed of a directional coupler and a splitter with two or more output connections. See also Tap.

NAUN—See Nearest active upstream neighbor.

Nearest active upstream neighbor—In the IBM Token-Ring, for any active ring station, the nearest active upstream neighbor is the active ring station sending tokens and frames to it.

Network administrator—A person who oversees the use and performs the maintenance of a network.

Network management—The activities determining how stations should be connected to or whether stations should be disconnected from a network.

Node—In a LAN, a LAN adapter and necessary LAN adapter software.

Node address—The address of an LAN adapter.

Noise—Any undesired signal in a communication system.

Noise figure—A measurement of the amount of noise contributed to a system by an amplifier.

Numbered frames—In the IBM Token-Ring, information segments arranged in numerical order for accountability.

Open—(1) To prepare an adapter for use. (2) An electrical circuit break.

Outbound—In broadband networks, the cable carrying signals away from the headend in a dual cable system.

Outlet—See Tap outlet.

Packet—A message unit processed by the transport layer. A packet contains control information, as well as user data.

Passive component—In broadband networks, a component that does not require electrical power to operate and which may cause flat loss.

Patch cable—In the IBM Token-Ring Network, a cable with IBM Cabling System connectors at both ends used to connect network components, devices, and cables.

Path—A route between any two network nodes.

Point to point—A connection between two and only two nodes on a network.

Programmed I/O (PIO)—A method of accessing input and output ports with specific instructions.

PROM—Programmable read-only memory.

Propagation delay—The time difference between when a signal is issued and when it is received.

Protocol—A set of rules or procedure for exchanging information between correspondents.

RAM—Random-access memory.

Receiver isolation—In broadband networks, the attenuation between any two receivers that are connected to a cable system.

Reflections—Secondary signals caused by the collision of the transmitted signal with objects in its path. In a cable system, such echoes can be created by impedance mismatches and cable discontinuities or irregularities. Also called echoes.

Remove—To stop an adapter from participating in network data exchange.

Return code—An adapter-provided value indicating the result of an adapter action.

Return loss—A measure of a component's reflection properties expressed in dB.

Return path—See Reverse direction.

Reverse direction—In broadband networks, the direction of signal flow in a cable system that is toward the CRF or headend.

Reverse path—See Reverse direction.

RF—Radio Frequency.

Ring in—On an IBM multistation access unit, the receive or input receptacle.

Ring out—On an IBM multistation access unit, the transmit or output receptacle.

Ring sequence—In the IBM Token-Ring, the physical connection order of components.

Ring status—In the IBM Token-Ring, the condition of a network.

Ring topology—A logically circular, unidirectional transmission path with distributed or centralized control.

ROM—Read-only memory.

Routing—In the IBM Token-Ring, the assigned path a message traverses to reach its destination.

SABME—See Set asynchronous balanced mode extended.

Segment—A portion of an IBM Token-Ring network possibly containing cables, components, and lobes.

Service access point—The logical point at which one communication layer acquires the services of an immediately higher layer. A single DLC SAP can have many links terminating in it. These link end-points are referred to in DLC literature as link stations.

Session—A communication connection resulting from a NetBIOS Call or DLC Link between two devices.

Set asynchronous balanced mode extended—A DLC command used to establish a link.

Signal egress—Undesirable signals emitted from a cable system.

Signal ingress—Undesirable signals that enter into a cable system from an outside source, such as an RF transmitting tower (AM or FM).

Signal level—The root-mean-square (rms) voltage measured during the peak of the RF signal. It is usually expressed in microvolts referred to an impedance of 75 ohms, or in dBmV.

Signal-to-noise ratio—The relative power of the information signal as opposed to noise present.

Single cable—A type of broadband local area network that uses a single branching-tree network to carry signals bidirectionally. See also Dual cable.

Single trunk bus—In broadband networks, a bus topology that uses a single cable to which all nodes connect with drop cables. The bus must extend to a tap within reach of a node.

Slope—In broadband networks, the difference between the signal levels at the highest frequency and the lowest frequency in a cable system. Also referred to as spectrum tilt.

Slope compensation—In broadband networks, the action of a slope-compensated gain control. The gain of an amplifier and the slope of its equalization are simultaneously changed to provide the correct cable equalization for different lengths of cable. This is normally specified in terms of cable loss.

Soft error—A network error that impairs a network's performance but, by itself, does not affect its reliability.

Splitter—In broadband networks, a passive device that divides the signal power of forward direction input signals into two or more output signals of lesser power before allowing the signal to continue in the forward direction. Splitters combine reverse direction input signals into a single signal and pass it toward the headend. Splitters pass through 60 Hz power to all lines.

Star wiring—A wiring arrangement in which an individual cable runs from each network device to a concentration point such as an IBM Multistation Access Unit.

Start delimiter—In the IBM Token-Ring, a specially formatted byte indicating the start of a token or frame.

Subsplit—In broadband networks, a frequency division scheme used in some two-way cable systems. Reverse path signals come to the headend between 5 to 30 MHz; forward path signals go from the headend between 54 to 400+ MHz. No signals are present between 30 and 54 MHz (the guard band).

Tap—In broadband networks, a passive device, normally installed in-line with a feeder cable. It removes a portion of the signal power from the distribution line and delivers it to the drop line. The amount of power tapped off the main line depends on the input power to the tap and the attenuation value of the tap. Only the information signal (and not any 60-Hz power, if present) goes to the outlet ports. See also Multitap.

Tap outlet—In broadband networks, an F-type connector port on a tap used to attach a drop line. The information signal is carried through this port. The number of outlets on a branch line tap usually varies from two to eight.

TDM—See Time division multiplexing.

Terminator—In broadband networks, a 75-ohm resistive connector that terminates the end of a cable or an unused tap port. The device is used to minimize cable reflections and minimize signal ingress. In the baseband PC

Network, a plug that is installed at the opposite end of a daisy chain from a wrap plug or network extender.

Thru loss—See Insertion loss.

Tilt compensation—See Slope compensation.

Time division multiplexing (TDM)—A method of sharing a single communication channel among several users by allowing each exclusive use of the channel for a short period of time in a well-defined manner.

Token—In the IBM Token-Ring, a bit sequence passed from station to station along the ring consisting of a starting delimiter, a frame control field, and an ending delimiter. The frame control field contains a token indicator bit indicating to a receiving station that the token is ready to accept information. If the station has data to send, it appends the data to the token. The token then becomes a frame.

Token-Ring—A network with a ring topology that passes tokens from station to station.

Translator—See Frequency translator.

Transmission medium—A physical carrier of signals.

Trunk amplifier—In broadband networks, a low-distortion amplifier that amplifies RF signals for long-distance transport.

Trunk cable—In broadband networks, coaxial cable used for distribution of RF signals over long distances throughout a cable system. Usually the widest diameter cable in the system.

Trunk line—In broadband networks, the major cable link(s) from the headend (or hub) to downstream branches. Also referred to as the main trunk.

Unity gain—In broadband networks, a design principle where amplifiers supply enough signal gain at appropriate frequencies to compensate for the system's cable signal loss and flat loss.

Unnumbered acknowledgment—A DLC command used in link establishment and DLC frame receipt indication.

Upstream—In the IBM Token-Ring, the opposite direction of data flow. Also, see Downstream.

Virtual circuit—A connection between two network nodes established by the transport layer and providing reliable data transfer between the nodes.

Virtual connection—See Virtual circuit.

Wire fault—An hard-error condition caused by a wire break or an electrical wiring short in a cable segment.

Wiring closet—An area containing one or more distribution panels connecting various cables together to form physical networks.

Index